101

GREAT WAYS
TO ENHANCE
YOUR CAREER

Selected and Introduced by

MICHELLE A. RIKLAN
AND DAVID RIKLAN

A PRODUCT OF

SELFGROWTH.COM

101 Great Ways to Enhance Your Career

By Michelle A. Riklan and David Riklan

Published by
Self Improvement Online, Inc.
http://www.SelfGrowth.com
200 Campus Drive, Suite D, Morganville, NJ 07751

Copyright © 2011 by Michelle A. Riklan and David Riklan
All rights reserved.
ISBN 978-0-9794992-7-2
Manufactured in the United States

*This book is dedicated in memory
of our brother/brother in-law,*

David H. Weintraub

who dreamed of being published.

ACKNOWLEDGMENTS

What inspires a person to pursue a project such as this? Self Improvement Online has published several volumes in its 101 series, including *101 Great Ways to Improve Your Life* (volumes 1, 2, and 3), *101 Great Ways to Improve Your Health,* and *Self Improvement: The Top 101 Experts*. Why careers?

As I attended the Career Thought Leaders Conference[1] in Baltimore last year, I had the good fortune of networking with many forward-thinking career experts, and a light bulb went off. Each expert has something to teach—different perspectives, resources, and suggestions—and the industry is filled with giving, collaborative professionals who are truly focused on assisting others in learning how to exist, survive, and climb upward within a difficult employment-career climate.

I hope that *101 Great Ways to Advance Your Career* will provide its audience with similar inspiration. Each contributor has a message to share, along with suggested strategies, expert advice, words of support, and relative anecdotes.

For every inspired project that comes to fruition, there are the people responsible for its execution and success:

- Thank you to our featured authors, Laura DeCarlo, Tory Johnson, Brian Tracy, and Charlotte Weeks, and to the ninety-seven additional author-experts who shared their pearls of wisdom.
- Without the support of the entire SelfGrowth.com team, this book could not have been created. To Sam Etkin, Adriene Hayes, Kristina Kanaley, Jamie Albert, Eric Taylor, Joe DePalma, Carlee Grabowski, and Christina Gangidino, your collaboration and efforts have been tremendous.
- Thank you to my sister Karen Weintraub for continual technical and moral support.
- Special thanks to my office manager, Robin Kugler, who makes sure that my business is well oiled, that details are not overlooked, and that I am well caffeinated every morning!

Many special thanks to my husband, David, and to my three incredibly smart and handsome/beautiful children, Joshua, Jonathan, and Rachel, who are forgiving when my multitasking skills fall short. *—Michelle A. Riklan*

[1] "Career Thought Leaders Consortium is a think tank of career industry leaders working collaboratively to support both our colleagues and job seekers worldwide by providing expert leadership and innovation throughout all phases of career development, job search, long-term career management, and career fulfillment"; http://www.careerthoughtleaders.com/.

TABLE OF CONTENTS

INTRODUCTION
By Michelle A. Riklan and David Riklan

"Your attitude, not your aptitude, will determine your altitude"
—ZigZiglar

In such a challenging workforce climate, "career enhancement" means many different things: procuring that first job, keeping an existing position, returning to the workforce after a long hiatus, riding the waves of unemployment, starting an entrepreneurial venture...

We are fortunate to have so many collaborative authors to share expertise, impart wisdom, and entertain us with relative anecdotes. In *101 Great Ways to Enhance Your Career*, we have compiled a thoughtful collection of 101 unique chapters from some of the industry's leading experts. Our experts are varied with impressive backgrounds and credentials from previously published authors and television personalities to coaches, business owners, and heads of associations. They are all stellar educators who have shared information on topics that are personally relevant and hope to inspire and motivate their readers.

Our mission in bringing to you *101 Great Ways to Enhance Your Career* is to offer chapters that speak to you on a personal level, and are useful to enhance your career or someone else's.

What You Can Learn From This Book

- You *can* find your passion and re-launch your career.
- You *can* network effectively and secure your next position.
- You *can* create a fabulous résumé and sell yourself in a difficult job-market.
- You *can* identify and act upon opportunities for change.
- You *can* fuel your own success.
- You *can* learn the most effective job search strategies.

And so much more! Whether you are seeking answers for yourself or working with a client on career objectives, this book offers solutions, suggestions, advice, and support on a wide range of topics including: retirement, business development, career branding, difficult work environments, effective communication, goals, job hunting, leadership résumé strategies, and telephone interviews. This book is a perfect tool for anyone who is looking to start a career, get ahead in their current position, return to the workforce, start their own business or is in a role that assists others with career development.

How the Book is Organized

We have organized this book by topic to simplify the information-gathering process. If you are looking for information on *Job Searching,* just go to the table of contents, locate the corresponding page numbers, and start reading! If you are seeking tips on how to ace the next *interview* or *leadership skills* that will help you to succeed, it's all right there. We tried to make it simple and hope you find this book easy to navigate.

Although not every chapter will relate to each individual's interests and needs, it is designed to be enjoyed like a cocktail hour – taste a little bit of this and a little bit of that. Find what you like, savor it, and digest it. If you haven't found what appeals to you yet, another tray of appetizing topics is just a page turn away. Every time you put it down and pick it back up, you can find new, meaningful messages, broken out into bite sized pieces.

Who Should Read This Book

101 Great Ways to Enhance Your Career is designed for a broad audience ranging from the recent college graduate to the retired professional seeking a second career. It is a clear, concise menu of information to choose from, featuring many of the industry's top experts.

How To Use This Book

This book can be used as a traditional reference guide. You can look up any of our top expert authors and find their contact information in their bios. Most have listed emails, websites and phone numbers.

The book can be read from cover-to-cover. Each chapter stands alone. Read it all the way through or out of sequence. Find what interests you today and go read something else tomorrow.

A PRODUCT OF SELFGROWTH.COM
AND
RIKLANRESOURCES.COM

Self Improvement Online, Inc. - Our Mission is to provide consumers with the single largest source of Self Improvement and Self Help information on the Internet, and to provide experts and business owners with a platform to get their message out and help others improve their lives. Our business is composed of four websites, SelfGrowth.com, NaturalHealthWeb.com, SelfImprovementNewsletters.com and SelfGrowthMarketing.com.com all dedicated to providing quality Self Improvement information.

Our websites receives over 1,300,000 unique visitors a month and our e-mail Newsletters or e-zines go to over 950,000 weekly subscribers. Our websites and newsletters are read in over 100 different countries, with the largest groups of readers and visitors coming from the United States, Canada, Australia, United Kingdom, and New Zealand.

Riklan Resources, LLC. – A career services firm for individuals and corporations.

For individuals: We offer résumé writing and related services, career coaching, interview training, and behavioral profiling.

For corporations and businesses: We offer a wide variety of customized training programs such as customer service, team building, supervisory, leadership, performance management, interviewing, diversity, sexual harassment awareness / hostile work-environment and more.

5 STAR QUALITIES

A-List Material: Top 5 Star Qualities Your Boss Looks for in a Star

Linda K. Sommer

Lady Gaga and Cher both made the A-list for the recent MTV Music Video Awards. Both ladies made newsworthy red carpet appearances. Lady Gaga was dressed in a gown made from raw meat, and Cher re-created her 1989 A-list appearance in an "If I Could Turn Back Time"–era jumpsuit of see-through lace.

I am not an expert at what makes you qualified for the A-list in Hollywood, but I do know some things that will get you and keep you on the A-list in the corporate world. There are universal qualities that management looks for when they are accessing who's a keeper and who's not. The good news is that you can learn to master these qualities. So if you are a young starlet or an industry icon, reviewing the list just might boost or save your career. Here's my corporate A-list: ability, agility, awareness, adaptability, and ambition.

Ability. First, you need to demonstrate that you have the technical ability to do the job. Managers are looking for people they can trust to do a good job with minimal supervision. They are looking for people who are competent and who want to stay that way. It's not enough to get your education and think your learning days are over. Star performers are lifelong learners. They seek out new knowledge, learn new skills, and develop new abilities.

Agility. Next, your boss is looking for someone who can maneuver through the interpersonal and organizational maze that is unique to your company. Your boss wants to know that you have the interpersonal skills to make things happen in the organization with or without formal authority. In other words, do people in the organization like you and want to work with you, and are they willing to do favors for you when needed?

Nothing is more valuable to a manager than an employee who can get things done because of his or her understanding of the formal and informal channels of communication, insight into the formal and informal power structure, and relationship with formal and informal decision makers. Your boss wants someone who can get around, over, and under interpersonal and interdepartmental barriers to get results.

Awareness. Your boss is looking for someone with the right technical skills and some social intelligence, but that's just the entry-level stuff. Research shows that the ability to understand your emotional intelligence is twice as important as mental IQ or technical skills for all levels of leadership.

What really sets you apart is the extent to which you know yourself. It is the ability to recognize and understand your moods, emotions, and drives as well as your emotional impact on other people. This self-awareness means that you have a realistic assessment of your strengths and weaknesses.

When you are self-aware, you know what you can do well, and you do it with self-confidence. You also know when you don't do things well and you are able to ask for help or you have strategies for working around your weak spots. When you get this, you will be comfortable in many different situations, and you'll be able to laugh at yourself as well as celebrate your wins! Bosses love people who know themselves and have a positive impact on others.

Adaptability. Being quick on your feet in the changing world of business is one form of adaptability. Quick thinking and action are often greatly rewarded. But what will really set you up is the ability to adapt or learn from your successful and not-so-successful experiences.

Lessons learned are not just for your project report. Real winners are able to learn from their circumstances and adapt their leadership style for future challenges. If you are not asking what you could have done differently, then you are missing out on getting an MBA from life. Employers, managers, and supervisors want people who learn from their mistakes and get better with each new experience.

Ambition. You have to want to be a star. Your boss is looking for you take charge, go where others are afraid to go, and pursue goals with energy and persistence. You can step it up by taking on assignments that others don't want or by taking on risk that others avoid. Your boss will take notice when you demonstrate a strong drive to achieve. She is looking for people who remain optimistic and believe it can be done, even in the face of setbacks.

And above all, your boss wants to know that you are willing to commit to the organization's success knowing that your success will follow. However, success for the sake of money and status is often short-lived.

A passion to work for reasons that go beyond money or status is the best fuel for sustained advancement. It pays to be doing something you love. A genuine strong drive to succeed is contagious and priceless.

So what does it take to outshine your coworkers? Apparently, not much these days. According to recent Gallup polls, only 30 percent of American workers reported that they were engaged in their work. But even more telling is that 52 percent were not engaged, and 18 percent were actively disengaged! That means that among your coworkers, most, a whopping 70 percent, don't care about their work, don't care about their boss's opinion of them, and don't care about getting ahead. They're zombies. That puts the odds in your favor from the get-go.

With 70 percent of your coworkers out of the way because they don't care, you can cultivate these five skills and soar to the top of the charts to get that promotion, raise, or bonus. If you want to be a star, it doesn't take wild stunts and crazy costumes like Lady Gaga and Cher. It just takes developing good character, sound work ethics, and a sense of self-worth—simple, but not easy.

So how did you do? Are you A-list material? If so, I'll see you on the red carpet.

BIO

With a background in clinical psychology and general management, Linda K. Sommer has over twenty-five years of international management and leadership consulting experience for large corporations, national governments, municipal governments, and entrepreneurial businesses. Linda has a MBA in leadership and management plus postgraduate certifications in executive development and executive coaching. She is president of Success Savvy LLC, an executive coaching and management consulting firm. She is a national speaker and author, including being the author of *Step It Up: An Insider's Guide to Career Advancement* (http://www.stepitupcareerdevelopment.com/). Contact Linda at lksommer@gmail.com or (719) 339-8223.

10 Attributes and Attitudes for Every Professional

᪥⁓᪥

Rabison Shumba

The modern business world is ever changing and more competitive and requires individuals who will stand and be counted as leaders above others. When you stand head and shoulders above your own colleagues, employers will rush for you, business will come your way, and your department will win all the prizes for good performance. As a professional in your own area of endeavor, know that your attitudes and attributes facilitate the well-being of your subordinates. This has a direct impact on the altitude to which the company's vision will rise. Do business like your entire life relies on it. If you are working for someone, take that business as your own, take responsibility for your area of endeavor, and do the work well. Many professionals go to work for the money and job security but behave as if they can't wait to leave the place of employment. They carry themselves like victims of the workplace, always demanding more without justifying their demands with results. In this article, you will learn some pointers that will separate you from others.

1. Determination. You need to have a "no matter what," "whatever it takes" attitude. Be determined to achieve that goal. Never be tempted to quit, never retire. You become the favorite of every employer when you show that you are a fighter. Even when you run your own business, determination carries the day. It separates wimps from achievers. Determination says "I may be standing in the fire now, but I am not moved by present pressure." This is first a mental position that then translates into a physical and tangible manifestation.

2. Diligent and detailed. This is when one pays attention to the tasks at hand. Diligent people follow procedures line by line. They do not invent or enjoy shortcuts. There is usually a desire to arrive at the destination immediately. The world is becoming faster each day. Microwave solutions lead to microwave disasters. If you maintain your diligence, your day of promotion will come, and you will go to the top, much to the amazement of those around you. Consider your diligence, and pay attention to every detail as a seed for promotion.

3. Dependable doer. When you can be trusted to be loyal, calling a spade a spade, being a person of your word, reliable and open, then you are positioned for promotion. No one wants to give power and influence to someone who is hard to understand, someone who shows signs of disloyalty and a lack of trust. When you are dependable, then everyone around you knows you do what you promise, and sometimes beyond. They know you go the extra mile to ensure that quality is achieved. Dependability purchases possibilities of leadership and promotion.

4. Destiny directed. No one would enjoy working with someone who has lost his or her moral, emotional, and psychological compass. Direction toward destiny speaks of focus, vision, and purposeful living. Every professional must answer the question on purpose succinctly: "Where am I now, and where am I going?" When you cannot answer this question without stammering then you are likely to be tossed around and shaken when others seem to make strides in their areas of endeavor. I have seen people spend years studying for a master's degree in international law or business only to decide after such investment that they want to be a professional musician or some other profession. I have no problem with this, as long as you don't live in regret over the time spent in your own professional wilderness hoping to please your college sponsor.

5. Distinctly different. You need to be separate, to stand up and stand out. You are treated in relation to the way you view and treat yourself. When you behave ordinarily, you should expect to be treated ordinarily. Carry yourself like a king, with dignity. Your uniqueness makes you uncommon. When you stop copying the identity of others and move toward originality in speech and action, then your uniqueness will draw employers toward you.

6. Disciplined delegator. When you commit to doing something, just do it. Why wait for other people to say "go ahead" unless such protocol is necessary in your culture? Be confident in who you are. Be secure in your role. You cannot skin a whole cow on your own. Provide the knives, advise the teams accordingly, and remain responsible for the outcome. Be hands-on, ask for feedback, and do not shun your own responsibilities. You remain disciplined in your delegation lest you lead your team astray. They may take their given roles seriously, but they will still look up to the leader to model and enforce discipline.

7. Daring dreamer. You need to have audacious, adventurous, bold, and courageous dreams and aspirations. You cannot be a professional who is not powered by dreams. What do you want to become in five years? You must be able to answer that in your sleep. Your dream is your blueprint on which your future hinges. If you won't dream, why wake up, as you have nothing to chase?

8. Deep-seated drive (passion). You cannot motivate those around you when your drive tank is low. I have personally tried it and realized it does not work. Always recharge your batteries before you meet or address your teams. Whenever you feel drained, discouraged, and bored, get someone else to lead while you resharpen and refresh. There is nothing as boring as a workmate or leader with no drive.

9. Decisively direct. You must be able to make decisions quickly and directly. Professionals who take long to make decisions tend to miss opportunities for promotion to leadership. Leadership is about making decisions that move the business forward. Modern business requires quick, direct decision making, as the world has become a lot faster. Information moves faster than it used to, and hence your decision-making processes have to be quicker and yet direct.

10. Dynamic deliverer. When you are dynamic, you are full of energy and new ideas. Every employer has one expectation for you as a professional: they want you to deliver results. When you deliver results, you make your company or department proud. Your attitude must be that of an achiever, a goal getter, and someone whose fruits are unquestionably evident.

BIO

Rabison Shumba is a young African entrepreneur who has interests in Information and Communication Technology, Agriculture and Mining. He is also a motivational speaker, trainer and author. His book, The Greatness Manual and various online articles are tools for personal and professional development. Rabison has a personal vision of impacting the lives of children in marginalized communities by creating platforms for career counsel and guidance, information empowerment and capacity building through the Greatness Factory Trust, where he currently holds the position of Chairman of the Board of Trustees and Acting Executive Director. Rabison believes that the effect of the lack of adequate information empowerment platforms has the potential to cause learners leaving schools to never realize an equitable chance at bettering their circumstances and therefore contributing to the downward spiral into poverty. He is actively involved in the organization of career enhancement and guidance colloquiums to propel and inspire both young and mature professionals to greatness. His areas of expertise include strategy, leadership, personal and professional development.

Rabison is married to Jackie, and they have two daughters. They reside in Harare, Zimbabwe. Visit him online at http://www.rabisonshumba.com/ or at http://greatnessmanual.wordpress.com/.

3

How to Leverage Your Happiness and Relaunch Your Career!

Ricky Powell

If you are like most people, you fall into one of five categories regarding your career:

1. You are unemployed.
2. You have a job, hate it, but stay to pay your bills.
3. You have a job, it's not your passion, but you stay because the money is good.
4. You have a job, you love it, and you would do it for free if you had to.
5. You are an entrepreneur and wouldn't take a job if your life depended on it.

Do any of these scenarios describe you? If so, or even if you're in a group I haven't mentioned, you can instantly improve the odds of success in your job, career, or business if you simply implement the ideas you are about to learn.

The exciting part is that what I'm about to share with you is just the beginning. Once you not only understand it but really "get" what I'm about to reveal to you, you will stand out from the crowd, and people will line up to hire you, promote you, or do business with you.

By the way, please don't expect to read it here once and be done. It's going to take some work on your part. Ugh, I used that four-letter word, didn't I? *Work.* It won't be that bad, I promise. This knowledge can change your life if you let it. It can even be fun!

You may not believe me at first because the idea sounds so simple. You need to believe it, though, because it's true. I know because I've experienced the benefits for years.

What is this super sexy secret to success in your career, not to mention your personal life? Be happy. Be really happy. Be so happy that you start getting known for it! I know it may sound simple on the surface, but let's dig a little deeper.

Do you like to be around whiners, complainers, victims, or grouches? Of course you don't. Guess what? *No one does*! At the same time, the opposite is also true. People *do* like to be around positive, forward-thinking people—the kind of people who are always asking, "How can I help?" They like to be around people who are always sporting a bright smile and a kind word.

Competition is fierce in the business world today. There are many qualified people out there who may do the job better, faster, or cheaper than you can. For this reason alone, it is imperative that you set yourself apart from the crowd. How is this possible?

Most people don't show up to work with this kind of positive, grateful attitude. Many employees show up to work with a feeling of entitlement. They are not interested in bringing more value to the table for their employer but rather in what their employer can do for them. Frankly, if you want to get ahead and really shine today, that's the wrong way to go.

I've spent over twenty years working for a major television network. Each day, I start over with a renewed sense of gratitude and bring a team-player, can-do, "how can I serve" attitude to the company. I've been very fortunate because that demeanor has not gone unnoticed. A few years ago, after undergoing a divisional structure change, I was offered a leadership role and was given a much broader scope of responsibility.

Apart from working for one of the largest media companies in the world for over twenty years, I have always had the entrepreneurial bug. I believe in multiple streams of income, including residual and passive income. In 2007, I launched i-choose-happiness.com, which became somewhat of a public service. I kept it up and running to demonstrate to the world that happiness is a choice you can make regardless of your outer circumstances. Currently I'm rebranding that space as LifelongHappiness.com, where you can learn tips, tools, and techniques that will help you incorporate a true sense of happiness into your life. There is also a social network, discussion board, forum, and blog, along with a plethora of information that will help you grow personally and professionally. I even offer group and private coaching through my Masterminds of Lifelong Happiness program.

Someone came up to me at work recently and asked if I'm the "happy guy" because he recognized me from a Google search he did on a term such as "choose happiness."

You should know that, now more than ever, your own personal brand speaks volumes. Why not stand out from the masses and be known not only for doing your job extremely well but for also being that positive individual who brings that all-important sense of happiness to everyone you touch? It has been proven that happiness is contagious. If you are going to spread something to others, why not make it something worth catching?

Taking this advice will only help you. I have yet to receive a complaint from someone saying, "Hey, Ricky, this happiness thing just isn't working for me!" I guarantee it.

BIO

Ricky Powell is a veteran of the entertainment industry, having spent over forty years in front of and behind the camera. The past several years, he has lectured on the importance of choosing happiness and how doing so can help you make more money, create stronger relationships, and live longer. His group and private coaching sessions will help you raise your "happiness set point" in every aspect of your life. You can contact Ricky through his website, http://www.LifelongHappiness.com/.

4

BEHAVIORAL METRICS

The Path to Your Pot of Gold

❧❦

Bob Kreisberg

Imagine for a moment that you are traveling along a path and have reached a fork in the road. In fact, as you are reading this book, you may well be at a "career fork in the road." In front of you are two distinct paths. One path is to attempt to fix everything that you perceive is wrong with you and then pursue fame and fortune. The other is to take advantage of everything that is right with you to find your "pot of gold." Which path would you take? Which journey would be more enjoyable? Which would yield quicker rewards?

Of course, the path that celebrates your natural talents is the one for you. That's the easy part, right? The hard part is clearly defining and articulating what your natural talents are. Surprise, surprise—owing to the tremendous advances in behavioral science and computer technology, metrics are available to provide you with the information you need to confidently follow your path to success.

Metrics are key parts of all business strategies. Too many "accounts receivable days outstanding" indicates that a business needs to tighten up its collection policies, or that perhaps it has some product defects (and that's why people are not paying). Either way, the metrics help define the strategy. The same is true with metrics that measure assets to liabilities, inventory turns, and myriad other business components.

Just as metrics are a key strategic element of a business, understanding your own metrics is key to your ability to enhance your career. Once you know what your behavioral talents are, you can then position them to good use.

The nomenclature I am using in this chapter has been developed by Professional Dynametrics Profiles Inc. (PDP), a company with which I have been affiliated for twenty plus years. PDP has leading-edge technology in this field.

So let's look at the information that is available to you and how you can use it. Behavioral metrics measure the following aspects of a personality:

- Dominance—also known as the control trait
- Extroversion—the social trait
- Pace/patience—the rate of motion trait
- Conformity—the structure and detail trait
- Logic—a fact-feeling orientation
- Energy level
- Energy style—i.e., are you more inner directed or outer directed, or steadfast and tenacious
- Behavioral adjustments—how you feel you need to be to succeed in your current endeavor
- Morale
- Energy drain—how much energy you are losing as a result of morale and behavioral adjustment factors

As you can see, that's a ton of metrics. The next obvious question is, why would you care? How would knowing these metrics about yourself allow you to choose the correct path to that pot of gold? Here's how:

- Contrary to popular belief, we are not all *great* at everything.
- There's more to gain by understanding your natural strengths and challenges than by ignoring them.
- You *can* adapt your style when you have to for relatively short periods of time.
- You can anticipate how you will respond to certain situations and consciously understand why you do what you do, and you can take corrective action, if necessary.
- You will be able to connect more effectively with the people who work for you and the person for whom you work.

Let's look at a few specific examples. Let's say that you really enjoy working with people, and you like a very positive, upbeat environment. Let's also say that you are much more comfortable with a consensus-oriented organization versus one that is highly confrontational. Great! A really good fit for you would be to work in a customer service area with a company that has excellent products. You'll enjoy helping people, and you can have confidence that they will like the product you represent.

Here's another example. Let's say you are a very competitive individual, and you like to be completely in charge of your own destiny. Nothing scares you, and you look forward to proving to yourself just how talented you are, every day. That's great, too, but you would *not* enjoy the customer service job. You should be out there on the front line, selling a product in a strong competitive market. You'll want to have a great product to sell, but it won't scare you if the competition also has a great product. It also won't bother you if you are looking for customers to be "first to buy." In fact, that situation would really get your juices flowing.

How about if you have a very strong process orientation? You like things tidy and neat. Let's also say that you enjoy being with people. You're a social person as well. What's the right fit for you? There could be plenty, but irrespective of the specific position, you need an organization that has a culture of high ethical values. It is very important to you that people are treated fairly and that customers, vendors, and employees are treated with respect.

When you find the right fit for your own personality style, then you can flourish. You can move forward with confidence, knowing that you bring the right stuff to the table. Make sense? Of course it does.

So how can you find out this information about yourself? You may be curious, but you're also not looking to take out a second mortgage on your house. Well, fortunately for you, this technology is now far more affordable than ever before. You can find out all of this about yourself—your natural personality style, your behavioral adjustments, energy drain, morale, and so forth—for less than $100, and in less than ten minutes. In fact, the offer we are making in this book is for you to be able to have the complete Personal Development Report (PDR) for $50. The PDR explains every aspect of your behavioral style, as described earlier—your four cornerstone traits (dominance, extroversion, pace, conformity), logic, morale, energy style, energy drain, and how the world gets to see you.

But that's still a fair chunk of change, and you will want to have confidence that the information is an accurate reflection of your strengths. Right, I agree. So here's what we are offering to you. You can receive, at *absolutely* no charge to you, the Initial Confirmation Report. This is very similar to the first page of the twenty-six-page PDR, and it spells out your composite personality but touches only on the four cornerstone traits. If you feel that the Initial Confirmation Report is an accurate reflection of your personality style, then, and only then, need you decide to order the longer report. In addition, for no additional charge, you will receive a one-page *Handy Guide to Understanding Personality Styles*. This will allow you to see the strengths and challenges of all the personality styles and will give you insight as to how to best communicate with each one.

What makes you tick? What are your strengths, likes, dislikes, motivators, and demotivators? Be proactive. Take this step you need to take to find out.

Simply visit our website at http://land.pdpworks.com/user/remote/entry/setup/0011-001.1/bob@opusproductivity.com,david@opusproductivity.com/200/, follow the simple instructions, and you're good to go. Although it is not a timed exercise, it likely will not take you more than a few minutes to complete. Let's get you on the right road to the pot of gold.

BIO

Robert S. Kreisberg is the president of OPUS Productivity Solutions, a company he formed in 1989 to help organizations maximize the results of the people they have on their teams. Prior to OPUS, Kreisberg spent seventeen years in industry, starting in sales and then gravitating toward sales management and general management. Bob is a graduate of Drexel University, with a degree in commerce and engineering. Bob's work has been featured in Robert Early Johnson's book *Kick Your Own Ass: The Will, Drill, and Skill to Sell More Than You Ever Thought Possible* and in two separate articles in *Inc.* magazine and one in the *Wall Street Journal*. Contact Bob at bob@opusproductivity.com or online at http://www.opusproductivity.com/.

5

BELIEFS

Program Your Subconscious Mind with Beliefs That Support Your Conscious Career Goals

≈≈≈≈

Tamera Rackham

The cat's out of the bag. With movies like *The Secret* and *What the Bleep Do We Know?,* understanding that we create our own reality is getting to be mainstream thinking, and many are learning that *our beliefs are the single most powerful force* that influences the creation of that reality. Beliefs determine how we see our lives and everything around us. They influence our thoughts, our emotions, our expectations, our actions, and our overall well-being. So just what are beliefs? According to FreeDictionary.com, they are "the mental acceptance of and conviction in the truth, actuality, or validity of something." Your belief system, along with your level of consciousness, *determines what you will experience in your life.*

Where do beliefs come from? According to Bruce Lipton, PhD, cellular biologist and author of *The Biology of Belief,* most of our beliefs are in place by the time we are five or six years of age, and some of our core beliefs, things like whether we think the world is a friendly place, can be programmed while we're still in the womb. Our beliefs come from interactions with our parents and the people around us during childhood, our religion, our community, or any traumatic event. We don't usually consciously choose what beliefs to hold. We soak them up from our life experiences when we're too small to have any way of evaluating them, and they become core components of how we see ourselves, other people, and the world.

We've all heard about the subconscious mind, but many people are stunned to learn that most of our behavioral and thought patterns are directed by it, not by the conscious mind. Many years of research have shown that 95 percent or more of our behavior is controlled by the subconscious mind. Though both parts of the mind are necessary for us to be fully functional, they are specialized in their capabilities and the way in which they process life's experiences. Let's take a quick look at the differences in the way they work. The conscious mind is volitional, whereas the

18

subconscious mind is habitual. The conscious mind sets goals, judges results, and is limited to processing one to three events at once, or about forty bits of information; in contrast, the subconscious mind can process thousands of events at once and millions of bits of information per second (e.g., monitoring all bodily functions). The conscious mind thinks abstractly and has a memory of about twenty seconds. The subconscious mind, on the other hand, is very literal and is where your long-term memory, attitudes, and values, and also your beliefs, are housed.

As you can see from its processing capacity alone, the subconscious mind plays an important role in your life. It is almost impossible to achieve a goal if you hold subconscious beliefs that are in conflict with that goal, no matter what it is. Even if you do achieve it, the subconscious will usually find or create a way to sabotage your success. Your subconscious programming takes over the moment your conscious mind becomes distracted and stops paying full attention. The fact is that as adults, we spend most of our time subconsciously reacting to life rather than consciously creating it. Fortunately, there are many ways to change your beliefs at the subconscious level. The one I work with is PSYCH-K®, which I'll tell you about later.

It's no surprise by now to hear me say that beliefs limiting personal prosperity and career growth are frequently embedded in the subconscious mind. They are counterproductive to achieving wealth, financial freedom, public recognition, or whatever personal career goal you might have and can also affect how fast you reach those goals. Beliefs such as "money is the root of all evil," "poverty is a virtue," "it's not OK/safe for me to have money," or "I don't deserve to have lots of money" are self-limiting when it comes to meeting your financial and career goals. Many people feel guilty about wanting or having money, or they believe that making money is hard, and for them, it most certainly will be. Beliefs can not only impede the accumulation of money but can undermine the management of money. If you spend it as fast as or faster than you make it, or make one bad investment decision after another, it's very likely that you have self-limiting subconscious beliefs about money.

In addition to limiting beliefs about money itself, beliefs that sabotage your self-esteem are often involved in your inability to move forward and reach your career goals. *Your self-esteem profoundly influences how others view you.* If your self-esteem is high, others will tend to like and trust you, and if your self-esteem is low, they will be more likely to respond with a lack of confidence and trust in you. *Your beliefs teach the world how to treat you,* and you know by now that the majority of them are subconscious. Another aspect of self-esteem is the concept of unworthiness. Some world religions teach us that we are fundamentally unworthy, and this is far too often unwittingly enforced by our parents, who were taught the same when they were children. Regardless of where they come from, such beliefs held on a subconscious level will most certainly create limitations when it comes to achieving your career goals.

The methods taught by self-help books and lecturers to reach our desired goals are to use positive thinking, positive self-talk, and lots of affirmations. These are all good methods, but they must be used for weeks, months, or sometimes years to gain results. There is another option though! With PSYCH-K belief change protocols, it is *fast, easy, and painless* to overwrite your self-limiting beliefs with ones that support you. PSYCH-K offers the following benefits:

- Most belief change balances are completed in three to five minutes.
- It is unnecessary to dig around in the past trying to find the unwanted beliefs.
- Permission protocols are always used to ensure the appropriateness of overwriting something within the subconscious.
- Immediately after the programming has taken place, it's checked to confirm the new belief on a conscious level.
- Sessions can be done over the phone.
- With the help of a facilitator, you can create very specific custom goals or beliefs and program them into your subconscious, stacking the deck even further in favor of accomplishing your career goals.

With PSYCH-K, you can *program beliefs of your choosing* and put your career into overdrive. Are you ready? Then find a PSYCH-K facilitator with whom to work today!

BIO

Tamera Rackham, as an Advanced PSYCH-K facilitator, has worked with clients throughout the United States, helping them align their subconscious beliefs with their conscious goals and desires. She helps further accelerate goal attainment as a *Fully Conscious Life* mentor coach and guide, helping clients to be fully conscious of what and how they are creating through their beliefs, thoughts, words, and actions, guiding them to create the lives of their choice. Learn more by visiting http://www.gracefulharmony.com/, or you can reach Tamera directly at (406) 363-4898. PSYCH-K® is a registered trademark of The Myrddin Corportation, Crestone, Colorado.

6

Beyond Retirement: Finding Satisfying Work When You're Not Over the Hill

Cathy Severson

Retirement is no longer considered a time without work. Research indicates that over 75 percent of baby boomers anticipate continuing to work beyond traditional retirement age. Many will need the income as increased life spans fail to match decreased pensions and savings. Some retirees are also motivated by the desire for new challenges, meaningful activities, and staying connected.

Finding work isn't easy as you approach your fifth or sixth decade. Many people find blatant discrimination as well as outdated policies and mind-sets. With that said, if you have the willingness to look at your job search in a new way, there are opportunities to make a contribution, even if you have gray in your hair.

Before you take pen to paper to update your résumé, spend time in self-reflection. You are not who you were forty years ago. What you want from work may have changed, as has what you have to offer. Don't approach looking for a job the way you did when you were first starting out.

Why do you want to work? What motivates you at this point in your life? What gives you satisfaction and personal fulfillment? These are questions related to your work values, a major component in your career success. Work values are those things that are most important to you. They often change as we get older.

Joan, a feisty woman, had worked most of her life as a bookkeeper. In her early seventies, she was looking for job as a result a corporate takeover. Frustrated in her search, she accused potential employers of age discrimination. On further reflection, she discovered an alternate explanation. When she took the time to look at her work values, Joan discovered that she no longer wanted to work as a bookkeeper. She had enjoyed the hustle and bustle of working in an office, but in recent years, her primary enjoyment had come from relationships. With more probing, Joan realized that she really wanted to work with homebound seniors, helping them with their household finances and providing companionship. This revelation shifted her approach in looking for work.

Work values are grouped into the following distinct categories:

Lifestyle. The need and desire to acquire money, status, security and other components connected to working but visible outside of work. It may also involve integration between the actual job and the environment in which the work is carried out.

Creativity. The expression of creativity and/or being in a creative environment. This often includes the need for less structure and more spontaneity.

Contribution. The desire to be part of something bigger than oneself. Usually, there is a need to show concern for others and be involved in social or political activities.

Achievement. This manifests in a compelling sense of purpose or a need for competence or recognition. Influencing, leading, and motivating others are included in this group.

Relationships. Building and maintaining meaningful relationships, sharing of oneself. This could be with the people served as well as with peers.

Search for meaning. Looking for a greater significance. This includes wisdom, spirituality, and feeling connected to a greater whole. It can also include self-transformation.

Though lifestyle and achievement are key motivators in the younger years, many older workers are eager to give up the long hours and stress associated with climbing the corporate ladder. Mature workers tend to want work where they use their creativity, build relationships, or make a contribution. Thinking about what you want will set the framework for your whole job search.

Once you have arrived at your work values, you will want to articulate your key strengths. What gifts and talents do you have to offer an organization? What kinds of problems do you want to solve?

When Jean called, it was clear from her voice that she was angry and aggravated. She had been unemployed for a year and didn't know why she couldn't get a job. Jean had accomplished amazing things. She had a three-page résumé listing her jobs as a cultural affairs director, nonprofit fund-raiser, journalist, and medical administrator. Her best experiences were at the bottom of the third page, as a volunteer. With so many diverse experiences and skills, nothing specific stood out. The résumé lacked focus and cohesiveness.

The mature worker often submits a résumé that is more a career obituary than a strong marketing piece. Jean made a mistake common for mature workers: not wanting to limit her options, she included all her experiences for the last twenty years. She thought a potential employer would see the many things she had done and view them as assets.

The key to your future lies buried in the nuggets of experience in your past. Completing the following C-A-R exercise will help you recognize your strengths.

First, think back over your life and identify activities in which you felt a sense of achievement, or those which were personally fulfilling, or from which you felt passion. Use achievements from childhood, adolescence, or adulthood in activities at work, leisure, hobbies, or home. Try to choose specific events and not milestones such as "graduating from college."

Then write at least a paragraph for each activity. Your description of each activity should include the following:

> **Challenge.** Begin with a problem, situation or activity in which you were directly involved and about which you feel a sense of pride and success. Write a description of the challenge, how it came into being, and how you became involved. Keep in mind that it was an activity you did well, enjoyed doing, and of which you are proud.

> **Action.** What action did take you to address the challenge? Provide details (who, what, when, where and how) of all aspects of the endeavor, from beginning to end. What responsibilities did you have? How were others involved in the process?

> **Results.** What were the results of challenge? The more you can quantify the results, the better. For example, ask yourself, how much money did I save? Did I increase profits? Enhance systems? Innovate processes? Improve products?

In coaching, Jean began to articulate her strengths. She started by listing her primary achievements. Jean was able to see the threads running through all her work and volunteer activities. She continually demonstrated great leadership and communication skills, but her real gift was the ability to enlist people in grand visions. On numerous occasions, she had recruited people to volunteer their time on projects requiring huge commitments. These projects were successful, winning accolades from superiors and the public. Consolidating this information resulted in a concise and focused list of skills that she wanted to use and that were also marketable to a potential employer.

Spend time in self-reflection as the first step in your job search. Identify your new work values and highlight your strengths. This will increase your self-confidence and feeling of empowerment. Armed with this information, you will be able to target potential employers to find rewarding work for this time in your life.

BIO

As founder of Passport to Purpose, a professional and personal development company, Cathy helps individuals find meaning and purpose in their lives and work. Cathy is creator of VISTa Life/Career Cards (http://www.VISTa-Cards.com), a counseling tool used around the world. As baby boomers approach retirement age, Cathy is taking a leadership role in redefining the process of "aging." Create a Great Retirement (http://www.CreateAGreatRetirement.com/) provides resources to help baby boomers lead fuller lives as they reach retirement age. Retirement Life Matters (http://www.RetiremetLifeMatters.com/) creates a community of support for people in transition.

7

Body Language for Success

Suzanne Masefield

Did you know that within five minutes of meeting someone, we decide whether we like, dislike, trust, or mistrust that person? We create a perception of others, and likewise, they read us, determining our credibility and whether they feel confident to do business with us. This is all determined through subtle messages sent to each other consciously and unconsciously.

*Communicating powerfully and authentically is pivotal to good relationships and career success.*Research shows that at least 55 percent of our communication is delivered via body language, 38 percent through tone of voice, and only 7 percent through the actual words we speak. The benefits of recognizing the subtle messages sent as well as projecting confidence and putting others at ease are huge and pivotal to becoming great communicators to enhance our careers.

Clients frequently ask me what is holding them back, often not realizing how they come across to others. They are unaware they shrink back, look nervous, or alternatively come across as aggressive or negative.

Strong, positive body language starts in childhood, when our parents teach us how to shake hands or make eye contact. Likewise, overcoming shy tendencies from the past increases positive results, whether it's finally daring to ask for a raise, applying for a new job, or admitting that we are overworked and assertively standing up for ourselves to create a win-win situation.

Leadership Presence

Good leaders adopt the natural body language of a director—maintaining an upright, open stance, looking down slightly, smiling less, carrying a strong sense of being in charge of themselves, with a more dominant stance to create a presence.

Adapting voice tone is a valuable technique used frequently by politicians and leaders alike. Women politicians are taught to lower their tone and speak more slowly. The depth of voice relates to body size; unconsciously, a lower, slower tone is heard as more dominant, authoritative, and commanding of greater respect.

Studies have revealed that the pitch of a woman's voice becomes more masculine as she becomes more liberated. By lowering their tone, strengthening their posture, centering their emotions, and grounding their bodies, women can reflect strong leadership qualities without forgoing their positive female attributes.

Seven Deadly Habits

Avoid the following habits if you want to get ahead:

- Slouching
- Crossing your arms
- Speaking too fast
- Fiddling with your hair
- Stroking your neck or arms
- Fidgeting or foot tapping
- Wringing your hands

Mirror, Mirror

One of the easiest ways to get on someone's good side is to reflect his or her body language and speech patterns, as we prefer people who are like us and behave similarly. This is called mirroring, and it's quick to learn. Practice on friends and colleagues, concentrating on posture, speech patterns, tone, and other nonverbal indications like breathing. Give it a go in the work environment, and notice how the rapport you create with others changes!

Be subtle, and don't go overboard—mirror positive, friendly body language without being intrusive or overly intimate. When we feel someone is like us, we feel safe and in control of the situation, which builds trust and rapport in relationships and interactions. This is what you want to aim for when mirroring others. Be sure you only mirror positive body language as reflecting back negative postures can be counterproductive.

Overcoming Conflict

When experiencing negative, invasive, or aggressive body language from others, rather than shrinking back or mirroring their gestures, try taking three deep breaths down to your stomach to allow yourself to recenter your emotions and get oxygen to the brain to think clearly. Feel your feet on the floor and bend your knees; this will help you feel grounded and safe to deal with the situation more effectively. Open your body posture, hold your hands together in a loose hold at your stomach, and expand your elbows to create some space between your arms and the sides of your body.

Often, in conflict situations, people hold their breath and close their body posture; this cuts off oxygen from the brain, arresting clear thinking and tightening and locking the body, which diminishes physical strength and the ability to act powerfully in a difficult situation. Remove yourself altogether if the situation is dangerous, but takc a few breaths to center yourself first to recharge.

Cultural Awareness

Cultural awareness is an important aspect of body language awareness as sensitivity to gestures that may differ considerably between cultures will help you get ahead in life. Eye contact is a great example as it is prized in most Western cultures yet is seen as invasive or aggressive in certain situations in Eastern cultures.

Communication is defined as "the process of sending and receiving messages in which 2 or more people achieve understanding" (*Oxford English Dictionary*). The first part of that equation is always *you*!

Developing and updating ourselves is the only true place in which we have complete power in life. Even if we believe we have an amazing ability to influence others, which many people do possess, that influence is increased tenfold when we focus on taking charge of ourselves first!

Leadership of Life Starts with Leadership of Yourself

Being in touch with yourself, your feelings, your thinking, and how you come across to others and updating your behavior to better serve yourself is pivotal to confidence levels, self-belief, and your ability to take charge of your career success in a powerful way.

Following is a simple technique to empower you to project confidence and encourage others to feel at ease in your presence. I call this technique POISE:

P   positive
O   open
I   in touch
S   smile
E   eye contact

Positive Focus

- Notice and center yourself
- Then notice the other person's body language and focus on something positive about him or her (if you do this alone, focus on something positive about yourself)
- Lean forward slightly to show you are engaged, and give a small nod to acknowledge the person

Open

- Body posture
- Stand tall
- Head up
- Shoulders back
- Chest out
- Stomach in
- Relax your breathing
- Move arms out approximately fifteen centimeters from your body, creating space along your sides
- Use your hands more confidently

In Touch

- Get in touch with yourself
- Put your hand on your stomach and take three deep breaths
- Calm your mind
- Center your emotions
- Bend your knees
- Feel your feet on the floor to ground your body

Smile

- Smile with your whole face and not just with your mouth
- Give a genuine warm welcome, and lift your mood in the process

Eye Contact

- Encourage open communication and build trust (not appropriate in all cultures)

Start each day and all interactions with the POISE technique to focus you, center your emotions, and ground your body, increasing your ability to take of the messages you are sending. Becoming more aware of others' messages developing confident body language will increase rapport-building skills to help become a greater communicator and increase success in your career.

Bio

Suzanne Masefield is director of Think Success Ltd. and Synergy Effect Coaching, amind-body analyst, a clinical hypnotherapist, a Reiki master, and an executive coach. She has facilitated conscious leadership for the last sixteen years with clients worldwide. Suzanne is a writer, inspirational speaker, and empowerment facilitator, training security, surveillance teams, and businesspeople in body language awareness. The Synergy Effect empowers you to take authentic leadership of life personally and professionally, generating core-level success. For more information on mind-body analysis or Body Language for Success courses or seminars, contact http://www.thinksuccess.co.nz/.

8

Effective Ways to Boost Your Career Online

≈≪∼≫≈

Scott A. Pete

A challenging economy underscores the need to maintain a competitive edge. Whatever business you are in, your ability to differentiate yourself from the competition is imperative. The Web offers tremendous opportunity to build your personal brand and boost your career. However, it can be challenging to sift through the vast number of resources that are rapidly growing and changing as you read this.

If you treat your personal brand like a business, you will find there are similar marketing approaches that can generate results to propel your career to new levels. Following are eleven ways to boost your career online.

1. Define your identity. To target your audience effectively and deliver relevant content to that group, it is essential for you to have a clear identity. Perhaps you are an expert management consultant, an accomplished author, or a medical device sales professional. Can your audience clearly see what you specialize in and what sets you apart from your competition?

2. Define your audience. Communicating your value proposition is not a one-size-fits-all endeavor. To be effective at engaging your audience, it is important to deliver a very relevant message. Which audience subsets (segments) exist, and how do their needs differ? To maximize relevance, it can be helpful to gain clarity about the audience that you are targeting. What need are they trying to solve? How do they search for solutions to that need?

3. Use tools to validate your assumptions. Understanding the behaviors and motivators of your audience can allow you to be more effective at engaging your audience. On the topic of search activity online, we can use Google Trends, Insights, and Analytics to understand search patterns for key search terms, look at trends over multiple years, or even understand geographic differences. This will help to prioritize and create the content that will most likely attract the audience we wish to reach.

4. Establish a "hub" for your personal brand. There are numerous online serv
that allow you to establish your own profile such as LinkedIn, Facebook, and oth
However, I strongly advise individuals to maintain their own personal websites. Th
will provide the greatest flexibility to tell your story and integrate links to your othe
profiles. Ultimately, this will give you the most control over your long-term image
versus being at the mercy of a service provider who can change its policies at any
time.

5. Focus on relationships, not followers. In recent years, there has been far too
much focus on metrics like "follower counts." Do those metrics even matter?
Actually, yes, they mean you have done a great job getting someone's attention and
making an initial impression. That is certainly a start. However, are you able to keep
the person's attention and get him or her to come back, and are you building a
trusting dialogue with him or her? Ultimately, it is the development of relationships,
not followers, that will produce results. Those relationships can more effectively
perpetuate a buzz, result in the endorsement of others, and even produce the referrals
you may be seeking.

6. Deliver unique content. Although there is value in forwarding a newly found best
practice, study, or insight to an associate, one should focus on producing unique
content as well. If you are a thought leader, your ideas may become a catalyst to
create positive change for others. If you do not consider yourself a thought leader,
perhaps putting your own spin on a subject will make it more meaningful to your
audience.

The authors of *Groundswell* (Li and Bernoff 2008) have identified six groupings of
online U.S. adults. One group, content creators, represents only 18 percent of online
U.S. adults, with 25 percent being critics and 48 percent spectators. By deciding to
deliver unique content, you will clearly set yourself apart as a member of the 18
percent minority.

7. Network, purposefully. With the recent explosion of social networking tools
across the business landscape, it is easy to get caught up in superficial metrics.
However, building an effective personal network goes beyond simple connections. It
takes time to build relationships, and with the fixed amount of time available to each
of us, it would only make sense that there are a limited number of true relationships
that we can maintain. According to a theory called Dunbar's number, each of us can
only manage around 150 social relationships. Arguments have been made, however,
to suggest that technology has allowed us to surpass that figure. Nevertheless, there
is a practical limit, and so when you reach out to make a connection, think about how
you will organize those connections, and clearly identify the relationships you want
to build.

build social equity. You have probably heard of the term *brand equity,* which relates to the value of a given brand name in a market. For an individual, a more useful term may be *social equity.* According to Wikipedia, *social equity* is defined as "the perceived value of an individual, organization, or brand's reputation and following online. This value increases or decreases based on the online buzz and conversations that take place across the various social media channels on the internet which ultimately transcend to the offline world."To build your social equity, look for ways to make meaningful contributions. This may include posting public content via your website, posting slides on Slideshare, or submitting comments on other blogs. An ongoing, consistent commitment to these types of contributions will go a long way toward building your social equity and online presence.

9. Integrate to magnify your results. Without integration, you leave it up to the individual to assemble the pieces of the puzzle to find you. A well-integrated strategy accomplishes a couple important things:

1. It connects the dots for people, allowing them to see your contributions across the multiple venues in which you participate. That helps build your personal brand image and provides value to your audience by connecting them with other people and resources that they may not otherwise have found.

2. It reduces your workload. Manually posting to each resource is time consuming and self-limiting. By implementing a well-thought-out and integrated strategy, you can magnify your efforts. For example, you can make a single post to Twitter that will automatically get replicated to Facebook and your website, after which an RSS feed can propagate it to other networks and subscribers.

10. Be genuine, and in for the long haul. Building trust online takes time, but losing that trust can happen quickly. We are all too familiar with those trying to make a quick buck or drive other very short term results. Remaining committed to your passion for the sake of creating positive impact will help build trust. Be genuine in your contributions, and others will be more likely to respond positively.

11. "Get in the ring" and build your confidence. One of the greatest benefits from jumping in with both feet is the knowledge and confidence you will gain from participating. Your contributions will have a positive impact on some, and their feedback will propel you. But as previously mentioned, remember that there are 25 percent critics out there, too, and you may hear from a few. Learn and grow from it, but don't let it stop you from advancing your career to the highest levels.

Reference

Li, C., and J. Bernoff. 2008. *Groundswell: Winning in a World Transformed Social Technologies*. Cambridge, MA: Harvard Business Press.

<u>Bio</u>

Scott A. Pete is a peak results strategist and coach, writer, and speaker who specializes in the application of business technologies to drive marketing results. He has worked with dozens of companies to translate strategic visions into practical implementation road maps to solve business challenges successfully. Scott can be reached at scott@peakresultscoaching.com, www.peakresultscoaching.com

9

BRIDGE the Gap in Your Career

✦

Dawn Quesnel

Once upon a time, you could get a degree, land a job with a great company that would take care of you, rise steadily through the ranks, and retire thirty years later with a sweet pension and a few great memories.

Unfortunately, that scenario exists today only in the employment history books and a few isolated corners of the business world. As anyone who watches the news can tell you, job security is no longer a given, no matter how hard you work. Rampant layoffs and corporate restructuring have kicked thousands of would-be lifers to the curb, and so employees have responded in kind, taking their job security and financial future into their own hands.

At any given time, 50 percent of the work force is seeking a new job or considering a career change. In May 2010, there were 3.2 million job openings in the United States but more than four million job separations (Bureau of Labor Statistics 2010). That means that either you, or the person standing next to you, is actively looking for a new job right now. It also means that whereas companies are picky about whom they hire and hold on to, individuals are being just as selective about where, and for whom, they work.

Becoming laser clear about what you want from your career is the first step to making it materialize. My BRIDGE career search strategy process is designed to help you do just that—and then to help you put this information to work for you.

BRIDGE is an acronym for the six steps in my highly successful career search strategy. The BRIDGE process is designed to help you bridge the gap between where you are and where you want to be so you can accelerate your career and love your life!

1. **Become clear** about what you're looking for. Can you clearly artic[ ] what you want in your career? If you're not sure, notice the differences [ ] tween these three responses:

   - "I am looking for a project manager position."
   - "I am looking for a project manager position in the advertising industry."
   - "I am looking for a project manager position in the advertising industry, working on health care accounts."

   The last response, of course, is the clearest—but don't stop there. Become clear on the type of company culture in which you want to work, the tasks and projects on which you want to be working, how long your commute will be, your salary, and what a day in a life in your new career will look like. Write these down, make lists, and write mission statements. Come up with a clear definition of your dream career. The more clearly you articulate what you're looking for, the more likely you will be to find it.

2. **Research** companies that hire for the specific positions in which you're interested. Take note of what key words they are using to describe the position, then look at your résumé: is it in alignment? This is very important. After all, you'd never set an account or marketing strategy without doing the research first, would you? Your career search is a business, too, so treat it like one. How can networking help you increase your contact list and get the word out?

3. **Identify** your target market. For which companies do you want to work? For which do you most definitely *not* want to work? Which companies can best utilize your expertise and skill sets?

4. **Develop** your résumé or CV and your list of contacts. Now that you have clearly defined the type of position you're after, and you've researched your target market, you will be better equipped to articulate your goals to your contacts. Ask your contacts if they know anyone in the companies you're targeting, and have your résumé close to hand.

   Also, don't forget to talk to your dentist, doctor, house cleaner, neighbors, relatives, recruiters, and even former boss. Utilize your alumni resources. You never know who might have a connection to a contact. You can expand your list of contacts by using tools like LinkedIn and Zoominfo.com.

5. **Get a game plan!** Set aside time to write out a game plan. This can be very simple, such as a bulleted list of items to support your search initiatives for the week, or it can be more complex. Whatever you choose, make sure it's specific. Instead of jotting down "send out résumés," try writing, "Go to office supply store to choose paper, send résumés to John and Beth, get fax number/e-mail for Company X." Keep track of when and where you've

sent résumés, and follow up. Attend networking events, and attend industry-specific association meetings and/or groups. Eighty percent of all jobs filled are filled through networking, 20 percent through ads; most people spend all their time sending out résumés from behind their computers and miss 80 percent of the opportunities. Conduct informational interviews, use article marketing to help you tap into the hidden job market, and develop new relationships.

6. **Execute and evaluate.** Remember that even the best plans need to have concrete action behind them to succeed. It's not going to happen by itself. Block off time in your calendar to execute, evaluate, and adjust your strategy as needed.

You are the sole driving force behind your life and career. When you take charge, make a plan, and work to follow through, you're stepping up to take the wheel of destiny and building your own bridges to a fantastic future.

Once you've built the BRIDGE, you'll want to be sure to avoid these *Top 5 Things That Can Kill Your Candidacy*:

1. **Not being up to date with technology.** If your skills are outdated, look into the many available classes, buy a book, or take a course online. Get up to date!

2. **Staying with the same company for too long.** Yes, I will be bold enough to say it because I see it all the time! This is not a myth; being with the same company beyond fifteen years, even if you have moved up the ranks, can hurt your personal brand. The concern often is that the person is stalled in his or her career and isn't expanding his or her skills aggressively enough and can be considered stale. Other times, the fear is that no matter how qualified the candidate is, he or she won't be able to adapt to a new company very easily.

3. **Applying for positions for which you are overqualified.** Some say it's a numbers game, but sending your résumé for just any open position, especially if you are over- or under qualified, doesn't make a good impression.

4. **Sending a generic cover letter.** The more you can target your cover letter to the specific skill set the prospective employer described in the job description, the better response you'll receive. Think about the objections the prospective employer might have when reviewing your résumé.

5. **Sharing your salary history.** Online forms and filling out applications can be tedious; however, if you fail to leave the salary section blank, employers can view you as unwilling to comply with guidelines, somewhat difficult, or unable to follow instructions. You never want to write in a specific number or give a range; instead write or respond with one of the following: "would

be happy to discuss in an interview," "open," or "negotiable." Do y~~~
search on where the salary for the position should be. Get the employ~~~
speak first about the range of the position, and ask for a job description.

Reference

Bureau of Labor Statistics. 2010. Jon openings and labor turnover–September 2010. Press release. http://www.bls.gov/news.release/pdf/jolts.pdf.

<u>BIO</u>

Dawn Quesnel, CPCC, PCC (aka Coach DQ), is a professional certified coach, speaker, radio show host, and workshop leader who helps sales, marketing, advertising, and creative entrepreneurs accelerate their careers so they'll love their lives! Before becoming a coach, Dawn was a record-breaking executive recruiter at two of Boston's premier agencies; now she uses her unique and powerful combination of skills to help clients reduce their job searches by half the time, while helping them take their careers and personal lives to the next level. Learn more about Dawn at http://www.coachdq.com.

10

BUSINESS DEVELOPMENT

The Fastest Way to Build a $100,000+ a Year Business

Discover the 7-Step Success Blueprint to Building a 6-Figure Business

Stephen Cabral

One of the scariest things about starting a new business or trying to build up the business of your dreams is not knowing whether it will succeed. Let's face it: you don't want to take an enormous risk that could leave you without the ability to pay your rent or mortgage.

The good news is that there is a solution to your concerns, and it involves following a step-by-step process that is tried and true. People have been using this powerful method for decades with amazing success.

I didn't personally discover this secret formula until just a few years back, and even then, I wasn't using it properly. Now that I've fine-tuned the process, I know that what I've developed will enable me never to have to worry about making money again.

Ever.

The reason I feel this way is because I've formulated a 7-Step Success Blueprint to Building a 6-Figure Business in under a year's time.

I know that may seem like an ad or something to that extent, but I can assure you it isn't. Plus, in just a few seconds from now, I'm going to reveal my entire blueprint to you so that you can copy my success.

As I've said before, it's worked for decades, and now that I've broken down system into manageable steps, you can enjoy the same business-building succ without having to go through all the trial and error that I had to.

Now, before we get into the system, I'm sure you're probably wondering why I'm giving away my coveted blueprint for building a $100,000+ a year business in this book. There are actually two reasons:

1. I know that the majority of the people who will read this will think that it is a great idea, but they'll find some excuse for why they can't start it or why it won't work for them. Remember, everyone wants to be wealthy, but only a select few actually take action. Unfortunately, I know very few people will ever use these strategies.

2. The second reason is that after you've achieved a high level of success, it is imperative that you give back. It truly is the only way to express your gratitude for how far you've come. If you hoard all your secrets and do not teach others, then you can't possibly expect to take your success to the next level. I consider my success articles like this one my way of giving back to people who are in the same position I was in not too long ago.

Now, let's get into how you will create your new six-figure business this year.

One of the worst ways to get new clients is to look desperate by going after them and asking them to buy from you. No one wants to do business with someone whom he or she doesn't perceive as already having an established business or clientele.

Therefore the first thing we need to do is establish you as the expert. The best way to do that is by having you publish your own book. Now, before you say there is no way you could ever write a book, we need to reframe your beliefs about what a book actually is and how you should be using it to promote your new business.

Most people believe that they need to sit down and write a four- to five-hundred-page novel, but nothing could be further from the truth. Plus, no one has time anymore to read long books—your customer wants the information he or she needs in under one to two hundred pages.

Remember, you're going to write a how-to or information-based publication that will help your ideal client or customer gain new knowledge on a topic he or she is trying to find answers to.

There are also many easy ways to write a book. You could simply speak into a recorder and then have the audio transcribed very inexpensively, or you could just

: a series of short articles or steps (chapters) outlining how to accomplish the
cific goal that your customer has in mind.

The other piece of this equation is that you can self-publish the book yourself and
have copies printed as needed (or even put it on Amazon.com). The other option is
just turning your book or "special report" into a PDF for online download. This may
also come as a shock, but the goal of publishing a book should never be to make
money on the book sales! I know that sounds crazy, and that's why very few people
know about this secret blueprint. The goal is actually to get your new publication
into as many people's hands as possible so that they can read your material and view
you as the expert in your field.

After they finish reading all the great content you put in your book, you'll make an
offer for the product to fix the problem that they are seeking answers to, or you'll
offer your coaching program on the last page of the book. Now, if you really don't
feel comfortable writing, you can always create a CD or DVD on which you give a
spoken presentation and then make the same offer at the end of your talk.

Now, let's quickly go through the 7-Step Success Blueprint:

Step 1. Offer a free or low-cost self-published book, CD, or DVD.

Step 2. Provide new and useful content to your ideal customer niche.

Step 3. Price the product that you will be selling at the end of your book
according to your niche's price threshold. Lower-end markets typically start
at $47, and higher-end coaching groups range all the way from $10,000 to
$25,000.

Step 4. Offer an e-mail address or Web link for more information on your
product or coaching program on the last page of your book so that customers can contact you for purchases.

Step 5. Deliver your product digitally right through your website, mail a
hard product to your new customer, or deliver your phone coaching sessions
on Skype.

Step 6. Figure out how many sales you will need to make $100,000 a year,
or whatever your specific goal is. Just eighty-six sales a month of a $97
product equals $100,000 a year, with no additional work on your part.
That's only 2.7 sales a day! If you sold a higher-end coaching program for
$497, you would only need seventeen sales a month! And if you sold a
program where the investment was $297 a month for three months, you

would only need 9.5 sales a month to make $100,000 a year! Do you see possibilities?

Step 7. When you multiply the formula I just laid out for you with additional product lines or service offerings, your profit potential is limitless, and all you have to do is do the math to calculate how many sales you would need to create a $250,000, $500,000, or $1,000,000+ business.

Don't believe for second that you can't do this—you can. Your new $100,000 business awaits you, and I truly hope my article served as a blueprint for you to begin. Remember, too, that if you use the formula I just outlined, then you will have clients coming directly to you already sold on your products and services—and that's the easiest and greatest type of business in the world.

I sincerely wish you all the best, and I can't wait to hear your success story soon!

BIO

For more free, complete details and resources on the 7-Step Success Blueprint as well as other helpful tips, go to http://www.CabralSuccessSolutions.com/. Stephen Cabral is an expert in the field of helping others create the businesses of their dreams. He focuses on breaking down the complex to allow his clients to use their passion for helping others, while building a highly profitable business. Stephen also offers an exclusive mentorship program on how to create a secure business future through multiple streams of income. For more information on Stephen Cabral's Exclusive Private Coaching Program, go to http://www.CabralSuccessSolutions.com/ for details.

11

Business Networking for Career Success

≈≈≈

Loretta Peters

Whatever employment situation you are in, you must network for career success. Because it is likely you already know many people, leveraging and expanding your network today will make searching for your next career opportunity much easier.

What Is Business Networking?

If you're still not clear what business networking is, let's just say that when you engage groups of like-minded people, business and employment opportunities have a tendency to be found, whether it's for your benefit or someone else's.

Getting Started

Family, friends, clients, prospects, your dentist and accountant, your boss, and the people in your office are part of your network. Having the awareness of who is in your network will help you when you have a specific need.

Organizing Your Network

Keep an active list of people in your network with phone numbers and e-mails so you can touch base regularly. Enter your list in a contact management tool. Then create categories or groups (e.g., clients, prospects, chamber members) that make it easy for searching and sending targeted communications such as e-newsletters. Manage your network by tracking how often you are in communication with each group.

Where to Build Your Business Network

Reaching your network through social media, blogs, and Skype, where messages can be sent to anyone around the world, is a way to stay connected daily. That said,

combining Internet networking methodologies with face-to-face business netwc
is a win-win strategy for business networking success.

Develop Your Strategy

Business networking is often strategic and involves a personal commitment. Having
a strategy or plan will help you generate better results, for example,

- Do you want to meet decision makers?
- Do you need resources in a vertical market?
- Are you looking for a new job?
- Do you need feedback on a new idea?

Knowing why you want to build your business network will help you stay focused
on accomplishing your goals. This includes choosing events that make the most
sense for you to attend or sponsor.

Networking at Chamber Events, Business Journal Events, Charitable Events, Trade Shows, and National and International Events

Being prepared before attending any business event is highly encouraged. Knowing
what the event is about and researching the industry beforehand will prepare you for
successful encounters with others. Expect industry experts to be in attendance, and
invest some time learning about current hot topics so that you feel comfortable
conversing with them.

Arrive early so you can see the name tags of those who are expected to attend.
Whenever possible, ask to see the attendee list. If you or your company is sponsoring
an event, the attendee list is usually included. Look for people who may know the
people you want to meet, then ask for an introduction.

Building Dialogue

Whether your introduction lasts for a few minutes or longer, asking questions that
will engage the other person will help in developing rapport. Business topics are an
easy way to establish mutual trust without getting too personal.

Your goal is to establish a connection, collect a business card, and move on to the
next person. This is a courtesy to the person you just met. Then it is your
responsibility to follow up within a few days and invest in building the relationship.
This is an important step to growing and sustaining your network that will pay off
over time.

Networking in Global, National, and Regional Organizations

...here can you find valuable connections? In your own organization! As you find ...pportunities in other departments at your company, how will you get in front of the executive team who will hire you?

If you need to learn how a department in which you are interested operates, ask some team members to lunch (this is networking). Listen for challenges that you could help solve if you were part of the team. The more knowledge you have about the department before meeting with the executive team puts you in a better position for the job.

Next, understanding how your talents, skills, and experience contribute to solving problems in the department for which you are applying is good information for your résumé. If you need help with this, e-mail me at the address given in the following bio. Also, as you grow your network internally, think whom you can ask for a reference.

Now think of how you will introduce yourself to the executive team. E-mail, interoffice mail, phone, through another colleague, or while attending an event is acceptable. In your conversation, mention a few ways you could help the team with your background, then send your résumé and cover letter and follow up weekly with another idea of how you could help the department. Whether you land the job, you will have established some credibility for yourself, and this could lead to another job referral from an executive.

Networking Using Social Media

Are you using social media regularly to build your business network? If not, you are missing out. LinkedIn is the preferred social media platform for business and is a great way to reach your network daily. I've scheduled several business meetings using LinkedIn and Facebook at 10:00 p.m., and you could too. You can learn everything about LinkedIn through its help center online. However, if you need help using these tools, e-mail me.

LinkedIn Groups for Business Networking

Much like organizing groups into a database, you can use LinkedIn groups to do the same. The only difference is that you invite LinkedIn members already within your network to join. Once members join your group, you can engage with them about specific business matters any time. You can also share links to specific information that demonstrates your thought leadership in a particular area of expertise. This is great for building your personal brand and replacing traditional e-mail.

Your Résumé as a Network Tool

Since employers and recruiters will most likely Google you after you send them résumé, using key words from your résumé in your LinkedIn profile and other social media is a way to use your résumé as a networking tool. If you are using more than one social media site, it is important that your message be consistent across platforms, or it could affect your chances of getting hired. Thinking about your online networking strategy so that it is consistent and generates the results you are expecting is the way to go.

Building a Business Network for Life:
10 Tips for Building and Sustaining Your Business Network

1. Network outside of your organization by attending or sponsoring local events.
2. Have a clear brand message that communicates what you do in ten seconds.
3. Reconnect with those from past jobs.
4. Stay in touch regularly.
5. Use a contact management system.
6. Find ways to help your network.
7. Be a thought leader in your industry.
8. Give more than you get.
9. Keep growing your network.
10. Always carry business cards.

Bio

Loretta leads personal brand marketing programs for businesses and professionals that include social media, networking, personal brand development, online identity management, and online brand awareness used for today's talent management, marketing, and advertising. Loretta graduated with a BA in business administration, with a minor in English. She maintains several certifications in personal branding, online identity management, and social media. Loretta is one of twenty-four Master Résumé Writers in the United States through the ResumeWritingAcademy and is a member of several associations. To learn more, visit http://www.EnterprisingCareers.com/.

12

Creating a Career Brand in the New Web 2.0 World

∻

Jessica Simko

The explosion of social media in today's society has created a whole new way of life—a new way to communicate, a new way of doing business, and even a new way of finding and keeping a job. Job seekers and employees are finding out that this new Web 2.0 world is nothing like what it used to be even as recently as two or three years ago. Whether you are out of work, looking for a different job, or striving for a promotion, the key to your success depends on you and your ability to create, build, and sustain a strong career brand.

Utilizing social media and understanding how, when, and why to use them is not everything, but it is a key component in building your career brand. The various social mediums can give you a tremendous advantage in your job search as they allow you to have more control over your own destiny. They give you the ability to literally "brand yourself" into your ideal job. However, if not used carefully, they can also sabotage any future opportunities and possibly even your career.

There are too many people who know so little about how social media come into play in a job search or in their work lives, or why they even need a career brand. Those who know little to nothing about social media are competing with those who do and are using them. How can the former measure up against the latter? They can't, and they don't.

What Is a Career Brand?

If you are utilizing social media tools, such as Facebook, LinkedIn, Twitter, YouTube, blogging platforms, or any other social media venue, you are creating your own personal brand—an online image of yourself. This can be an intentional process, but for many, it is an unintentional process. Whatever public content you have posted or published online creates your personal brand or your online image.

46

Seventy to eighty percent of employers are using search engines to seek out information about potential employees and consider the findings as part of their recruiting processes. Doing so now gives employers the opportunity to learn more about you and your personal life, and it can make or break you in the job market. Your personal brand must be managed properly, or it will be a struggle (if not impossible) for you to find and keep the right job.

A career brand does not consist ofall the unique things you do and say online that ultimately create your online image; those are the elements that make up your personal brand. Rather a career brand is*you* positioning yourself at the center of your career interests, passions, talents, and strengths and building a strong presence through which you can showcase your expertise and gain interest and trust from employers and clients.

A career brand consists of anything and everything that has to do with how you present yourself in relation to your career and/or career goals. To a potential employer, your career brand may start with a Google search which could allow them to learn more about you, but once you pass that test, it then leads to a conversation on the phone, in-person interviews, salary negotiations, and ultimately, the onboarding process. You will then continuously be assessed and evaluated until the day you leave the company.

ne anyone is assessing or evaluating you, you must be conscious about
ing a strong brand for yourself. Your ability to advance in a company and to be
ognized as a leader depends entirely on how you present yourself. Consider how
u want to be perceived, and what your career goals are as that will be your starting
oint when creating your career brand.

Your Two Online Brands

Many people do have two online brands. You can have an online brand that is only a
personal brand, a combination of a personal and career brand, or only a career brand.
Whether your brand is a personal brand, a career brand, or a combination of both
depends on whether you create and post content that is related to your personal life,
your professional life, or both.

While your career brand does go far past your online presence, you can and should
have an online career brand to add value to your personal brand. You can create an
online career brand around your current job and company, or you can create one
around the career niche you are trying to obtain (e.g., creating a leadership brand if
you are trying to become a manager). Whatever you create it around, it is essential
that you work toward creating a career brand that is centered around your career
passions because spending your days doing work you love doing is a key component
to creating a rewarding and fulfilling life.

It should go without saying that your brand should present you as a positive,
energetic, self-motivated, and career-minded professional. However, many people
utilize social media without much thought at all. When posting content in a public
venue, that content should represent the best of who you are, and if your current
manager or potential employer should view it, he or she should walk away feeling
more confident in you and your abilities rather than unimpressed and concerned
about your character.

If you post high-level content online, it can have a huge benefit in your job search
and career. For example, you can create a blog around your career and/or brand.
You can also join career-related discussions in the various LinkedIn groups, answer
questions, or even create YouTube videos around professional topics of interest.
Intentionally creating high-level content that can be found by your employer or a
potential employer is very powerful because it allows you to brand yourself as an
expert in your field and be recognized as one by the very people who have the
ability to provide you with potential opportunities. Online networking, when done
properly, can open up doors and provide opportunities that simply can't be found
any other way.

The Elements of a Career Brand

There are ten elements that make up your total career brand. It is important understand that only two of the ten elements are actually created and built entirely online. There are many other critical factors that must be considered to build a strong and effective brand:

1. Online career brand (your intentional efforts to brand yourself into your career niche)

2. Online personal brand (the combination of everything that Google can find out about you online)

3. Job search strategy

4. Résumé and cover letter

5. Interview skills

6. Personal appearance

7. Work style (how you plan, implement, and execute; how well you work with others; leadership skills)

8. Attitude (beliefs, behaviors, morals, and values; emotional intelligence)

9. Education and training

10. Groups and associations (where you are or should be a member, including any speaking engagements that may result)

Why Is Career Branding Important?

Whether you are striving for your first job, a new job, a career change, or a promotion, building a strong and sustainable career brand will position you at the center of your interests, skills, and talents and enable you to drive your career on your own terms.. By utilizing various social media resources, you have the ability to freely showcase all your knowledge on any topic and even be seen as an expert in a field in which you have never worked before. By being mindful of your work style, attitude, and appearance, you can brand yourself as a leader at work whether or not you are in a management role. By networking in professional groups and associations, you can brand yourself as an expert, earn respect from influential leaders and ultimately become one yourself.

The key to career branding is making the right people aware of who you are and what you have to offer. Above all else, you must work hard and make yourself stand out. A strong career brand, with all its components, will cause the right people to take notice and will bring new opportunities. Managing your personal and career

nas to be a conscious and continuous process as you gain new skills and
ience.

member, this is *your* life and *your* career. Creating and building a strong and
sustainable brand will help you maximize your true potential and allow you to reap
the benefits that only an enjoyable and meaningful career can bring. This is a plan
that is easily attainable! We are not meant to have a career created by chance or by
others. There is no better time than now to make the decision to take control of your
future. Decide to drive down your own path, on your own terms, and simply choose
to pursue a career in the way that will bring you the highest levels of happiness,
achievement, and success.

BIO

Jessica Simko is a seasoned senior-level human resources professional with over
fifteen years of experience in all facets of human resources management. She is a
career coach and consultant specializing in helping all levels of professionals create,
build, and sustain a strong career brand. She strives to help connect people to their
passions and to leverage their brands in their job searches and careers. Utilizing the
career branding model, she offers job search and career branding articles and tips and
a variety of coaching and consulting services at the Career Branding Guide
(http://www.careerbrandingguide.com/).

13

Should I Stay or Update My Résumé?
Knowing When It's Time to Go

≈⤳

Leslie Attwooll

Are You Ready for a Career Change?

If you are one of the 50 percent of people who do not like their jobs, read on. Even if your career transition is not by choice, this is your invitation to have a more rewarding future. Career transition involves effectively managing your career. It requires knowing and honoring yourself. We often get into a position, get comfy, and neglect to conduct periodic self-evaluations. This chapter outlines the steps of making a successful career transition and also shows you how to recognize when it's time to go.

What's Your Job Stage?

As a career coach, I usually meet clients at the last stages of their jobs—you know, where the straw is breaking the camel's back. Understanding job stages will help you become aware of when to initiate your next move. Think back to when you started your job. It was new and, I hope, exciting. There was some angst navigating the new terrain as you were learning the nuts and bolts of your job. You gradually became masterful, gaining institutional knowledge to get things done. Being actively engaged at this stage can cause delays in your thinking ahead. The last stage is when you are confident in your role, your boss gets out of your way, and even brings coffee. Don't wait for this last stage to start strategizing. The middle stage of gaining mastery is when to start preparing next steps.

Google's Red Pushpin

I recently visited rural Texas and the red pushpin on my Google map app was invaluable. What a great feeling to arrive at the dirt road of my journey (which was also red). Think about it: to move forward in your career, you must first know where

are. Put aside the water cooler gossip, the antics on *Housewives*, and whatever
y be distracting you; get your red pushpin and map ready; and start your career
urney, which begins with self-exploration.

What do you value? What's important to you? What are you good at? List the
achievements, work preferences, and skills that are transferable to other careers. This
insight will help you make a sound decision on whether to stay in your current
position, change jobs, or even change professions.

A big plus of self-exploration is that you will interview better. A job candidate who
knows his or her strengths can effectively communicate what he or she will offer a
prospective employer, thus having a better shot at getting hired. To download some
free self-exploration exercises, go to http://www.CareerLunchBag.com/101GreatWays.

Current Job "Pulse Check"

- **The job.** Do you enjoy your work? Are you learning or stagnating? Is your
  field or industry growing? Is there a sense of accomplishment, meaning,
  and/or purpose?
- **Compensation and benefits.** Are you paid fairly for the work you perform
  and the hours you put in? Are you earning enough to support your lifestyle?
  Can you prepare for retirement?
- **Relationships with management.** Do you receive regular feedback? Does
  management show by their actions that they care? Are organizational goals
  and your role clearly communicated?
- **Relationships with colleagues.** Do you like the people with whom you
  work? Are colleagues cooperative and fun?
- **Company.** Do your values line up with those of the company? Are you
  proud to work there? Is the company committed to providing exceptional
  customer service?

Which Way Do I Go?

Two excellent career evaluation tools include conducting Yellow Pages research and
informational interviews.

The Yellow Pages can help you scope out interesting corporate, nonprofit, educational,
and government entities. Grab a copy or go to http://www.SuperPages.com.

1. Review each category and note any you find interesting.
2. Narrow your selections to ten, then to five.
3. Of the five, get contact information of three businesses from each category.

Conducting informational interviews expands your network, which can lead
offers. To ensure successful interviews, determine with whom you should spea
owner or manager, or a person in the role under consideration), and have
questions ready. Consider inquiring about the person's career journey, recommenc
education, important skills, most and least satisfying role aspects, work-life balanc
and earning potential. Ask to keep in touch to update the person on your progress.
This can open the door to an ongoing professional relationship.

Making Your Decision

After completing the exercises and looking at your options, what have you
discovered? What is your inner wisdom telling you? You may decide to stay where
you are. This could be an affirmation to remain in your profession but with another
company. You might decide to enter a brand-new field. My company, Balanced 6
Coaching, is based on a philosophy that integrates Career, Financial, Physical,
Relationships, Spirituality, and Self-Growth and Fun. As you weigh your career
options, consider each.

The Pros and Cons

This decision-making tool compares each career option against identified values,
needs, and skills. To complete the worksheet, follow these steps:

1.   Create a Values/Needs/Skills column. In each row, note what is important
     to have in a job. Be specific. If you need a window view or a 20-minute
     commute, write it down.

2.   To the right of the Values/Needs/Skills column, add a new column for each
     career option.

3.   Look at each row containing a value, need, or skill and compare these to
     each career option. Place a checkmark for each career that meets that value,
     need, or skill.

4.   Total your columns. What career has the highest score? What is this telling
     you?

ե:

Values, Needs & Skills	Career A *Designer*	Career B *Realtor*	Career C *Programmer*
Customer interaction	X	X	
Being creative	X		X
Solve complex problems	X		X
Manage people	X		
etc.			
TOTAL	4	1	2

Knowing When It's Time to Go

The following questions will help you evaluate whether it's time to update your résumé:

1. Are your contributions not appreciated?
2. Is it harder to get motivated?
3. Are your skills, talents, and abilities not utilized?
4. Do you have an internal battle between feeling OK and being angry?
5. Are your opinions not solicited or valued?
6. Is your industry or job changing for the worse?
7. Is the culture negative or toxic?
8. Are your ethics or values being compromised?
9. Do you desire a new challenge?
10. Have you developed a hopeless or helpless feeling about work?

If you answered yes to six or more questions, isn't it time for your exit strategy?

What If I Can't Decide?

If, after completing these exercises, you are still unsure of what career direction to pursue, I recommend taking an online vocational assessment. Go to http://www.CareerLunchBag.com/assessment and, for a reasonable fee, you will receive an extensive report giving you specific career options. Also, consider hiring your own personal career coach. Leverage his or her expertise and get quicker results.

Action-Cubed Goals

With your decision and career map in hand, your next steps will determine ho
serious you are about enhancing your career.

- **Staying?** What *three things* can give you greater job satisfaction?
- **Updating?** What *three things* will get you closer to your career goals?

Brainstorm, add these things to your calendar, and do them! These Action-Cubed
Goals (Action, Action, Action) involve taking three daily *action* steps. I emphasize
the word *action* because to arrive at your career destination, you must take action. To
assist you, connect with other readers via Twitter by tweeting your three Action-
Cubed goals and including #101Action in your tweets.

In conclusion, career transitions are a delightful journey. Be curious, face your fears,
and ask for directions along the way. Be committed to having career satisfaction.
Build a supportive network—it's easier than going it alone. Age is irrelevant (think
Betty White). Applaud short-term wins. Never ask permission to have the career you
want, and always ask for the job!

<u>BIO</u>

Leslie Attwooll is a career management expert, a national speaker, and author of
Should I Stay or Update My Resume? Take 5 Lunch Hours to Decide. She helps
individuals take control of their professional lives to identify, assess, decide on,
pursue, and secure rewarding jobs they love. As a certified professional coach, a
former headhunter, and an employee engagement manager at a Fortune 50 company,
Leslie offers a unique perspective on how to successfully manage one's career. In
addition to working with clients individually, she also delivers fun and engaging
workshops on career transition, career management, career satisfaction, and job
search skills. For more info and to receive Leslie's *free* career newsletter, go to
http://www.CareerLunchBag.com. Find Leslie on Twitter: @LeslieAttwooll.

14

The Masterpiece Job Search

꿿꿿

Michael Vignery

Most of us want our lives to have purpose and meaning, so let's give the word *job* a very practical definition. Regardless of what anyone says, your job is where you spend most of your life on this planet (at least, Monday through Friday, for thirty to fifty years). Your job, like it does for most people, represents where you make the largest share of your income during that thirty- to fifty-year period. With these two incredibly important facts in mind—and make no mistake about it, they are facts— doesn't it make sense to engineer your career with a *specific* strategy?

The question everyone asks is, how? How do I move forward with *my* particular set of circumstances? By the time you finish this article, the answer to this question will be delivered in an inspiring, true story, "The Masterpiece Job Search."

What Are the Benefits of Controlling Your Career?

- Living a quality of life that is full of passion
- Seeing a dramatic increase in self-esteem and confidence
- On Sunday, looking forward to Monday
- Interviewing with high-level people whom you select
- Avoiding phantom positions on the Web
- Not being at the mercy of who's hiring
- Eliminating repeated down-sizing
- Remaining current with changes in the marketplace
- Moving toward your potential versus "getting a job"
- Being proactive, not reactive
- Operating on an exclusive playing field
- Achieving balance between work and home

Working at something you don't care about is the very best way to waste your life. You will never be successful—truly successful—at a job you don't like. With these truths in mind, doesn't it make sense to reach out for your career potential? I assure you that most of your competition will be following our time-honored mant "I gotta get a job."

How Do You Control Your Career?

You can construct a masterpiece job search on a designed, creative basis. The following key checkpoints, which I call the Five-Step Blueprint, have worked repeatedly, year after year.

1. Install the belief that you have a very strong influence over your career. Without the belief that you—yes, you—are in charge, the other steps will never happen. The great thinkers are in agreement. The absolute number one skill you can develop is an awareness of how to master *your* mind. The best way to install this belief is focused, concentrated study on the unlimited power of your mind. Inner-world thoughts create your outer-world environment, *guaranteed.* Robert Collier, the great author, wrote, "Your chances of success in any undertaking can always be measured by your belief in yourself."

2. Create a crystal-clear vision of your ideal job. The number one reason the working population is uninspired is that people never decide what they want to accomplish in their professions. Absolutely no passion is involved. They simply want a job instead of finding meaning in their work.

You really need to answer these questions in terms of true meaning for your career:

- What am I truly passionate about?
- What industry do I want to work in, and why? (The *why* is big here!)
- What company or organization is my target? (It doesn't matter if it has advertised openings.)
- Where do I—or we—want to live?
- What is the ideal work environment for me on a day-to-day basis?
- What kind of income now, and potentially, would be satisfying?
- What do I do best from a *skill* standpoint?
- *What is the next step, based on my current set of circumstances?*

Well-thought-out answers to these questions will bring clarity to your end result. Remember that this is about what you *want*—not just what you *think* you can have.

3. Market your value. This is critical. What do employers want? *Return on investment*! Outstanding offers will appear when the decision maker realizes you can provide one or more of the following assets:

- Affecting the bottom line profitably
- Providing a competitive edge
- Increasing market share
- Improving internal processes
- Affecting morale positively
- Instituting creative problem solving

I can assure you that helping the employer with these challenges is very exhilarating, as opposed to limping along to the next job vacancy.

4. Begin at the finish line—the *top* of the organization. All of us have been programmed to pursue vacancies in the black hole of cyberspace. And who is your competition? Millions of job seekers. These numbers make the lottery look efficient.Take your solutions to the senior executive or business owner. Making a *positive impact on them* means you are hired!It is critical that you place yourself on this playing field. It is *exclusive*!

5. Constantly evaluate trends in the global marketplace. The career winds of change are blowing. This means you will have a phenomenal number of opportunities to reach your potential—more opportunities than we have ever seen in history. Once you, in fact, obtain your position, the strategy really begins. Keep moving forward. The openings are unlimited! Decide where you want to go in the years ahead, and be bold.

Stay current. Your opportunities will be incredible. You will see and feel the surge in all facets of your life.

Hard work and bumps in the road are part of this scenario. However, you can, and must, create your openings. Maintain your newly installed belief system, and you will succeed.

In any endeavor, there are classic performances; the arts, business, and sports have all seen events or creations that are ingenious. The sphere of activity called "job searching" is identical. The following story is characterized by enduring excellence. It brings all five steps of our blueprint together in a way that will greatly enhance your own personal search. The masterpiece is found in a great book by Napoleon Hill, *Think and Grow Rich*. Our star is a man named Edwin C. Barnes.

Masterpiece Job Search

Mr. Barnes climbed down from a freight train in Orange, New Jersey, toward the end of the twentieth century looking for a job. Reportedly, he resembled "a tramp," but apparently, he thought like a king. He did not know Thomas Edison, the famous inventor, and could not even pay the railroad fare to his destination in New Jersey. However, as he made his way from the railroad tracks to Thomas Edison's office, his mind was one of undeniable intent. He saw himself standing in Edison's presence. He heard himself asking Mr. Edison for an opportunity to carry out the one consuming obsession of his life: a burning desire to become the business associate of the great inventor! Barnes's desire was not a *hope*. It was not a *wish*. It was *definite*.

His desire was not a sudden impulse when he approached Edison. It had been Barnes's dominating desire for a long period of time. In the beginning, it may have been—probably was—only a wish, but it was no mere wish when he made contact.

According to Edison, "he looked like an ordinary tramp, but there was something in the expression of his face which conveyed that he was determined to get what he had come after. I gave him the opportunity he asked for, because I saw he had made up his mind to stand by until he succeeded." A few years later, Barnes was in business with Edison.

When the opportunity did come, it came in a way totally unexpected, which is very common and why many opportunities are missed. Thomas Edison had just perfected a dictating machine, and his sales staff were not overly enthusiastic about it. Basically, they thought it could not be sold without great effort. Barnes, however, knew he could sell the dictating machine and suggested this to Edison. He promptly got his chance. He was so successful at selling the machine that Edison gave him an exclusive contract to distribute and market it nationwide. Out of that business association, Barnes made himself rich from his partnership with Edison. Obviously, Barnes did not become the partner of Thomas Edison the day he arrived. He was content to start in the most menial position, as long as it provided an *opportunity* to take even one step toward his ultimate goal.

Let's take an exhilarating snapshot of what happened. Edwin Barnes was a penniless, tramplike individual with no education and no connections. He became a business partner of who could be considered the Bill Gates–type figure of that era. In the process he became financially independent for the rest of his life. It is stimulating to look at the Five-Step Blueprint in relation to Edwin Barnes's accomplishments:

1. Did he have a total belief and burning desire to control his career? Absolutely yes.

2. Did Barnes create a crystal clear vision of his ideal job? Again, without a doubt, yes.

3. Did this ordinary citizen market his *value* to solve his problems? Yes!! Even though he did not have tangible skills, Edison recognized his possible benefit because of the way he presented himself (burning desire, absolute

certainty about what he wanted to do.) Did Edison have any advertised vacancy? No. Barnes created his own opportunity.

4. Did he *begin* at the finish line: the top of the organization? Without question. Edison had the authority to offer him a position immediately. Barnes' first contact was at the pinnacle.

5. Did our overachiever constantly evaluate changing trends? Obviously. When the opportunity arose, Barnes pounced on the chance. The reason? He had been carefully scrutinizing tendencies within the organization for five years. His entire life changed because he was patient and observant. The other employees were simply content being employed.

This Five-Step Blueprint can change your life if it is followed intently. I'm sure you don't face the hardships Mr. Barnes did; however, if you do, it's important to know that they can be overcome due to the limitless power of your mind.

Mr. Barnes was not a hero. He was an ordinary chap sufficiently motivated to reach challenging goals. You can do the same, and more, if you choose! Never lose sight that *you will attract exactly what you think you deserve and expect.*

Now, let me nudge you a little. I sincerely hope that you will continue to dig into the five steps that we have discussed. (Really get to work with that shovel, because you are digging for pure gold.) Earnestly apply these steps to *your own* set of circumstances. When you do, you will change your quality of life and create your own Masterpiece Job Search.

BIO

Mr. Vignery's background features over thirty years of executive leadership at the Fortune 500 level. After a distinguished career in financial services, he transitioned into the career management industry. During the past eighteen years, he has successfully helped individuals engineer their own career paths and currently works with national and international clients. Contact Michael Vignery at vigneryintl@pcisys.net, or visit his website at http://www.MasterYourMind.org/.

15

Enhance Your Career by Changing It!

How to Make Sure Your Career Change Really Happens

❧❧❧

Cherry Douglas

One great way of enhancing your career is to change it! Leave the job you hate and make a fresh start in something that will inspire and motivate you.

Sounds great, doesn't it? But I'll bet there are quite a few of you who are thinking rather cynically, "Yeah, right! Easier said than done." Changing a career is not a quick-fix exercise—it takes time, effort, and motivation, and it is the motivation bit that often seems to scupper the most well-intentioned career changer.

We all have days when motivation wavers and doubt creeps in, but motivation typically operates on a scale from low to high, and you will find yourself at different points on that scale from day to day. Your challenge is to understand what influences your motivation and to begin to manage these more consciously.

What Influences Your Motivation?

Attitude to Change

What is your experience of change in your life so far? Do you see change as something to be welcomed and expect that it will lead to positive results, or do you regard change with suspicion?

Take a look at your own attitude and be ready to challenge it if it is holding you back. Look for evidence of changes that have worked in your life to boost your commitment to pushing forward with your career change plans.

Limiting Beliefs

Limiting beliefs are habitual ways of thinking, often expressed using words such as *must*, *always*, and *never*:

- Work is hard.
- Anything less than the best is failure.
- I must do what is expected of me.
- I'm not good enough.

These beliefs can often lie behind your failing motivation. However, although they are well ingrained, they are still within your control. The best way to overcome these beliefs is to actively challenge them and seek positive alternative beliefs to replace them. Take each of your limiting beliefs and ask,

- What evidence is there for this belief? Do words like *must*, *always*, and *never* really apply?
- In what way is this belief unhelpful to my career change plans?
- What would be a more helpful, alternative belief?
- What can I do to build up evidence for this alternative belief?

Use these questions to dispute your negative beliefs, and whenever you find your old thinking habits stopping you, consciously apply your new alternative beliefs instead.

Fear

This is the biggie—you are afraid of all the things that could go wrong. How come we spend so much time imagining the negatives instead of working on how we can realize the positives?

Feeling fear when you are facing a charging bull is very valid, but letting fear that you might be charged by a bull stop you from taking a country walk is not. Yet it is a fear of *what has not yet happened* that holds so many of us back.

Evaluate the realistic probability of what you fear about career change actually happening. Put your fears in their place, and then focus on what you can do to make positive outcomes more likely.

Other People

Sometimes your friends and family can be your worst enemies. They want to keep you safe, and so they discourage you from being bold and striking out in a new direction. They try to impose their limiting beliefs on you—with the best o. intentions, of course.

Your challenge is to seek out people who will energize and support you, friends who are enthusiastic about your plans and to whom you can turn for a boost when your motivation is flagging. Make sure you spend more time with these people to counteract the naysayers in your circle.

Lack of Time

We are all so frantically busy these days that it is easy to believe that you just don't have the time to make the changes you want. Take a look at how you spend your time. Create a timetable of what you do each day for a week or so, and see where your time really goes. Then rate the activities on a 1–4 scale for importance and begin to question the time you spend on each. Who else could do some of those tasks, and what would happen if some of them were never done? I'll bet you have more time than you thought and that some of that could go toward your career change plans.

Self-Motivation Techniques

Look for Patterns

Become a curious observer of your own motivation levels and moods. Look back to situations when you were motivated. What gave you that energy boost? Was it that you had positive people around you? Or that you were very clear about what you were trying to achieve? Or maybe you'd just had a good night's sleep for a change! What can you do now to re-create more of the positive mood states that you have felt in the past?

Talk to Your "Stuck Self"

You may realize that there's a part of you that is resisting change. What do you do about it?

Start by visualizing that "stuck" part of you. Make it as real as you can. Ask yourself what feelings that stuck part of you is communicating (e.g., I'm afraid, I'm angry, I'm overwhelmed). Then talk with this stuck part:

- What are you afraid of?
- What do you need?
- What is difficult for you?
- What would help you get moving again?

e gently curious and supportive of your stuck self, and see what emerges. Negotiate
a way forward that will allow you to take some small actions but still acknowledge
the underlying feelings.

Reward Yourself

You can also boost your motivation using rewards as an incentive. Choose
something you can give yourself when you have made some progress. This could be
as small as a cup of coffee and a chocolate chip cookie after you have made one
phone call, or it could be a weekend away when you have researched and chosen the
training course you will take to prepare for your new career. Generally, small
rewards for small steps are the most effective if you are feeling a bit stuck.

Record Your Progress

A long journey like a career change is made up of many small steps and successes.
They may not feel all that significant at the time, and so it is easy to feel that you are
not achieving much. This can leave you feeling discouraged.

One of my favorite techniques to keep motivation levels up is to keep a success
diary. Each evening, record at least three things you have achieved toward your goal.
They do not have to be big things—any moves in the right direction are worthwhile.
Recording these actions will help confirm that you *are* progressing, and looking back
through your list can give you a real boost when you think you are getting nowhere.

Reconnect with Your Career Change Goal

Possibly the most inspiring of self-motivation techniques is to revisit what originally
prompted your career change plans:

- What started you on this career change journey? What spurred you into
  action, and what will be the benefits when you have made the change?
- Imagine yourself in five years' time, happily settled into your new work.
  Now write a letter *in the presenttense* to a friend describing how your life is
  now. Make it feel real!

Ask yourself, *how will I feel next year if I give up and just go back to where I was
before?*

BIO

Cherry Douglas is your Career Change Guide. She has worked as a career professional for twenty-five years and has supported many clients through successful career transitions. Building on her own experience of career change as well as on her professional expertise, she has created the How to Change Careers website (http://www.how-to-change-careers.com/), a self-help site for career changers worldwide. She is the author of *Know Your Personality, Know Your Career* and *The CV & Resume Workbook* and of numerous articles on career change issues. She runs her own career coaching practice in the United Kingdom (http://www.career-plan-coaching.com/).

16

Three Awesome Ways to Enhance Your Career

(As Seen through the Eyes of a Flight Attendant)

Bettina "Sparkles" Obernuefemann

1. Chicken or Beef?

Most flight attendants enjoying their work in the sky these days are not aware of the deluxe service that was available before they came along. Years ago, flight attendants gave the same free, premium service to everyone on the entire airplane, not just to those seated in first class. Now, here they are, given the job of sellingpackaged food, instead of serving free, full-course meals, including choices. Many of those in client-service positions in varied industries are facing the same challenge: selling a product that was once part of a bundled package. How can we deal with this current challenge?

Like those in many positions, as a flight attendant, my colleagues and I were hired for our pleasant personalities and promises to meet customer satisfaction. Soon after, we were given training and a basic understanding of cost-efficient practices. We then combined our training with common sense. In today's economy, in which yesterday's standards (complimentary meals, free luggage, entertainment) have become luxuries, how can we exceed client expectations? When companies do not necessarily provide the same tools, training, and investment in their current-day employees, what can we, as employees, do to enhance our offered services within present-day standards?

Though standards and available resources have changed, people have not. Whether one is riding on a plane for business or pleasure, or a client is purchasing a given product or service, all people basically have the same needs as yesterday—and always.

Pretend you are sitting in a passenger seat on a flight, and think about how you would like to be treated. I'll bet the first thing that comes to mind is that you would really like to feel welcome. It is up to you in any client-service-oriented position to play your role well and *serve* cheerfulness. A caring smile and a friendly tone in your hello are a good start.

2. Will I Be There in Time to Make My Connection?

As a flight attendant, this and other critical questions that concern your flying guests are constantly coming your way. As in any industry, we are often challenged with deadlines that may not be met, projects that are slow to come to fruition, and client conflicts that need to be solved. What is the best way to handle these issues? Immediately speak positively, indicating that there is a solution to your client's problem. This gives you time to get informed and the client a chance to calm down. Say to your client, "I understand your concern, and I am doing such-and-such to solve your problem as quickly as possible." It's that simple. You can do it!

3. Congratulations!

Congratulations—you are established in your given career, and now you have discovered that not everything about your work is quite what you had dreamed it would be. Here is another ingredient to help you enhance your career: talk to yourself about appreciation. "I am glad I am here, and I am glad the client is here."

This will make you feel good and will help you treat both your internal and external customers with grace and kindness. Now you have created a win-win situation, and everyone is happy. That's the only way to fly!

Review of Three Awesome Ways to Enhance Your Career

1. Make each and every customer or client feel welcome.

2. Treat your clients as if they were guests, and let them know that you are available to help them.

3. Let appreciation be your guide.

I enjoyed contributing the preceding advice to my fellow flight attendants everywhere and feel that these basic principles are transferable to so many other careers. I experienced many ups and downs (no pun intended) during my years as a flight attendant from 1965 to 2003. This career offered many obstacles that I turned into opportunities for self-growth.

BIO

Bettina "Sparkles" Obernuefemann was born in Germany and presently lives in the north central Ozarks of Arkansas with her husband, Michael. She retired on July 31, 2003, after a thirty-eight-year flying career. She is devoting her new "free" time to writing, a creative effort, blending her love for flying with her dedication to her recovery from posttraumatic stress disorder. Visit her online at http://www.bettinasparkles.com/.

17

CAREER LEADERSHIP

Are You Leading Your Career?

❧~❧

Cari Kraft

In a recent article, I focused on the top ten qualities of "what makes an exceptional leader." The focus was the following:

A Leader

- **Creates trust.** A leader's colleagues and clients can count on his or her motives and know that they come from a place of worthy intent. Leaders also build trust by establishing credibility and demonstrating that they have the needed skills and capabilities.
- **Invents the future.** A leader excels at creating a vision for the future and communicating that vision to his or her team.
- **Enrolls and inspires.** A leader is able to have his or her team see the possibilities for themselves and how they can contribute to the organization. This is more than just inspiring action because a leader can actually be inspiring inaction (as in the case of a cease-fire situation).
- **Serves.** A leader serves his or her team, providing them with the tools, resources, and coaching they need to succeed.
- **Takes ultimate responsibility.** In the end, how it goes rests on the leader's shoulders. Was the goal achieved? Was it the right one? Was the team satisfied with the process? A leader takes complete ownership.
- **Develops leaders.** This is a trait that is a key differentiator between good leaders and great leaders. Great leaders build leaders and take pride when their team members excel and are promoted.
- **Creates the context.** A leader knows how to start from a blank slate and create an empowering vision for those working with him or her.
- **Focuses on solutions.** A leader always asks the question, "How can we . . . ?" versus "Why can't this be done?" A leader relates to failure as a bump in the road and realizes that he or she is one step closer to achieving his or her objective.

- **Lives with integrity.** A leader commits to his or her word and does what he or she says he or she will do, even when no one is looking.
- **Builds lasting relationships.** A leader moves up the relationship ladder, building strong professional bonds that turn into a team of trusted advisors.

These same characteristics apply to someone who is leading his or her career and can help you assess who is driving yours. Do you

- **Create trust?** Can your managers and peers count on you? Are you known as someone of high credibility within the organization?
- **Invent the future?** Do you know where you want to go? Are you driving your career by taking positions to gain the skills and experiences needed to get there?
- **Enroll and inspire?** Are you someone whom your managers and peers seek out for projects? Is everyone with whom you work invested in your success?
- **Serve?** Are you constantly supporting those around you? Do you take the opportunity to contribute to others without being asked, simply because you can? Do the people around you want to help you because you have always helped them?
- **Take ultimate responsibility?** Do you feel like you are the one in the driver's seat of your career? Are you sitting back and waiting for something to happen to you, or are you causing your next promotion and moving up the ladder?
- **Develop leaders?** Do you develop the people who report to you? Are you happy to promote them from your team even to a peer or manager level? By doing this, you create an exceptionally strong network of people who can attribute their success to you.
- **Create a context?** Can you tell a compelling story about your career? Do you know how your current position fits into the overall picture? Do you know what move is next and why you are going there?
- **Focus on solutions?** Are you an optimistic player whom everyone wants on his or her team? Do you contribute to how results will be achieved without spending energy on why something won't happen? What happens when you fail? Are you stopped in your tracks, or do you pick yourself up and continue toward your goal?
- **Live with integrity?** Are you known as someone to be counted on? Do you hold yourself accountable for your actions regardless of who is keeping track?
- **Build lasting relationships?** Do you build strong bonds with everyone with whom you work? Do you have the type of rapport whereby you can call and ask for help?

Some find it helpful to review this list and analyze themselves according to these attributes. As you review, give yourself a 1–10 score (10 being the highest) to see how you rank as a career leader. If your total is below 35, you definitely want to do an overhaul. It is easy to fall into a reactive state with your career, only paying attention when you have an issue with your current position. Be careful: with today's economy, you might find yourself suddenly without a job when you haven't built a strong foundation for finding your next role. If you scored between 36 and 75, you have some of the basics in place but are likely lacking a committed focus. With a score of 76 and over, congratulations: you are definitely leading your career—it is not leading you.

Another approach is to review the brand you have created for yourself. What value do you bring to the table? How you are perceived by others? Begin paying close attention when you are being introduced to someone new. What words do they use to describe you? Does everyone use the same words? How do those words differ from how you would describe yourself? This will prepare you to answer "tell me about you"-type questions. A great answer format is "I am a ———, ———, ——— [three adjectives] ——— [functional area] professional." Those three adjectives describe your brand.

What steps can you take to get in front of your career? First, assess where you are and build a clear plan on where you want to go. Next, develop a career story that explains the reasons for your moves and shows how you are driving your career. Review your résumé and make sure it reflects that compelling story with specific accomplishments for support. Finally, build your internal and external networks, focusing on creating lasting relationships with as many people as possible. Seek out mentors to both guide you and help you make connections. Assist as many people as possible in achieving their success. Go back and right any professional relationships that have ended on a not-so-great note so that you will have stellar references from all places.

Once you do this work, be sure to keep a continued leadership focus by establishing a structure for reviewing your career. Your format can vary based on personal preference. Some establish a time to review their careers weekly and put reminders on their calendars to make sure it happens. Others create an action plan related specifically to the preceding steps. Those who are completely committed find someone to enroll as a career buddy who will hold them accountable. The process you create doesn't matter, as long as you develop a structure to keep yourself honest and focused on leading your career.

<u>Bio</u>

Cari Kraft is the president of Jacobs Management Group Inc. (http://www.jacobsmgt.com/), an executive recruiting organization with twenty years of hiring success. Ms. Kraft has held positions in Sales, Marketing, Business Development, and Operations over a twenty-year period. Prior to her association with JMG Inc., Ms. Kraft held positions at Omicron, Packard Press, and the Strategic Management Group, where she taught business based on the Wharton Business Simulation Game. Ms. Kraft holds a Bachelor of Science degree from the University of Pennsylvania's Wharton School, with a concurrent Bachelor of Arts degree in economics. Ms. Kraft can be reached at ckraft@jacobsmgt.com.

18

Navigating the White Waters of Career Change with Values as Your Compass

Judith Joyce

Has everything you thought was nailed down in your career come loose? Have you lost your job? Or have you become so overworked due to others being laid off that your health is compromised? Has looking for a job in your current field led to nothing but dead ends?

If nothing seems to be working, a course correction may be in order. Whether that course correction is your choice or has been made for you, deciding whether you want another job in your same field, a job in a different field, or to be self-employed is your next step.

Creating a Values-Based Foundation for Your Life and Career

Where do you start? Start by clarifying your values to gain clarity and direction for what you want to create going forward.

Values are the guideposts for your life and your career or business. Values describe your deepest desires, talents, and abilities. They provide the elasticity for you to live more in the flow of the present moment, lessening fears and gaining confidence. Defining the values that you've identified is paramount to accessing your best guidance and support for generating the life, career, and/or business of your dreams.

Many of the values by which we have lived were embedded during childhood from families, religions, and teachers. I was in my forties and going through some major life changes before I really looked at my values to see if they still applied to the adult I had become. I found that even though some of the values' names hadn't changed, my definitions for them were dramatically different and have continued to change as I grow and expand.

Clarify and Define

1. Look at the choices you've made over the past year. What values have driven those choices? Write the first words that come to mind. Don't over think this.

2. Review the list, adding others that come to mind.

3. Define each value.

4. Read each definition, asking, for example, "Truth—does this value fully support my life at this time?" Feel the lightness or heaviness in your body. If you feel lighter, that is your truth; feeling heavier is a lie for you. Continue to refine and revise until you deeply resonate with the list and definitions as the foundation for *your* life, not the expectations or values of others.

Integrate

Values are the compass for your life and career choices. Periodic reviews identify how things are going and what shifts are needed. Useful insights can be gained by asking questions such as the following:

- Which values am I living?
- Which values am I not living?
- How often am I using my values to guide my choices?
- What do I do the rest of the time?
- What gets in the way?

Stress, which undermines mental, physical, and spiritual health, indicates that you have disconnected from your values. Explore the causes of your stress, noticing how they affect your quality of life. What or who else is affected by stress? Are you using your values to relate to what is causing your stress? What adjustments are needed to reduce or eliminate the stress?

As you consider the career, job, or business that will enrich and nurture you, use your values to inform your considerations. Research the companies that place a high priority on having values as key drivers for how they do business. And when interviewing for a position, always ask what the business's values are and how they are integrated into the company's business practices and policies. Little else will give you the clarity you need to determine if the opportunity is best for you.

In the 1980s, company values were in. Beautifully framed values were hung in companies' reception areas while owners and employees walked quickly by them each day. To this day, I know of no business plan format that includes clarifying values as the first step in the creation of a plan. So few, if any, leaders and employees actually saw and used those values as key components to guide personal and business decisions, support marketing and customer service behaviors, and inform relationships with customers, suppliers, distributors, and employees, while providing the foundation for policies and working environments. That disconnect between stated values and actions was a major component of the economic meltdown.

During my corporate career, I worked for five different companies. The second was an international company in which the senior executive staff meetings were called "blood baths," describing the way the CEO "went for the jugular" of one or more of those attending. The tension employees felt as they entered the building each morning indicated whether the CEO was in the building. While the values of the company were not stated, it was clear that politics and ruthlessness were highly valued. The fourth company valued the appearance of hard work seen as working very long hours ideally six days a week in the office. The president frequently said that "the most important assets of the company rode up and down in the elevator each day." Yet he never spoke to any of those assets when he rode the elevator with them. After I left that company to start my business in 1993, I knew that if I were ever to work for someone else again, it would have to be with a company whose values resonated with mine. And sure enough, that's what happened nine years later. My desire to work for a values-based company appeared when a well-known environmentally focused company was looking for a human resources leader to create a values-based workplace community. The company's president was deeply committed to a work environment that included active employee participation in all aspects of the business plus employee policies and benefits that supported best practices. Because the company was widely known for making a difference in people's lives, the applicants who clamored to work there weren't looking for a job—they wanted to be part of a larger mission and vision to change the world. It was by far the most alive, creative, engaged working environment I have ever experienced.

An Arizona hospital that wrote its values and mission statement over twenty years ago still has them prominently placed throughout all hospital buildings. The first agenda item at high-level weekly staff meetings is sharing how each attendee and department has lived those values. This is a great integration example!

Reap the Benefits

If you choose to start your own business, integrating your values at the start of your business-planning process will ensure that they will guide all aspects of your business relationships and culture, giving you the advantage of uniqueness and quality that will reap many rewards, including becoming an employer of choice for many job seekers.

Continuing to ask which choice feels lighter (truth) and which feels heavier (lie) will ensure that your life, career, and/or business will be based on what's true for you and release fears that arise. Allowing your values to guide your actions will reduce stress while increasing confidence, vitality, creativity, perspective, flexibility, and well-being.

Enjoy the space, freedom, sense of internal security, and potency that will be available as you more easily transform the white waters of change into balance, joy, and fun!

B<small>IO</small>

Judith Joyce, owner of Journey beyond Belief, supports people in building a strong foundation for their future based on what they value. She has more than thirty-five years of experience in coaching, training, management, and consulting as a corporate human resources executive and entrepreneur, in addition to certifications as a Conscious Relationship, Body-Mind Vibrance Coach, Access Bars Facilitator, Past Life Regression Counselor, and ordained interfaith minister. Her intuitive, integrated body–mind–spirit approach to private sessions and classes, plus her extensive toolbox, assists clients with enhancing the vibrance of their lives, relationships, careers, and businesses. Visit Journey beyond Belief online at http://www.journeybeyondbelief.com/.

19

CAREER OVERHAUL

Career Transition

Finding Purpose and Passion

❦

Laura Allan

Leaving the Familiar, Embracing the Unknown

Martha sits at her desk, dreading yet another day of angry customers and a boss who's impossible to please, and knows that by the end of the day, she'll have eaten too many snacks to fill the empty hole within her. "Surely, there must be more to life than this—where's that feeling of pleasure I used to feel in just doing the best job I could do?" she catches herself asking.

Dr. Lewis twirls around in his chair to view the X-rays while his assistant sets up for a procedure. "I wonder how many fillings I've done in my career," he asks himself, "and how many more I'm going to do before I retire." He's surprised at the melancholy that washes over him, but really, these feelings have become increasingly frequent. "I worked so hard and was so proud to become a dentist. This used to be enough—what's happened? What's changed?"

Martha and Dr. Lewis are both experiencing the first seeds of awareness that something needs to change in their careers. They're both experiencing the first hint that things are not as they should be.

A famous line from a Robert Frost poem reads, "And if you're lost enough to find yourself . . . " One could certainly imagine this applying to considering a career change—and the exploration that goes along with it! For it's this feeling of being lost that often precludes a period of learning and growth, exciting new directions in our careers and the most wonderful discoveries within ourselves. It's both exhilarating and scary to begin this search for passion and purpose in our work lives—and it's well worth exploring.

Career Exploration as a Life Transition

There's no doubt that career exploration is a transitional period in your life, and whether planned or unplanned, it carries with it conflicting emotions.

If it is a planned process, such as graduation from college or the desire for a new career, there is an undercurrent of excitement to be sure. This doesn't mean that doubt won't crowd your mind from time to time, however. And even as you are moving toward a future that thrills and inspires you, you may suffer a feeling of loss at leaving behind the familiar and comfortable.

If your career transition was unplanned and precipitated by something such as job loss or the death of a spouse, the challenges are all the more difficult. You will need to work through the grief arising from such a loss, while at the same time opening yourself to the potential for finding a new life of purpose and passion.

Limiting Beliefs and Fears

Being open to possibility can be the most difficult of tasks. We each have many perceived limitations placed on us by family and friends, society, and—most important of all—ourselves. When beginning an exploration to uncover purpose and passion in your life, it is essential to set aside these limitations and preconceived notions about what you *should* be doing in your career and to focus on what you *want* to be doing.

Many fears can also accompany the prospect of a new career. Some of these are logistical: wondering if you can continue to support yourself or how you will manage going back to school and working at the same time.

Other concerns may include a fear that you are incapable of learning something new, that no one will hire someone your age, or that *you will make the wrong choice of career.*

You can trust that if you follow your purpose and passion when choosing your new career, it will not be the wrong choice. A career that brings a sense of meaning, joy, and satisfaction to you guarantees that it will be the right choice.

Finding Purpose and Passion

What if you don't know what your purpose is? What if there's nothing you can think of that you feel passionate about? Are you doomed to have a career that at best is so-

so and at worst may be miserable? Absolutely not! Everyone has a purpose, and on some level, we each already know what it is.

A good starting place to finding purpose and passion is to think about what you loved to do as a child. What was your favorite game or toy? What emotions did this play evoke in you? Did you love sports? If so, which were your favorites, and why? How did it feel to be part of a team or to be physically active? What specifically did you love about it? What did you want to be when you grew up? What about that career appealed to you?

You can also make a list of all the things you loved in your previous jobs. Does there seem to be a theme? Or conversely, make a list of all the things you hated in previous jobs and look at the opposites of those things.

Remember that these are blue-sky exercises, in which the sky's the limit! For now, don't get bogged down in thoughts like "I don't know how that could be a career" or "I could never make enough money doing that" or "what would my mother think?" Right now, you are just reconnecting with what brings you joy, passion, and a sense of fulfillment. There is plenty of time later to whittle and hone to find the career within your sense of purpose and passion.

You can also ask family and friends about what they see that you enjoy, or imagine you might enjoy. Parents will have memories of things in which you were very interested (maybe even mildly obsessed with) as a child; this can be very helpful and insightful information.

Beware friends who start with "I think you'd be good at . . . " or who suggest things because you have done them well in the past. This is not about what you do well but rather what brings you a sense of accomplishment, satisfaction, and happiness. Aptitude tests can be misleading for the same reason. There are many people who excel at their jobs but are still unhappy in them.

Purpose Statement

As you go through the suggested exercises, an idea of your purpose will begin to form. It might be pretty specific, as in "I love to teach dance and share in my students' passion for movement," or it may be more general, such as "I enjoy teaching others and seeing them learn and grow." Or your purpose could be extremely general: "I feel passionate about physical movement in the company of others." Regardless of the specificity, you have discovered your purpose!

Most people feel quite exhilarated when they discover their purpose. Although there is still work that must be done to decide the exact direction you want to take and embark on that journey, knowing your purpose and the passion it evokes within you will keep you moving in the right direction.

BIO

Laura Allan is a psychotherapist and life coach. After making a mid-life career change, she is happily living her ideal career. Laura's purpose is to share her experience, insights, and wisdom for the benefit of others, while continuously learning, growing, and expanding her awareness. She is passionate about helping clients use their own experiences and inner wisdom to evolve into the best versions of themselves and live happy and fulfilling lives. You can find Laura at http://www.BestSeattleCareerCounseling.com/.

20

CAREER STRATEGIES

A Business Plan for Career Success

Craig Frazier

In today's crowded job market, differentiating yourself by building your personal brand within your organization is paramount to separating yourself from the pack and jump-starting your career opportunities. Learn how to "think like a boss"—turn your ideas into company assets and your colleagues into evangelists for your brand. Find out where most people stop short and how your initiative and follow-through can put your career over the top.

Here are several keys to implementing a strategy based on initiative that will positively affect your career and make you an asset to any organization—or give you the experience you need to advance your career by becoming your own boss!

Give Your Idea *Wings*

Want to know how to get exposure within your organization and build your personal brand? Give your idea *wings* by turning it into a ready-made solution. A man named Edwin Perkins used this principle when, in 1927, he developed a powdered version of his product Fruit Smack, which he then renamed Kool-Ade, and later changed the spelling to the brand that most of us easily recognize today as Kool-Aid. Kool-Aid was a hit, in large part because of its convenience. By 1964, the presweetened packets were formulated so that all busy moms had to do was add water. It was an easy and cheap alternative drink that was convenient and met a need (Hastings Museum 2010). When your ideas can be presented in such a way that the hard work and planning is already done, then all upper management has to do is add the water.

Practice thinking through the problems you see within your organization and come up with workable solutions rather than just complaining about what you don't agree with. Take action by building a strategy or business plan around areas where your company could expand or grow. "Think like the boss" when you develop your plan by making decisions and projections part of your analysis.

If a particular process or idea is complicated or will require a large investment, take the extra effort and build a business plan around the strategy, and include projections and researched data. Successful careers are made by those who are willing to put together and implement a good idea. Putting it down on paper in business-plan format will make a strong case for the project and will certainly get the attention of upper management. Find a business-plan template and insert your research and data. Once it is ready, schedule a meeting to review it with your boss and any other appropriate management personnel, and watch your influence begin to grow within the company.

For Every Problem, There Is a Solution

I have managed many types of employees, but they all fall into one of two categories: the ones who constantly have complaints they are looking to off-load on someone else (usually me) and the ones who bring me their problems along with proposed solutions ready to discuss. Guess which of those employees I would rather manage? If you are the kind of employee who presents solutions to your problems, your manager will quickly realize that you know how to think through an issue, and your influence will grow. Work to be the type of employee whom you would want to manage if you were in the position of authority.

Avoid Entitlement Syndrome

It is easy to feel like the company for which you work owes you something, whether it is benefits, a bonus, or time off. The entitlement attitude is a dangerous enemy to the growth of your career and the influence of your initiative.

Think for a minute about your cost to the company for which you work. Add up your salary or hourly wage for a year, and then add in an estimated cost for health insurance and any other benefits your company may provide. You may be surprised to learn that according to statistics, workers pay an average of $3,997 toward family health coverage, but the actual cost of that coverage is $13,770, which is generally subsidized by the employer (Wojcik 2010). Once you have your figures totaled up, ask yourself a simple question—do I generate more revenue than what I cost my company?

Find ways to give back to the company by volunteering for different committees or just going above and beyond in your everyday work.

The Pathway to Promotion

Many people avoid additional work and actually spend a great deal of time and energy appearing to be busy when the reality is the opposite. When you have the opportunity to be involved in a project or take on additional work, use that additional responsibility to expand your influence within the organization. Positioning yourself as a person who is willing to accept greater responsibility will signal to others within the organization that your attitude is right and that you are a team player.

I remember that several years ago, I had the opportunity to help another department with technical support for a new software module that was built to take enrollments. I became the go-to person for solving problems with this integral piece of software, and as a result, when a key management position was vacated, I was asked to take the job. This new role amounted to a substantial raise and an increase in responsibility, but there was no way I would have gotten that opportunity had I not been willing to take on the additional work initially.

Build "pathways to promotion" by taking the initiative to accept and master the additional work or new experiences that come your way. The knowledge and experience you gain will help develop your personal brand within the company and will build a level of job security that will help keep your job safe in a downsizing economy.

Be a Student of the Industry

Be intentional about learning your business or industry. Get involved in projects that enable you to learn about different areas of the business from where you work every day. When you are recognized as a person who has a wide range of experience within the company, you will build your résumé and make a strong case for consideration of future promotions. A wider understanding of your company and industry will help you gain a big-picture view of where your company is and where it needs to go. This understanding will greatly influence your project plans and the receptivity of those in management to your new ideas.

The difference between being where you are and being where you want to be is the ability to finish. It is very easy to be critical; in fact, for some of us, it is second nature. Using that to then improve the situation is a step most of us rarely take because that part isn't so easy. The test of a good businessperson is not whether you can notice a problem or point out a flaw but rather whether you can take the next step to offer a solution or help develop the fix. Anyone can have a good idea; however, if you can take the initiative to build a plan around your solution, it will become a company asset—and you will become an asset along with it.

References

Hastings Museum. 2010. History: Kool-Aid: Hastings Museum.
http://www.hastingsmuseum.org/koolaid/kahistory.htm.

Wojcik, Joanne. 2010. Cost-shifting rises in poor economy. *Business Insurance*,
September 6.

BIO

Craig Frazier is an entrepreneur at heart and has helped start, manage, and improve
many small businesses over the last decade. To learn more about developing a
business plan to enhance your career or even to take your idea and start your own
small business, visit http://www.Business-Plan-Examples.com/. Find the business-
plan templates you need to help take the guesswork out of creating a solid business
plan for any small business by visiting our website.

21

Get to the Top of the Promotion List and Stay Off the Layoff List

Bud Bilanich

Creating the career success you want and deserve can be difficult and confusing. I know. I had to learn how to navigate the choppy career waters on my own. Early in my career, I was frustrated. I was dedicated to my job but I wasn't moving up. The promotions I wanted kept eluding me.

Let me back up and tell you a little about me and my career journey. Neither of my parents got anywhere near a college, but education was a big thing in our house. All I heard growing up was "go to college." I worked hard, got good grades in high school, and went to Penn State. I followed that by getting a master's degree from the University of Colorado.

Then I got my first job in business. I figured I was on my way to the top. I worked hard, did a good job—and kept getting passed over for promotion. The reasons were vague—"you've only been here a little while," "the hiring manager thought the other person was a better fit," "you need to polish up some of those rough edges."

So I found another job. I worked hard, did a good job, got good performance reviews—and no promotions. I was frustrated. In my heart of hearts, I knew I was as good as, or better, than the people who were moving ahead while I was standing still.

I decided that maybe more school would be the answer. I quit my job and enrolled in a PhD program at Harvard. I decided to use my situation as a lab. I was surrounded by high performers at Harvard—people who had achieved a lot at an early age and seemed destined to achieve even more. I decided that maybe I should pay some attention to these folks.

I got one of those marble-covered notebooks. I made a list of all the people I admired at Harvard, and all the people who got the promotions I didn't, and all the people who were my role models. I started reading biographies of successful people. I created a page for each person. I wrote down the characteristics that I observed in each person.

When I was finished, I had a notebook full of what I observed in successful people. It was a long list, so I started looking for patterns. I found four distinct characteristics that the successful people I studied all had in common. They all...

- Had a clearly defined purpose and direction for their lives.
- Were committed to succeeding. They faced obstacles and overcame them. They didn't blame others when things went wrong.
- Were self-confident. They knew they were going to succeed and continue to succeed as they went through life.
- Shared some basic competencies:
  o They knew how to present themselves in a favorable light. Other people were attracted to them and wanted to be around them.
  o They were high performers.
  o They were great communicators.
  o They were good at building relationships.

Once I finished my degree, I took a job with a Fortune 50 company in New York City. I started applying the lessons I learned from observing successful people—and I began getting promotions I craved. I became the confidant of several senior executives, and I began coaching up-and-comers in the company—teaching them the basic principles I discovered by writing my observations in that marble-covered notebook.

I kept refining my ideas, making them easier for others to understand and apply. I became the most sought-after internal coach in that company.

Then I opened up a small consulting, coaching, and speaking business. The idea was to reach an even greater number of people with what I knew about creating life and career success.

I thrived as a corporate consultant for many years. Then I got cancer—and survived. My cancer experience helped me realize that there is more to life than working as a high-paid consultant. I realized that I had an opportunity to reach even more people with my common-sense message about career success—people I would never get a chance to meet working one on one with executives in very large companies.

That's why I created my Career Success GPS System (http://www.careersuccessgps.com/). That's why I'm on a mission to make everything I know about life and career success widely available. That's why I've written several books on life and career success. That's why I've written the chapter you're reading.

I want to help as many people as I can create the life and career success they want and deserve. I survived a cancer scare, and now I want to share my career success knowledge and wisdom with as many people as I can.

It's all based on four simple but powerful common-sense ideas:

1. Clarity of purpose and direction
2. Commitment to taking personal responsibility for your life and career
3. Unshakeable self-confidence
4. Four specific competencies you must master to succeed:
   a. Positive personal impact
   b. Outstanding performance
   c. Dynamic communication
   d. Relationship building

These four *Cs*—clarity, commitment, confidence, and competence—have guided me on my success journey. I'm sharing them with you so they can guide you on your personal journey to the life and career success you want and deserve. Let's look at them in a little more detail.

- There are three keys to developing your clarity of purpose and direction:
- Define what success means to you personally.
- Create a vivid mental picture of yourself as a success.
- Clarify your personal values.

There are three keys to committing to your success:

- Take personal responsibility for your success.
- Set high goals—and do whatever it takes to achieve them.
- Choose to respond positively to people and events, especially negative people and events.

There are three keys to becoming self-confident:

- Choose optimism—believe in your heart of hearts that today will be better than yesterday and that tomorrow will be better than today.
- Face your fears and act—don't let your fears paralyze you into inaction.
- Surround yourself with positive people—jettison the naysayers in your life.

Finally, there are four key success competencies you must develop:

- Learn how to create positive personal impact.
- Learn how to become an outstanding performer.
- Learn how to become a dynamic communicator—in conversation, writing, and presenting.
- Learn how to build strong relationships with the important people in your life.

I know this can sound overwhelming when you see and hear it like this. That's why I wrote a little book called *Success Tweets: 140 Bits of Common Sense Career Success Advice, All in 140 Characters or Less*. You can download a free copy of *Success Tweets* at http://www.SuccessTweets.com/. The tweets will help you create the life and career success you want and deserve. I explain each tweet in detail on the Success Tweets blog (http://www.SuccessTweets.com/blog/).

Download a copy of *Success Tweets*. Read the blog. Put the ideas to work, and you'll be on your way to creating the career success you want and deserve.

BIO

Bud Bilanich, the *Common Sense Guy*, is a career success coach, motivational speaker, author, and blogger. He helps his clients succeed by applying their common sense. He has been featured in the *Wall Street Journal*, *Success Magazine*, and *Self Improvement Magazine*. He is the Official Guide for Career Development on SelfGrowth.com and the Preferred Partner for Career Development at Success IQ University. Dr. Bilanich is Harvard educated but has a no-nonsense approach to his work that goes back to his roots in the steel country of western Pennsylvania. His approach to career success is a result of over thirty-five years of business experience, a lifetime of research and study of successful people, and the application of common sense. Bud is a published author, is a cancer survivor, and lives in Denver, Colorado, with his wife, Cathy. He is a retired rugby player, an avid cyclist, and a Penn State and Pittsburgh Steelers football fan. He enjoys independent film, live theater, and crime fiction. Visit http://www.BudBilanich.com/.

22

5 Steps to Career Success as a Leader

Why Help *Is Not a Dirty Word*

꧁ ~ ꧂

Mike Myatt

In working with numerous C-level executives and entrepreneurs, I have found that there are a few things that distinguish those who achieve the highest levels of career success and those who don't. Moreover, as much as some want to confuse the issue for personal gain, it really isn't too difficult to stand apart from your peers and competitors if you consistently pay attention to a few key items. In this chapter, I'll share a commonsense approach to achieving career success that isn't just more tired rhetoric, but rather time tested advice.

As much as some people won't want to hear this, *help* is not a dirty word; rather asking for help is a sign of maturity as a leader. So my question is this: are you easy to help? Think about it. Do you make it easy for others to want to help you, or is your demeanor such that most people won't lift a finger to assist you in a time of need? How many times during the course of your career have you witnessed executives and entrepreneurs who desperately need help but either don't recognize it or, worse yet, make it virtually impossible for someone to help them? If you take one thing from this chapter, it should be that *it is critically important that you learn to position yourself to be helped.*

If your pride, ego, arrogance, ignorance, the way you were raised, or any other excuse (yes, I did say excuse) keeps you from asking for help, it is precisely those traits that will keep you from maximizing your potential. I hate to break it to you, but you don't know everything or everybody, so why even bother pretending that you couldn't use a bit of help? No single person can or should go it alone in today's business world. The more partners, sympathizers, champions, allies, supporters, enablers, influencers, advisers, mentors, friends, and family you have helping you succeed, the faster you will achieve your goals. Without question, the most successful business people on the planet are those who have learned to blow through self-imposed barriers to openly harness the power of broader spheres of influence.

I don't know about you, but I am so tired of all the "self-made man" propaganda floating around business circles. I sincerely believe that there is no such thing as a "self-made man." While I take complete responsibility for all my failures and shortcomings, I take very little credit for my own success. Virtually all the good things that have happened to me over the years have been the result of the collaborative efforts of many. I don't see asking for help as a sign of weakness; rather I see it as a very smart thing to do, and I therefore tend to seek out help wherever I can find it. I have long made it a practice to encourage others to help me succeed. My personal and professional networks are far more important to my success than my individual competencies. My clients hire me not solely on the basis of what I can personally do for them in a vacuum but rather because of what the collective influence of my network and resources can accomplish for them when I operate outside of my own personal bubble.

If you desire to enlist others in your success, the following items are the five basic prerequisites for getting others to help you:

1. **Don't be a jerk.** Though people don't necessarily have to like you to help you, it certainly doesn't hurt. However, I can promise you that if you're perceived as a jerk, people will not only go out of their way not to help you succeed but they will do everything possible to impede your success. I have long been a believer that contrary to popular opinion, nice guys (and gals) do in fact finish first. Be sincere, honest, humble, and likeable—avoid being the arrogant know-it-all if you want to be successful.

2. **Go out of your way to help others.** *Do unto others, what goes around comes around, you reap what you sow,* and any number of other statements to that effect ring true more often than not. If you are sincerely interested in helping others, and make it a habit to go out of your way to do so, then those people will likely be inclined to reciprocate.

3. **Know what you want, and focus your efforts to that end.** You must develop a clear picture of what it is that you want to accomplish and then apply laser-like focus in the pursuit of your goals.

4. **Make your goals known to those who can help you.** It is not only impor-tant to communicate your vision to those in a position to help you succeed but always to make sure to ask for their help. Don't be bashful or embar-rassed; rather confidently recruit others to become enablers and evangelists of your cause. You need to believe that one of your top priorities is team building and consistently seek out greater numbers of people to champion your cause and scale your efforts.

5. **Execute.** Becoming accomplished at all four of the preceding items will certainly help you advance your career, but if you don't perform, if you can't execute, or if you fail to deliver on your commitments, it will be a career ender. Like it or not, when it comes to advancing your career, you are likely to be evaluated on the hard realities or based on what you do or do not accomplish. Say what you mean, mean what you say, and deliver on your commitments. Do this one thing, and many of the typical career woes will simply disappear.

In the final analysis, it's really all a matter of perspective: you can either view yourself as part of a hierarchical world sitting at the top of the organizational chart, puffing your chest and propping up your ego, or you can view yourself as the hub at the center of a large and diverse network. The latter view is both more profitable and enjoyable than the former. You can choose to build your personal brand and your success either at the expense of others or by helping others. The easiest way to help others is to make it easy for people to want to help you by helping them.

BIO

Mike Myatt is a top CEO coach, author of *Leadership Matters . . . The CEO Survival Manual,* and managing director and chief strategy officer at N2growth. His theories and practices have been taught at many of the nation's top business schools, and his work has been noted in several publications, including *Psychology Today, Washington Post, Wall Street Journal, Entrepreneur, Chicago Sun Times, Personal Branding, Institutional Investor,* and *CIO Magazine.* He is also the author and moderator of the *N2growth Blog,* which was recognized as the number one consulting blog of 2009 by Postrank. Follow Mike Myatt on Twitter @mikemyatt, or e-mail Mike Myatt at m.myatt@n2growth.com.

23

Career Transition

≈⌒⌒≈

Helen P. Bressler

Making a career transition is often seen like, and felt to be, a huge step. Many are reluctant to take it, settling instead for a seemingly easier but less satisfying career. Regardless of whether you feel forced into making a career change due to shifting economies or technological advancements or have been considering a new career for some time, this chapter sets out simple steps to systematically take you from where you are now to where you want to be.

Step 1. Emotional Health

Whether you want to return to the workforce or have chosen to make a career change, the first step is to consider your emotional health. If there is unresolved stress, anxiety, doubt, low self-esteem, a reduced sense of self-efficacy, or another issue, then this will cloud your decision making and jeopardize your plans.

In my experience, one of the most effective ways to resolve negative emotions and diminish self-limiting beliefs is to use emotional freedom techniques (EFT) (for more information on EFT, visit http://www.optimumevolution.com/). Even if making the career move is something you've been planning for a long time, unresolved issues and self-limiting beliefs *will* hold you back, so use EFT to resolve these first. Once emotional health is addressed, simply follow steps 2–5. Furthermore, look at this career change positively; see it as an opportunity for growth and fulfillment.

Step 2. Knowing What You Want

Now that your emotions and self-confidence are in check, you'll want to consider what you *really want* out of a career and what *you're willing* to put into it. By answering the following questions, you'll become more aware of yourself in relation to work and career (make a note of your answers so that you can refer back to them later):

1. What are/were you doing that you feel isn't/wasn't really you?

2. Why exactly doesn't/didn't the work suit you?

3. What don't/didn't you like about the work? Include the following: environment, tasks, responsibility and accountability, people, supervisor or boss, who answers/answered to you, location, hours per week, time off per month or annum, benefits, remuneration, training and promotion opportunities.

4. How much work-related stress do/did you encounter on a daily basis?

5. Are/were you challenged in a positive way that encourages/encouraged both personal and professional development? If not, why?

6. Do/did you feel valued, respected, and happy on a daily basis? If not, why?

7. Do/did you get a sense of satisfaction and achievement?

8. How does/did your work affect your quality of life or desired lifestyle?

9. How does/did your work affect your sense of self-efficacy and self-esteem?

Though most of the preceding questions seem to focus on the *negative* aspects of your current or past work, understanding what you don't want will provide you with clarity on what you *do* want. Many times, clients give *general* answers when I ask them what they want out of a new career; this makes setting clear goals and creating a definite plan of action almost impossible. The preceding exercise clarifies what you want and generates an understanding of what you're prepared to do to get you there. So now, go through your answers and make a note of exactly what you *do* want. The next step is to prioritize what is *most important* to you at this time and what you perceive as important in five years, ten years, and so on.

Step 3. Guidance

I included this section because I've seen folks wait for guidance, especially in regard to life-altering decisions such as a career change. They wait for the guidance—and they wait and wait and wait. They are waiting for the message that tells them exactly what they should do. However, what they fail to see is that guidance is really *an affirmation of what they really want.* What's more, guidance is happening all the time; they just tend to miss it! The exercise you've just done is guidance. Your emotions act as guidance. Think about this for a moment: what are your emotions telling you? For example, jealousy confirms that someone has something you wish you had. If you step aside from the *feeling* of jealousy and step aside from the *person* of whom you feel jealous, then what you are left with is the recognition that there is a qualification, a title, a lifestyle, or something else that you want but do not yet have. Now consider regret. What is regret except an emotion telling you that a decision you once made would now be made differently? Decide what you would do *now*, forgive yourself, and move on.

Of course, there are practical considerations to make when transitioning careers. Some of these are mentioned in our next section. It may also be useful to see a career's advisor or coach. However, do learn to become aware of your own guidance. Become aware of your emotions and reactions with regard to your current, past, or potential career.

Step 4. Practicalities

So now it's time to get practical. What do you *need* to get you to the career you want? Do you require extra training, qualifications, or help with marketing or résumé writing? Start making a list of practicalities. Include skills, experience, and qualifications that you already possess as well as those you need. Additionally, ask yourself the following:

- What career do I *specifically* want?
- Do I want a specific title?
- Do I want job security, to work for myself, to be situated in one locale, to travel, or to be able to move around as I want?
- Do I want to be an employee, self-employed, an investor, or a business owner?
- How does this career suit my personality?
- How does this career suit my goals, ambitions, and (desired) lifestyle?
- What are the challenges to beginning this (new) career?
- What do I already have to enable me to meet these challenges?
- What do I need to meet these challenges?
- Who else, if anyone, is involved?

You may want to use resources such as the U.S. Bureau of Labor Statistics (http://www.bls.gov/) to research required qualifications, projected career growth, and expected income. It's also important to check out professional organizations for additional requirements and licensing prerequisites, as necessary.

Step 5. Be SMART

Once you've completed steps 1–4, it's time to be SMART (Wheeler and Grice 2000). To achieve your main objective (starting your new career), you need to break this up into smaller goals. Doing so will remove any feeling of being overwhelmed and will create a series of manageable steps. Take one step at a time, and ensure that each is SMART:

Specific

Measureable

Achievable

Realistic

Time bound

Once you've clarified your SMART steps, you may find that you have a list of finite goals (to reach your objective of getting the new career) as well as ongoing ones. The latter will be especially helpful once you've reached your objective and you want to further advance your career. Perhaps there are ongoing skills, training, or personal development opportunities that will set you apart from the rest and lead to even more exciting opportunities.

Use my five steps to transitioning between careers, and you'll be clearer and more focused about what you want and how to get there. Enjoy your journey.

Reference

Wheeler, N., and D. Grice. 2000. *Management in health care*. Cheltenham, UK: StanleyThornes.

Bio

Helen is a Professional Personal Development Coach. She is certified in EFT, Professional Coaching, NLP, and Clinical Hypnotherapy. She is also a registered nurse and ordained minister. Helen has over two decades of experience in the area of self-development and has helped hundreds transform their lives. She uses a powerful combination of EFT, NLP, and professional life coaching to help people improve health and relationships, unleash potential, and clarify and achieve goals. Furthermore, she expertly uncovers and resolves core issues responsible for procrastination, lack of direction, low self-esteem, unhappiness, and more. Helen expertly creates tailor-made sessions that perfectly suit the needs of her clients. Career transition coaching is part of this service. Visit her website at http://www.optimumevolution.com/, or e-mail Helen at optimumevolution@gmail.com.

24

How to Know If the Opportunity
Is Right for Change

≈≈≈≈≈

Cathy McCann

So you've created a winning résumé, perfected your interview skills, and identified some suitable employment opportunities. All goes well, and you receive a job offer. How do you know that this is the right job for *you*?

Whether you're considering a new job, a promotion, a transfer, or a career change, it's important to evaluate the opportunity in relation to your whole life and the people closest to you. Every decision that you make affects other areas of your life—even when it's a positive change such as a long-awaited promotion or much sought-after job. These types of life changes can be easier to navigate if you are aware of their impact and prepare in advance.

We all seek to achieve and maintain some level of balance in our lives. The definition of *balance* is different for everyone, but one thing is true for all: change requires movement, and movement affects your balance. We all fear losing our balance; therefore risk accompanies nearly every decision you make. But ultimately, change is good for us, and we need the momentum it provides to grow, improve, and succeed.

Is This the Right Opportunity for Me?

How do you evaluate whether an opportunity is right for you? You can start by asking yourself these three questions:

- Will this position bring me fulfillment in keeping with my personal values?
- Am I willing to make the sacrifices required?
- Do I have the support that I need to make this change?

Try answering these questions as your honest, true, authentic self, and listen to your intuition. The authentic self understands your abilities and personal limitations. Remember that true instinct happens automatically, whereas the process of analysis and deliberation is filtered through social conditioning, habituation from your upbringing, and past experiences. Everyone has intuition; the problem is that we don't listen to it. We overanalyze, second-guess ourselves, and worry about what others want and expect from us. Your own values are the only thing that will bring you fulfillment.

Personal Fulfillment and Growth

Most of us spend the majority of our waking hours at work. Therefore it's important that your job allows you to live authentically and maintain your personal integrity. You should consider the following:

- What am I doing at the times when I feel happiest? What am I good at? What do others like or admire about me?
- Will this position fulfill my need for growth and development?
- Do I feel drawn to this position?

Chances are that the more certain you feel that the job will bring personal fulfillment, the more willing you will be to make sacrifices to have it.

Change and Growth Requires Sacrifice

We all recognize that there are a limited number of hours in each day. But no matter how skilled you are at multitasking, adding to your responsibilities in one area of your life means that there must be sacrifices in another. For instance, the promotion might mean more money but also longer hours and more stress. That dream job may offer the career growth potential you've been seeking but will also require more travel and time away from your family. You must give to get.

When considering the sacrifice that will be necessary for the new position, you can ask yourself the following:

- Is the position in keeping with my personal values?
- Does this job matter to me enough that I am willing to make sacrifices for it?
- One year from now, will I feel satisfied with the decision that I've made?

Only you know whether an opportunity is worth the sacrifice, and you must make this decision for yourself. Sometimes a change may seem like a great sacrifice on the surface, but if you consider the whole-life impact, you can see that it is not really much of a sacrifice at all. For instance, if you decide to take a job that requires more travel, at first glance, you might think that the extra time away from your children is too much to give. But when you consider that the job you currently hold makes you so unhappy that the extra time you have with your children is tainted by your stress and tension, you might decide that quality is worth more than quantity and that your happiness will ultimately benefit your children.

Get the Support You Need

Be sure that your family and friends understand your goals and current priorities, and ask them for their support and encouragement. Explain the changes that you are expecting and how those changes might affect them. Be candid. Approach the situation objectively and from a distance to lower your emotional response. People are afraid of the unknown and are therefore afraid of change because the outcome is uncertain. By limiting your emotional reaction, you can assist them in limiting their fears. It may be a good idea, especially if you have children, to take time to write out a plan. When you have a plan in place, making a change is a whole lot less threatening.

Once you've made your decision, try not to feel guilty. Guilt is a wasteful emotion that arises from an unresolved past. Guilt steals time and energy from what you're doing right now. If you address the challenges that you are facing and prepare for them, there is no reason to feel guilty.

Be prepared to ask for help when needed, whether from family, friends, or a trusted mentor. Enlist a support team. These might be other people with the same or similar goals. Perhaps it's your family and friends. Make sure that the people you choose are encouraging of your goals and will support your efforts even when it means change to your normal routine. State your goals out loud and share them with others—this action makes them real, imprints them in your consciousness, and holds you accountable.

Remember that it's always the right time to make a change. Change is growth, and growth is essential to your health and happiness. When you embark on a path of change, the unknown may scare you most. If possible, carefully plan through your change. Think about all the possible scenarios and outcomes—positive or negative— then make a plan. When you have a plan, you'll ease your fears of the unknown. Change is going to find you one way or another, and learning how to better adapt to change can improve all aspects of your life.

Bio

Cathy McCann is a certified life coach who specializes in assisting people in transition. Her life-coaching programs help her clients see things in a new perspective, discover their life purposes, identify and define goals, establish a systematic process for achieving those goals, and provide support and encouragement. Cathy spent more than twenty years in the corporate and legal worlds and is intimately familiar with the struggles her clients face in balancing work and family, managing stress, and achieving their goals. She is passionate about helping others actively choose their life paths and realize happiness and success. Visit http://www.CreatingYourPerfectLife.com/.

25

COACHES/MENTORS

How to Win the Super Bowl of Your Career

Carol Wenom

Every team has them, whether they're pro, college, Little League, or bush league, and although they don't take the field and score the points, the team couldn't win without them. Of course, we're talking about the coaches. They're such an integral part of sports that a team without them would be almost unthinkable. These are the folks who stand behind the team 100 percent. They love them whether they're up or down and have their best interests always at heart. They're ready and willing to give advice, constructive criticism, motivation, and inspiration. When it comes to your career, do you have a coach standing at the sidelines cheering you on? Think of yourself as the star quarterback of your career. Every day on the job is like another Sunday on the field. Wouldn't it be nice to have someone to call in the plays, scope out the competition, keep you from fumbling the ball, and then cheer on your successes? This could happen for you if you choose the right career coach.

Think of a career coach as a mentor—someone either inside or outside your company who always keeps an eye on your career and helps you to keep gaining yardage without fumbling—at least not too much. This will be someone who is truly interested in your growth and success and will really make a difference in accelerating your ability to achieve your goals.

A mentor can be someone in your company who has been there, done that on the same career path that you're following. He or she has fought the same corporate battles, seen the unsuccessful go away, and survived and thrived in the organization. A mentor has a wealth of knowledge about career paths and options that could be open to you. He or she challenges you to stretch your boundaries and consider career options that you might not have thought possible.

Alternatively, a mentor might be someone outside your company. For example, a mentor could be someone who is in the same professional field as you but in a similar company or industry. Perhaps a mentor could be someone who used to work at your company but has now gone on to another opportunity in the same field.

Here's a really great idea—why not cultivate a relationship with a recruiting professional as a mentor or career coach? This would be someone who specializes in search in your profession or industry. A really good search consultant will do a whole lot more than just be there when you need to change jobs. After all, who is better positioned to have a bird's-eye view of *lots* of professionals in your same shoes? And for sure they've seen *lots* of successes and failures in the industry. Better yet, they know the good companies from the bad, they follow the market trends, and they can give you great advice with historical perspective about the industry, your career path, your competition, or your compensation. They're really available to *consult* with you—virtually always free of charge to you!

Some people have several mentors concurrently for different parts of their lives or careers. Perhaps you could have one for your financial planning, one for your career, one for your favorite hobby, or one for just about any facet of your life. Think about these people as comprising your very own board of directors—a whole staff of folks dedicated to making the corporation that is *you* very profitable and successful.

Regardless of whom you choose or how many, following are a few key criteria to remember:

1. You must choose someone with whom you can communicate completely and openly. Neither you nor the coach should have a hidden agenda—the coach really has to have your best interests at heart.

2. Typically, a coach-mentor is someone older and wiser, or at least someone who has walked in your shoes enough times before that he or she can speak with some authority about your actions and their potential consequences.

3. Pick someone from whom you know you can not only hear the truth but take the truth. Sometimes the advice you get may not always be what you want to hear, so the mentor needs to feel comfortable that you're not going to shoot the messenger or negatively affect your relationship.

4. Choose someone whom you admire for his or her career progression and/or personal accomplishments and integrity. After all, you want to pattern yourself after someone who has grown and succeeded and not after someone who lives in a world of would-have, could-have, should-have.

5. Just as important, pick someone who has seen his or her share of failures and hard knocks—someone who has been through rough patches and come through them not just as a survivor but as a thriver.

Well, now you're thinking, "Gee, this is simple. I'll find a great mentor, and that person will help me pave my way to glory until I retire." Unfortunately, this is typically not the case. More often than not, as your career progresses or as you make career decisions that change your path, you may well outgrow your mentor. Most people find that it's far more common to have several mentors through the course of their careers. For example, you may have one mentor who helps you early in your career to get established and figure out your career direction. But say you decide to move into management and that mentor has never been in management. Now you need to find a new mentor who has had that management experience to teach you how to get there and how to avoid the pitfalls that come with management. So you rock along for a while, skyrocketing in your career, and then you decide you want to ditch the corporate world and go into consulting or write a book. Now you need yet another mentor who has had *that* experience to take you to that next place. One of the key characteristics of a great mentor is someone who has the capacity to know when you need more than he or she can offer and will push you out of the nest and encourage you, or even assist you, in finding your next mentor.

So as you prepare to take the field each day of your career, don't be the person who ends up sitting on the sidelines while someone else marches down the field to career glory. Build a team of great career coaches and mentors, and prepare yourself to get inducted into your own career hall of fame.

BIO

Ms. Wenom began her recruiting career in 1978 with one of the nation's largest engineering placement firms based in Houston. She became manager of a major technical recruiting firm in Dallas for six years, before returning to Houston as vice president of Whitaker Technical Services in 1989. Ms. Wenom has achieved "preferred provider" or "exclusive provider" status with many of her clients.

Consistently a top producer in the recruiting industry, Ms. Wenom has been recognized with numerous honors and awards at local, state, and national levels, including, most recently, her induction into the Pinnacle Society—the nation's premier consortium of top recruiters within the permanent placement and search industry. In 1985 and 1992, respectively, she was awarded the Certified Personnel Consultant (CPC) and Certified Temporary Staffing Specialist (CTS) designations, attesting to her continued commitment to the highest standards of legal and ethical business practice. She was honored in 1992 as the Houston area "Consultant of the Year" and "CTS of the Year" by the State Professional Association (TAPC). In 1994, Ms. Wenom was also recognized by the National Association of Personnel Services as "CPC of the Year." In 2003, the Houston Area Association recognized Ms. Wenom for Outstanding Contributions to the Professional Staffing Industry. Ms. Wenom currently serves as past chair of the Board of the National Association of Personnel Services (NAPS) and served as its chairperson from 2008 to 2010. She is also a founder and director of the Rocky Mountain Association of Recruiters.

In addition to her operational roles at Whitaker, Ms. Wenom serves as vice president of training and organizational development. She conducts both new-hire and ongoing training for all divisions and offices of the company. Additionally, she has developed a series of training videos introducing the fundamentals of the staffing industry that is now being offered throughout the industry nationwide.

As a noted industry speaker and trainer, Ms. Wenom's credentials include the National Association of Personnel Services, ACSESS (the national Canadian Staffing Association), the ASA, the National Personnel Association (NPA), and the International Personnel Association (IPA), as well as "guest appearances" for the Society of Human Resource Managers. She has also spoken at many engineering and technical professional association meetings and conferences.

Ms. Wenom received her bachelor's degree from Syracuse University in 1973 with a dual major in English and communications. Prior to her career in recruiting, Ms. Wenom worked in both technical and training positions for the Western Geophysical Company of America, based in Houston.

26

Communicating Confidence
in the Job Interview

Nancy Daniels

> If you doubt yourself, then indeed you stand on shaky ground.
> —Henrik Ibsen

Today, competition for employment is fierce. To secure an interview and then sell yourself in that interview is extremely challenging. For some, just the thought of being interviewed is frightening. With the number of applicants seeking the same position, older workers may feel quite intimidated going up against a younger generation, whereas those fresh out of college may feel their own inadequacies due to lack of experience.

So how do both younger and older prospective employees vie for the same position? By honing their interview and communication skills and presenting themselves in a professional manner, no matter what their age.

It is known that a weak handshake generates a less favorable opinion than a firm grip. The same holds true about your vocal delivery and body language. If you enter the interview room timidly, with your shoulders slouched and your head hung low, then your body is screaming that even you doubt your capabilities. Perhaps you are unable to make eye contact with those to whom you are speaking—definitely a sign that you are uncomfortable—or maybe your voice quivers as you desperately try to express yourself. Unfortunately, a quivering voice is informing your listeners that you cannot control your nervousness. Any one of these three scenarios is telling those who control the bucks that they shouldn't spend their money on you.

If there are two candidates for a job and both have equal education and experience, but one speaks with confidence and the other does not, who gets the job? The answer is obvious. Now, let's look at a different situation. There are two candidates: one is slightly better educated and has a bit more experience than the other individual;

however, the more educated candidate's confidence and communication skills are sadly lacking. Not as well educated and less experienced, the second candidate is very strong in his communication skills. He conveys confidence in himself as well as in his abilities. Who gets the job in this case? More than likely, an employer will be more impressed with the confident individual than with the one whose communication skills are weak.

Recently a young man named Aiden phoned me. I thought I was talking to a woman. He told me that during one of his job interviews, the man in charge advised him to do something about his voice. A few weeks after taking my course in voice improvement, Aiden was not only offered a job with that same company but was offered a better job than that for which he had applied. His future boss said to him, "The change in your verbal articulation is significant; I feel as if you have matured ten years!"

Though most men do not sound like women when they speak, there are many other problems that may be associated with your voice, whether you are a man or a woman. If you are soft-spoken and are asked to repeat yourself constantly during the interview, you will not be hired: if your words are not being heard, your message will be lost. On the other hand, if you speak so loudly that others cringe when you speak, the interview may end sooner than you would have desired.

Speaking too quickly or too slowly is also a characteristic that will not endear you to those doing the hiring. If you speak at a hundred miles an hour, you will tire your listeners. Likewise, maundering along at a snail's pace will try their patience.

If you speak like a valley girl so that the pitch of your voice rises at the end of each sentence, you will not be looked on as professional. The rising inflection sounds immature—definitely not the image you want to project.

Perhaps you speak in monotone, displaying no emotion, no life, no animation in your delivery. If your response is going to put the interviewer to sleep, then you should consider working on putting some life into your voice. This is known as color and is heard not only in the vocal variety of your voice but in your facial expression and body language as well.

Speaking indistinctly is another problem that needs to be resolved. Whether you mumble or speak with an accent or dialect, it is your responsibility to enunciate your words clearly so that all can understand what you are saying the first time you say it. Your voice, along with your speech, is the vehicle by which you must sell yourself.

Think back to the last time you heard yourself on your voicemail or some other form of recording equipment. Did you like what you heard? It is important to understand that the voice you hear in your head is sound traveling through the solid and liquid of the brain—distorted sound. In that sense, it is a lie. What you hear on your voicemail, however, is the truth. That is the sound by which everyone else recognizes you. What does *that* voice say about you? Is your sound, your manner of speech, and/or your delivery an asset or a liability?

Candidates who express themselves with the most confidence are the ones who prospective employers consider most seriously.

A good exercise to do before your next interview is to video-record yourself in a mock interview session. Research the firm for which you have an interview so that you know more about them than they know about you. With that information in hand, compose the questions you feel they may ask, especially the one in which they want to hear about your greatest weakness. Practice your answers by recording yourself, and then study the playback. Make a list of what you need to work on, and then do it. If your voice is a liability, consider a course in voice training.

After graduate school, I applied for a position with G. Schirmer—at the time, the largest publisher of classical sheet music in the United States. Though my music education was obviously a strength, my business background was nonexistent. In addition, there is no doubt that the other candidates were definitely more experienced than I. However, I got the job because of my voice. I sounded confident when I spoke. I sounded like I knew what I was talking about.

Yes, your education and ability are most valuable; however, the candidate who lands the coveted position is the one whose confidence is unquestioned. Arm yourself with the best communication skills training possible. Walk with purpose. Make eye contact. Be expressive. Believe in yourself. And discover your "real" voice. You may find it to be your greatest asset. You will sound better; you will probably look better; and you most definitely will feel better about yourself—undoubtedly the best way to communicate confidence in the job interview.

Bio

After graduating from GettysburgCollege with a bachelor's degree in music, the Voice Lady, Nancy Daniels, discovered her real voice while pursuing graduate studies at AmericanUniversity. In addition to her guest speaking engagements, she offers private, group, and corporate workshops in voice and presentation skills as well as *Voicing It!,* the only video training program on voice improvement. Visit http://www.voicedynamic.com/ and discover how you can sound more mature, eliminate vocal abuse, increase your volume without shouting, speak in living color, and control your nervousness in any form of public speaking.

27

Embrace Conflict and Embrace Success

❦

Margaret Meloni

When you think of conflict, do you conjure up negative images? Do you imagine power struggles and battles? Or do you think great, bring it on? Maybe you think that if it were not for other people, you would never have to deal with conflict. *Avoiding human contact at work is not a great career-enhancing technique*! Even if you work in a laboratory by yourself all day long, at some point, you have to emerge and share your results and convince your investors to keep your work alive.

What is conflict? Conflict is a condition in which people's concerns appear to be incompatible. Since you and your coworkers are not intellectual and emotional clones of one another, conflict is inevitable. Conflict is a natural by-product of our environment. *A complete lack of conflict is not normal.*

Conflict is not inherently bad or evil. Conflict does not have to lead to fighting. Conflict handled well can strengthen our relationships and lead to a healthier work environment.

The key to enhancing your career is through strong, mutually supportive relationships. Truly strong relationships are those in which the people involved walk through conflict together and emerge with even more trust and respect for one another than they had prior to the conflict. How you deal with conflict shapes who you are as a professional and as a person. How you manage conflict is a direct reflection of who you are and is directly related to the success that you and your team experience. *Your team needs to see you resolve conflict.* The time to start is now; the place to start is within.

Understand Your Conflict Resolution Mode

The first step in strengthening your conflict resolution skills is to understand how you prefer to face conflict. When you understand how you handle conflict, you can begin to understand when your approach is effective and when it is not. Then you can learn to adapt your behavior and draw from different conflict resolutions styles, as needed.

Most of us identify with one of the five conflict-handling modes identified in theTKI, or Thomas-Kilmann Conflict Mode Instrument. The TKI is a questionnaire designed to measure how you tend to handle interpersonal conflict. This is expressed using five modes and two dimensions:

- **Assertiveness.** This is the degree to which you try to satisfy your own concerns when faced with a conflict.
- **Cooperativeness.** This is the degree to which you try to satisfy the other person's concerns when faced with a conflict.

Take a look at the five modes and see if you can identify your go-to method of handling conflict. *There are no right or wrong answers; there is only you and your way of being.*

Competing. This mode is considered to be very assertive and very uncooperative. Sometimes the term *power oriented* is associated with this mode. This can be an individual who pursues his or her beliefs at another person's expense, using whatever power is appropriate to win his or her position. Although there might be some negative connotations to the way this mode is described, there are absolutely times when it is the best and most effective way to resolve a conflict. How do you know if this is your mode? Consider these statements; do they ring true for you?

- In a conflict situation, you like to feel you are winning.
- You will try to get your way; in fact, it is very important to you that things go your way.
- You like to convince people that your approach is the best and only approach—you might use logic and show the benefits of your approach to win your position.

Accommodating. The exact opposite of competing, accommodating is unassertive and highly cooperative. You might neglect your own concerns to satisfy the concerns of another person. This could be self-sacrificing, but it can also represent selfless generosity or obeying orders when you would prefer not to. Is this you? Review the statements below; is there a fit?

- I try to emphasize the things we agree on rather than negotiate what we disagree on.
- I might try to soothe the other person's feelings for the sake of our relationship.
- Sometimes I will sacrifice for the wishes of others.
- I try not to hurt people's feelings.
- I try to be considerate of the other person's feelings.
- If someone's wishes seemed really important to him or her, I would try to let the person have his or her way.

Avoiding. This is unassertive and uncooperative. You are not pursuing your concerns, you are not pursuing the concerns of the other person, and you are not addressing the conflict. You might be doing this for diplomatic reasons or to wait until a better time, or maybe you are withdrawing from a threatening situation. Here are some statements that identify conflict avoidance:

- There are times when I let others take responsibility for solving the problem.
- I try to avoid useless tensions.
- I try to avoid creating unpleasantness for myself.
- I might avoid taking a position that I know would cause controversy.

Collaborating. This is assertive and cooperative, and it is the opposite of avoiding. You work with the other person to find a solution that satisfies both your concerns. Together you dig into the issue and identify both your underlying concerns. You might work to understand each other's needs and perspectives so that together, you can find creative solutions. These are the statements that fit a collaborator:

- I try to deal with all our concerns, yours and mine.
- I like to seek out others to help find a solution.
- I like to get all issues and concerns out in the open right away.
- I share my ideas and ask others to do the same.
- I try to work through our differences.
- I am concerned with satisfying all our wishes.

Compromising. This is the middle ground in terms of assertiveness and cooperativeness. You work to find a mutual solution that partially satisfies both of you. You give up more than you would when you are in competitive mode, but less than you would if you were accommodating. You address the issue more directly than avoiding, but you don't give it as much attention and analysis as you do with collaborating. If this is you, these statements will feel comfortable:

- I look for a compromise.
- I will give up some points in exchange for others.
- I will let the other person have some of his or her points in exchange for some of mine.
- I propose a middle ground.
- I try to get the other person to settle for a compromise.

Honesty and Self-Awareness Set the Stage

Each of the preceding conflict resolution modes has pros and cons. That is why it is so important for you to be honest with yourself about your approach. This is the foundation to your ability to resolve conflict. A shaky foundation equals an unreliable structure (or relationships), whereas a strong solid foundation upholds your professional self and supports lasting professional relationships.

BIO

Do you want to end your day in pieces or at peace? Margaret Meloni is dedicated to helping professionals become free from the work-related conflict that prevents them from experiencing peace. You spend so much time at work; what you do and say to others (or what they do and say to you) can make a difference. Margaret's passion is to support you as you navigate the workplace and forge your very own path to peace. Her approach includes inspirational writing, speaking, self-study programs, and coaching. Visit Margaret at http://www.MargaretMeloni.com/, and join her community today!

28

CORE VALUES

Core Values

❦

Ayman Hamid

Are you reading this as you're looking for your first job, your next job, or the job that is going to make you successful? As someone who has made a living helping people become more successful than they thought they could be, I can tell you that it's not the job that makes you successful; rather it's you and what you stand for that make you successful—your *core values.*

In the past ten years, I have fielded two questions over and over: what does it take to be successful, and what characteristics do I see in successful employees? My answer is the same now as it was ten years ago: *know who you are and what you stand for.* You might be tempted to offer a vague answer like "to be an overachiever," "to set and hit my goals," or "to be competitive." Though these reasons may sound valid, they each fail to explain precisely why you are doing what you are doing. The first step to achieving your goals and becoming successful is to figure out what you really stand for. Do you have a clear grasp on your core values?

Though I do not know what your core values are, I can describe the values of successful individuals who definitely knew theirs. These individuals represent a wide spectrum of experience, from the entry-level employee to the CEO of a multi-billion-dollar company. They all share a set of core values that guided their lives and their work: *integrity, work ethic,* and *self-development.*

Integrity, in its simplest iteration, is doing what's right when no one is watching. It's easy to see why this characteristic would be shared by successful individuals, and of course, there are many obvious moments when doing the right thing is clear, though not always easy. What may not be as simple to identify are those situations in which your integrity is being tested, those moments when both the dilemma and your reaction to it are equally overlooked. A colleague put it this way: how many times do you pass by your pet's empty water bowl and not fill it up? Your pet will not truly suffer if you postpone filling her bowl, and she certainly will not get on your case if you pass her bowl without topping off her water. However, you know it needs to be done, whether anyone tells you and whether anyone notices. Living a life of *integrity* means that you will do what's right when no one is watching! Think about all the times you've walked by the empty bowl in your career and simply not stopped to fill it up. Instead, let *integrity* guide your actions. See the empty bowls in your career as opportunities to demonstrate *integrity,* even if the only person to whom you are demonstrating it is yourself.

Integrity shapes and goes hand in hand with *work ethic.* In the early years of my career, I knew that a strong *work ethic* was a key characteristic to becoming successful. I am consistently amazed that individuals work hard in school to get good grades and successfully network—neither of which pay you any money—to land the "job." But once they get the job, they show up from 8:00 a.m. to 5:00 p.m. and do not put forth the extraordinary effort they expended to get the job to excel at the job. These individuals do not achieve their potential because they simply do not take the time to learn what they are not taught at work. Refuse just to coast when you land the job; put in the effort to ensure your success! Figure out what is going on in the industry, who the competitors are, how they are doing, and why they are better or worse than the company for which you work. Most people don't realize that it's not that some people are smarter than others; it's that some work harder than others. Develop a strong *work ethic,* and let it guide your life and work—you will set yourself up for success!

Finally, *integrity* and a solid *work ethic* alone cannot guarantee that you achieve the level of success you would like. However, if you add to these qualities a drive to improve yourself continuously, you will have the core values to ensure a successful career. *Self-development,* when practiced properly, is the key value that will enable your constant growth, personally and professionally. Once you make a commitment to yourself to improve, you'll be amazed at the amount of support and number of opportunities that are available to you. The unsolicited responses you will receive from others once you make the commitment to improve yourself will more than justify the decision. We've heard our entire lives that people want to "associate with successful people" and that "success breeds success"—my experiences tell me that these statements are never more true than when the value of *self-development* is demonstrated.

To enhance your career, to achieve and exceed your potential, you must first determine what your core values are, then simply work by them! The three I have briefly described here are simply the ones that have helped guide my career, and the careers of those with whom I work. I recommend these values to any and all who will listen: *integrity, work ethic,* and *self-development.* In other words, do what's right when no one is looking, work harder than everyone feels is necessary, and consciously work on your own development.

<u>Bio</u>

Ayman Hamid is a director of operations for Aerotek Inc., a leading employment agency providing technical, professional, and industrial recruiting and staffing services. Prior to joining Aerotek, he enjoyed a career as a professional soccer player. He holds a bachelor's degree in mathematics from California State University, Bakersfield and is certified as a Senior Professional in Human Resources (SPHR).

29

Dealing Effectively with Criticism in the Workplace

Brock Hansen

Criticism, despite its negative connotations, is one of the most common, necessary, and creative events in the working environment. The importance of giving and receiving honest feedback along the management chain and within teams of colleagues cannot be overstressed. The issue is how to do it effectively.

In a perfect world, all workplace criticism would be clear, constructive, and carefully expressed. The critic would be able to say, "These are my expectations, this is why I think they are important, and this is what I think you should do or how you should change to meet my expectations. If you don't understand or agree, let's talk about it." The expectations themselves would be SMART (specific, measurable, attainable, realistic, and timely). The person receiving the criticism would be calm and rational—evaluating the criticism, giving appropriate counterproposals for discussion, and then committing to mutually agreed-upon changes.

In the real world, however, criticism is usually delivered in situations defined by stress for both parties, triggering powerful survival emotions of fear, anger, and shame and driving important interchanges in irrational and destructive directions. A supervisor may feel irritated by a worker's project performance but anxious about her potential reaction to criticism. A worker may experience criticism as an overt attack on his abilities, intelligence, character, reputation, or wage security and react with anger or anxiety, clouding his ability to assess and accept the criticism appropriately. Systematic approaches to performance evaluation, intended to reduce friction over careless or poorly defined criticism, may be minefields of emotional reaction. All of these can lead to power struggles that absorb enormous amounts of energy and interfere with creativity, cooperation, and productive outcomes.

Our responses to criticism are driven by powerful survival emotions. Our brains, programmed by evolution in our animal past, can react to criticism as to a life-threatening attack. In addition, many of us have grown up with carelessly delivered or abusive criticism, causing us to develop painful expectations and habitual emotional reactions, many of which we don't consciously recognize. This is why a well-meaning supervisor can be baffled when an otherwise reasonable and cooperative employee reacts with stubborn defensiveness or anger to criticism intended to be positive and helpful. A careless supervisor can exacerbate the problem by voicing criticism in public, thereby adding shame, another primal emotion, to the mix and increasing the likelihood of halfhearted compliance or stubborn resistance on the part of the employee. Other team members, viewing or hearing about the exchange, may also respond with a variety of negative reactions. Once work relationships are deeply scarred by careless or ineffectual criticism, confident cooperation within an entire work unit can be difficult to reestablish.

No matter where you are in the office pecking order, you can enhance your reputation and effectiveness by knowing how to sidestep potential power struggles to learn from critical interchanges. Everyone can avoid much of the wasted time and energy inherent in irrational responses to criticism if he or she understands the emotional traps involved and prepares in advance to deliver and accept criticism with sensitivity and clarity. Neither is as easy as it sounds, but expanding emotional intelligence skills to successfully deal with workplace criticism is well worth the effort.

So how do people prepare themselves to successfully give and receive criticism? Is that even possible? Don't these things just come up spontaneously? How do you know how you will react under different circumstances? The first rule of achieving any degree of emotional intelligence is to *know yourself*. The second is to *learn how to manage your emotions under varying circumstances*, particularly those in which you know you are vulnerable. To a greater or lesser degree, everyone is vulnerable to primal emotions in criticism situations.

In most interchanges, it is the person delivering the criticism who has primary control of the situation and thus primary responsibility to do it well. This person must understand that serious criticism requires serious thought before it is delivered. It pays to prepare for giving criticism by asking yourself this question: what would this criticism sound like if it were

- delivered thoughtfully at an appropriate time and place?
- constructed in all particulars as a SMART request for change?
- framed for mutual discussion and creative feedback?

The person giving the criticism is in control of all these criteria unless he or she responds impulsively to stress and fails to prepare. Impatience, irritation, and confusion can undermine the ability to deliver effective criticism. Then any number of mistakes can interfere with the effectiveness of the criticism. It may be blurted out at a time and place where the recipient is embarrassed or distracted or unpleasantly surprised and therefore unable to listen thoughtfully. It may come out as a vague, unrealistic, rambling, open-ended, and overwhelming demand that confuses and intimidates the recipient. It may show up as a dictatorial announcement that does not ask for or allow any response from the recipient, completely cutting off the critic from the opportunity to get the recipient's point of view or negotiate. If you feel the urge to complain, criticize, or command, the emotionally intelligent move is to pause and think: what is the change that I want the other person to make? Can I describe it in SMART terms? When is the best time and where is the best place to talk about this? Am I in control of my emotions generally right now? Am I prepared to listen to questions and feedback in an effort to complete this communication successfully? And yes, it does take time to practice the self-calming and centering skills needed to reduce these impediments, but it saves more time than it costs in the end.

The potential recipient of workplace criticism, that is, everyone who works, has a significantly tougher job. Accepting criticism is never easy and rarely pleasant, but it cannot be avoided. Furthermore, accepting criticism and learning from it is enormously important in understanding your role in the work to be done and achieving success in your career. Because criticism can come at you anytime or anywhere, and you cannot depend on the critic being sensitive, centered, or SMART, you need to know about your own emotional reactions to criticism and how to manage them. If you know that you habitually respond to criticism with fear, anger, or shame, and that these emotions tend to compel negative overreaction, you must prepare yourself with quieting skills that will allow you to take a deep breath, rise above the immediate emotional response, and ask yourself, "What can I learn from this to make my work more effective, and what will I need to do, either now or in the future, to make that happen?"

Some may think it absurdly unrealistic to aspire to this degree of emotional self-control, but in fact, most of us have met someone who remains calm and focused when criticized and whom we can observe as a role model. Anticipating potential criticism situations, honestly observing your emotional reactions, and practicing self-calming techniques—even rehearsing with a friend or spouse—does work. If old wounds or emotional baggage present a special handicap in mastering these skills, there are counselors and coaches who stand ready to help.

<u>Bio</u>

Brock Hansen, LCSW—author of *Shame and Anger: The Criticism Connection*—is a therapist and personal effectiveness coach with over thirty years of counseling experience. Based in Washington, D.C., he is available for telephone or Skype video coaching and personal effectiveness training. Visit http://www.change-for-good.org/.

30

DIFFICULT WORK ENVIRONMENTS

Navigating Difficult Work Environments

~~~

Mary-Jeanne "MJ" Cabanel

You used to love your job, but it seems like the earthquake that is the economic climate keeps sending aftershocks that shake your foundation and keep you ducking in case there are any other damaging debris flying around out there. Maybe the business has been restructured, likely layoffs have occurred, and certainly there is more work to do with fewer people doing it. So you've done what any reasonable person would do: you put your head down and kept on working. You miss the joy, though, and wonder if you should look around. The thing is, you like the company, and part of you keeps hoping it will go back to what it was in the good old days, when you were happy to go to work and when what you did really did make a difference. So how do you survive, much less thrive, at work when the environment is challenging or worse?

Separate Who You Are from What You Do

If you are used to putting in an eighty-hour workweek (whether for love or money or both)and can't remember the last time you had a hobby, much less a passion, it is definitely time to get a life outside the office. Take a yellow sticky and paste it over your job title, and imagine yourself without it. Who are you now? What is important to you? What do you love? What do you thrill to? Look backward. What did you adore doing when you were five years old? Look inside. You must be in there somewhere. Taking time to get to know yourself again will protect you from overly relying on work to fill your emotional needs. Reinforcing your sense of self will add to your confidence, which experts cite as the key factor to surviving at work in troubled times. Follow through and commit to reengage with one of your passions—join the local softball team, dust off that cello and play. Doing an activity that you love will give you the space you need from your job to find new perspectives. Think of it as an energy and confidence infusion rather than as time stolen from work.

Forgive and Forget

Change is the rule, not the exception, these days. Projects get abandoned, entire departments get cut, managers have a revolving door, and nothing whatsoever is static. As much as possible, take nothing personally. Most of the time, a troubling situation is not about you at all but rather concerns a much bigger picture such as returning the company to profitability or even saving the organization. Avoid blaming the enterprise as it only dehumanizes the situation and puts you in a "me against the system" perspective that leaves little room for adaptability or change. Remember that people are behind corporate decisions and that people are human and imperfect. They also have different values. Indeed, many times, what is perceived by one executive as an act of treason by another is simply a mismatch in values. Though Mr. X might value employee retention, for example, Ms. Y might value achievement and so may be driven to diminish the head count to meet company targets. She doesn't mean it personally at all; it is simply an unfortunate means to an end. Understanding these differences, seeing the fallible, imperfect human behind decisions and forgiving him or her will free you up and give you the power to see what opportunities this flux has brought.

Wake Up and Smell the Opportunity!

Now that you've purged any anger and blame, pick your head up off the desk, come out from your cubicle, and walk into the light that is shining on the new possibilities that are available to you. As Einstein said, "In the middle of difficulty lies opportunity." What is the spirit of the company now? Where is the energy being focused? What is exciting for you in the present circumstances? What are the problems that you can help solve? Taking the pulse of an organization can provide insight on how you can reorganize, reframe, and remotivate yourself to be part of the solution. Connect with the vision that inspires you, and focus on aligning yourself to it. This will help you sail the winds of change rather than fight against them.

Have the Conversation

Once you begin to see the vision and opportunities to realigning with the organization, it is time to communicate your interest and intentions, and perhaps your change of heart. Start by looking up. Request a meeting with your boss or the person spearheading the new movement (or cleaning up the mess). This conversation may not be easy—especially if your emotional intelligence slipped during the trying times and you let comments fly like an errant baseball through a neighbor's window. Stop pretending you don't see the broken glass. Get over yourself and apologize. Executive coach and author Marshall Goldsmith calls apologizing "the most magical, healing, restorative gesture human beings can make." Think of it as clearing the rubble out of the way and opening up the path to a new future and a new direction.

Ask for What You Want (and Wait Around to See If You Have to Negotiate)

Depending on your situation, this conversation and the preceding one may take place at two different times. The important thing is to demonstrate how you are on board and ready to lend a hand. Speak clearly and enthusiastically about what you want. Articulate from a place of openness and flexibility. Then be quiet and listen to the answer. Remember, if it is not the answer you want to hear, do not take it personally. Rather, keep cool and get curious. Ask open-ended questions to find out what management plans are and how you might fit in. What does the company need from you now? How does your boss see your role evolving? What does it take to earn the role you've just described? This can be helpful to pull the manager down from a bird's-eye view into the specifics. There may even be more of an opportunity to help out than you previously thought.

Be Patient

Survival of the fittest generally takes longer than a weekend. Change takes time to unfurl, whether it is from an organizational or individual perspective. Each one of the points outlined here is a process that will unfold over a period rather than in a moment in time. Even though it may be uncomfortable, wait it out. Ask most leaders the secret to their success, and they will nearly always cite tenacity: the ability to hang in there over the long term. This doesn't mean you have to do it alone. Ask for help. Find a coach, mentor, or confidant to help you move forward even when waters are choppy. Always remember that you have a choice in any situation. Aligning your personal rudder with who you truly are will help you weather even the most difficult of storms.

BIO

Mary-Jeanne "MJ" Cabanel, MBA, CPCC, is an executive coach and leadership trainer living in Geneva, Switzerland. She works with executives from multinational corporations, non governmental organizations, and entrepreneurial ventures. Her passion is helping people thrive at work, and she fervently believes that everyone has an inner leader eager to get out. Prior to becoming a coach, MJ spent twenty years in sales and marketing for leading financial and other institutions. She is a member of the International Coaching Federation and is a Certified Professional Co-active Coach from the Coaches Training Institute. For more on MJ, please see http://www.mjcabanel.com/.

31

DiSC – Behavioral Styles

The Winning Edge:
Hidden DISCoveries That Set You Apart

Susan Cullen

Do you ever wonder what makes some people seem to almost magically advance their careers, while others, with similar backgrounds, go unnoticed? What makes them so special? How can you discover what gives them the hidden edge?

We hear it said that "It's not *what* you know, it's *who* you know," right? But that's only part of the truth. It's really about the way you connect with who you know. This is true if you desire to move ahead in your current job, if you are looking for your next career move, or even if you are anticipating a job interview.

About Behavioral Styles

We know that there are some people with whom we just click and others with whom we don't. What we don't always remember, however, is that each of us approaches the world differently and has different behavioral style tendencies. There's one hidden truth at which winners excel: they are masterful communicators and adapt their approaches to the needs of other people.

For example, if we were to go to any other country whose citizens didn't speak English, we would be crazy to expect them all to learn to speak English just because we were visiting there! It just wouldn't happen. We would get frustrated, they would get frustrated, and neither of us would understand each other.

If, instead, we learned to speak their language when we were visiting their country, we would be able to communicate and connect with them much more easily. This doesn't mean we would give up our native tongue; rather it just means that we would be willing to adapt our approach to most effectively engage with the inhabitants. Adapting our behavioral styles is the same way. It's one of the highest signs of

120

respect to be willing to put the other person's behavioral style needs first—and it can give you a hidden edge to accomplish your own career goals.

There are four different behavioral styles. While we can each use all four of them, we will tend to use one or two most frequently:

- Dominance
- Influence
- Steadiness
- Conscientiousness

This approach to understanding behavioral styles is frequently referred to as DISC, because of the first letter of each style. In the following paragraphs, I provide descriptions of each style. As you review them, ask yourself which ones you think best describe you.

The Dominance Style (D)

People demonstrating the "D" style thrive on the challenge of accomplishing results and tend to be quick decision makers. They don't wait to be given authority; they take it. They like being in control. They are primarily interested in the bottom line and the big picture. They couldn't care less about all those details! They hate feeling micromanaged and work best when they are free from lots of supervision. They're not afraid to try something new if it will get results. They seek an environment that includes power, authority, prestige, challenge, opportunity, scope, freedom, and variety.

The Influence Style (I)

People demonstrating the "I" style are often thought of as "People-People." They prefer to be around others and tend to be very enthusiastic and entertaining. They enjoy contacting people, making a favorable impression, speaking articulately, creating a motivational environment and participating in groups. They seek an environment that includes social recognition, freedom of expression, group activities, freedom from control and detail, coaching and counseling skills, and positive interactions with others.

The Steadiness Style (S)

Those demonstrating the "S" style take a much more deliberate approach and don't like frequent change. They are patient and loyal. They have a real desire to be of service and help others. They are also very good at calming people when they get upset or during a conflict. They seek an environment that includes security, predictability, minimal work infringement on home life, sincere appreciation, identification with a group, and minimal conflict.

The Conscientiousness Style (C)

The "C" style of behavior tends to focus on details. In fact, they pick up the tiniest, most minute items that others miss and keep the nondetailed people out of trouble! Unless quality will be improved, this style doesn't like sudden or abrupt changes. They tend to be very systematic, critical thinkers. They seek an environment with a focus on quality, accuracy, and access to the latest, most up-to-date information.

Leverage Your Own Style's Strengths

Remember that there's no one best style. In fact, in any job, you probably need to use all of the styles at different times, depending on the situation. You might need to use one style when you are looking at detailed reports, another when you are leading a team, another when you are supporting other team members, and another when you are championing a new corporate initiative. In fact, the best teams are made up of the greatest diversity of styles. That's because one person's liability is another person's strength.

So take full advantage of your behavioral style strengths. Know what they are and when to use them. Then learn to adapt your approach to the needs of the other styles when the situation requires.

How to Adapt to Other Behavioral Styles

The main thing to remember when adapting to others' behavioral styles is to be like them. Approach them in the manner they would approach you. Here are some quick tips that can help you:

- **With the "D" style.** Tell them the results you need, and let them figure out how to get it done. Don't try to force your will on them or micromanage them. Don't give long, detailed explanations. Focus on the bottom line in a quick, direct way.
- **With the "I" style.** Approach them in a personable, relaxed, upbeat manner. Don't shower them with details or be too serious. Use humor. Let them know you like them and value them.
- **With the "S" style.** Approach them in a warm but deliberate manner. Explain step-by-step methods for best getting things done. Let them know they can count on you. Follow up when you say you will. Don't change

things just for the sake of change. Be as dependable with them as they would be with you.

- **With the "C" style.** Give them the details they need and ask for. Don't be vague in response to their questions. Know what you're talking about, and be able to back it up with facts.

The Winning Edge

When you adapt your style to others, it will help you build much better bridges to them. They will respect your approach (because, after all, it's like theirs). They will trust you more. They will think more highly of you.

In any competitive endeavor, this will give you a winning edge that others might not know about. After all, it's not just what you know. It's not just who you know. It's how others think and feel about you that makes all the difference.

BIO

Susan Cullen is president of Quantum Learning Solutions Inc. She provides a variety of DISC-based self-improvement training programs for management and leadership development, team building, sales, and customer service. For over twenty years, she's successfully helped people like you gain that winning edge. To receive your own DISC profile to learn about your own behavioral style, experience a DISC e-learning program, or learn about additional resources, contact (800) 683-0681 or http://www.quantumlearn.com/. Join the thousands of people Susan has helped to distinguish themselves and advance their careers.

32

Corporate Culture That Embraces Diversity

❧

Paul Lawrence Vann

Want to discover what it takes to become a diversity trainer and consultant? Diversity and inclusion experts are on the cutting edge of corporate change—it's by far one of the most dynamic fields.

People who choose to become diversity train-the-trainers and consultants are some of the most in-demand people in the world. This article provides a snapshot of what it's like to be on the leading edge of diversity and inclusion in the corporate world.

To become a successful diversity trainer and consultant, one needs to learn diversity content; one requires teaching and facilitation skills to guide participants' learning and have a good feel for emotionally charged discussions that occur in diversity sessions.

Diversity trainers can be outside consultants or in-house staff members who work with managerial and line staff. Discover what your role is: leading organizations to understand corporate culture that embraces diversity.

America is and always will be one of the most diverse countries in the world, with a population of over 309 million and counting. A lot of the current population growth can be attributed to and is the result of a massive influx of immigrants from all corners of the world.

Over the past decade, corporate America has been trending to a more diverse workforce, and as a result, companies and organizations that want to survive understand that progress is impossible without change. Demographic trends are accelerating change in the culture of organizations, and they include a psychological climate that is open and valuing of differences.

As a diversity trainer, your role entails your awareness of your being; it takes into account your issues, values, and assumptions about diversity and inclusion. Effective diversity trainers do not have an axe to grind; in other words, you are a tool for the people you train.

Given that diversity training represents a set of beliefs on which to build, diversity is an inside job. In other words, one needs to find comfort and security inside oneself to deal with difference. Understand that diversity implies inclusion, tolerance, adaptation, and equality, and as a trainer, you must subscribe to these values.

Another important aspect of being an effective diversity trainer is to have content knowledge. Why? Diversity as a body of knowledge requires some comfort with theories drawn from anthropology, psychology, and sociology. Diversity examines human behavior in groups and individually. It also focuses on awareness of stereotypes and prejudice, culture as a shaper of behavior, and management skills adapted to heterogeneous, pluralistic organizations.

Your role as a diversity trainer is to lead organizations to create and understand that inclusivity is a place where people have a diverse work environment. It implies a comprehensive openness and, more specifically, an environment that welcomes any person who can do the job, regardless of race, age, gender, sexual preference, religion, ethnicity, or physical ability.

Skill sets required to become an effective diversity trainer include platform and facilitation skills. You need to be able to instruct, inspire, and hold people's attention, provoke thought and discussions. On the other hand, facilitation skills are the ability to structure the group's processes and design an involving session around complex issues. A good facilitator also affords dignity and respect to all participants and keeps the group on task, while also being flexible enough to change direction as needed.

As referenced earlier, one of the top goals of an organization should be to create an inclusive work environment; in an exclusive environment, what counts is a person's ability to do the job, and no one is disadvantaged because of background. Suffice it to say that smart leaders and managers know the value of creating an inclusive environment.

The fact of the matter is that organizational leaders know the value of creating an inclusive environment, and they know it is not easy to achieve one. A few gains from an inclusive environment include productivity and commitment. In the end, organizations must ask themselves, what's in it for them to embrace diversity?

As the world becomes smaller as a result of more efficient travel, organizations that are the most resourceful, talented, and productive will yield better performance and productivity and will increase with a rich staff mix. Diversity trainers know that interaction between cultures has always been a source of knowledge, growth, and progress.

Perhaps the most beneficial aspect of a diverse workforce is the problem-solving results. Inclusive organizations know that the reason for this is the differences that occur in thinking, and work groups see it in the problem definitions and solutions.

One of the most amazing aspects of an inclusive environment is that each person is accepted for who he or she is and is valued for the talent he or she brings to the task at hand. Any time there is an atmosphere of acceptance of a person's genuine self, it represents an atmosphere that will get top performance from staff.

A few barriers to corporate cultures embracing diversity include the cost of implementation, fear of hiring under skilled and uneducated employees, annoyance at reverse discrimination, diversity not being seen as a top priority, and the need to dismantle existing systems to accommodate diversity. To effectively implement diversity in an organization, the organization must be open to change. If an organization doesn't see a need to change, it is likely that it will not survive. Diversity is about remaining competitive in your industry, while understanding the need to be adaptive, flexible, and open to new ideas.

Good diversity trainers are aware that there will be resistance and that the people in some organizations will resist change for a number of reasons; unfortunately, this results from fear of loss. To overcome this barrier, organizations will need to come face-to-face with the losses people fear.

Prior to creating an organization that embraces diversity, losses and gains need to be dealt with and acknowledged. The primary question to ask is, what do I stand to gain and lose in a more diverse organization?

Some of the perceived losses during change include loss of attachments; in other words, a change in the workforce means you can no longer count on the people with whom you work, people who are a mirror image of you. Loss of turf is another perceived loss from a position of power, dominance, and organizational influence. Loss of structure pertains to organizational systems such as promotional, accountability, and reward systems.

Loss of the future involves a perception of a direct hit on the career opportunities of those who have been favored in the past. Loss of meaning is also a perceived loss in that a person feels a lack of loyalty and that a new employee will benefit more. Last, people feel as though they have lost control as a result of an increase in diversity.

There are several phases an organization goes through when it comes to change, specifically as it pertains to diversity. Stage I is shock and denial because of the changing workforce composition. It has to do with coming to terms with a new reality. Some aspects of this phase include refusing to talk about the need to become more inclusive, acting as if everything is business as usual, showing no feelings, and acting and feeling bewildered.

Stage II behaviors consist of increased absenteeism, angry outbursts, seeing only the negative, and performance drop-offs. Stage III behaviors reflect a surge of energy and ceased complaining about change. Increased communications exist, as does a can-do attitude.

It's important in your role as a diversity trainer or consultant to understand that getting through the three stages is not going to be easy. When it comes to change, the bottom line is that you never learn to change culture; rather you work with it, and in the end, the results will speak positively for themselves.

Bio

Paul Lawrence Vann is president of the Wealth Building Academy LLC. He is a certified diversity train-the-trainer who provides dynamic interactive training, focus group studies, and leadership capacity building assessments for his clients. His company consults with Fortune 500 companies, government agencies, associations, military organizations, and educational institutions. He is the author of the book Living on Higher Ground. Paul can be reached online at http://www.paullawrencevann.com/, via e-mail at paul@paullawrencevann.com, or at (240) 416-5077.

33

Let Them Fall in Love First, *before* You Tell Them What Kind of Ring You Need!

Interview Hints from a Recruiting Pro:
The Dos, the Don'ts, and the Don't Even Think about Its!

❦

Ann Zaslow-Rethaber

As a job seeker, it can be exciting yet daunting when you get a call from one of the companies on the top of your list to set up a job interview with you. In many cases, how you prepare for and conduct your first interview will determine whether you close the deal and get the job.

Where to start, you ask? How about approaching it as a first date, where instead of getting a second *date*, you get that second *interview*, which can then lead to a final job offer.

Following are some basic steps to improving your interviewing skills to land that job you desire.

Do your homework. Just as you would want to do a casual background check on someone you are about to date, a company background check is that and so much more. Start by reviewing the company's website to locate its main headquarters and the names of key company representatives. Research recent news on the company, and get general information about the industry.

Check out other resources. Hoovers (http://www.hoovers.com/) can be a terrific source of information—it will not only provide you with information on the company itself but will also give you industry trends and other information. Also visit LinkedIn (http://www.linkedin.com/) and look up current and past employees— this can be a fantastic place to try to connect with someone who may be able to give you the inside scoop on corporate culture and similar matters.

Dress the part and be prepared. Suit and tie for men, dresses or suits for women. *Be sure to turn your cell phone off*, and bring a pad of paper and pen to take good notes. Bring a copy of the job description discreetly in your notepad for reference. By studying the job description and requirements beforehand, you can make a point of emphasizing the skills that you want to highlight during your interview, matching them to the job's mandatory requirements. Do your best to have that job description and its requirements virtually memorized prior to your interview.

Bring copies of your résumé, along with letters of reference. It can be very powerful to bring printed letters of reference that you can leave, along with copies of your résumé. Be sure to bring one for every person you will be meeting so that each person can have a copy of the materials during the interview. Take the time to print them on nice paper, and always bring extras just in case you are able to meet with additional people. Remember that the most effective résumés focus on *job accomplishments* rather than on *job descriptions*.

Be prepared for the questions that you will be asked. If you have a spotty job history, rest assured that you will be asked your reasons for leaving each position, so be sure to have ready replies that are brief and positive. The more you can prepare yourself for a variety of questions, the better you will do in the interview. And remember, *never* interrupt the interviewer!

Prolong any talk of salary. When it comes to money, defer the topic as long as possible. You already know the salary range from when you applied for the position. Other than that range, you should not be talking about what it would take to get you, until an offer is made. Statistically, we have found that the longer you can put off talking specifics, the more money you will get.

Let them fall in love first, *before* you tell them what kind of ring you need. You get the picture—you are not going to open the door for your first date and tell your date that it will take a three-carat, unblemished stone, top grade, and so on, for you to date him. In the same way, you do not want to tell the interviewer that it will take the top end of the salary range and endless benefits to get you interested in the position. We have had candidates do that, and it never fails—for the entire interview, the interviewer is comparing that candidate to others in the pipeline, thinking, is this person worth it? Is this person that much better than the other candidates? It is much smarter to focus on making sure the position and corporate culture are a great fit, then on selling *them* on *you*. Get the offer, and then you can push for more money. "Let them eat the steak *before* you give them the bill."

Close the deal. You want to end the interview on a positive note. Be sure to thank the interviewer for his or her time and let the interviewer know how you feel about the job and why you are interested in working for the company. Recap the main points of why you are qualified for the job, and while it can be intimidating at times, ask the interviewer directly, in a sincere way, if the interviewer sees you as a good fit for the position. If he or she says no, find out the reasons for objection and try to overcome them. If he or she says yes, ask for the interviewer's next steps. Last, be sure to get a business card from the interviewer as well as a correct address to send a thank-you card. You always want to send a thank-you note to all the persons with whom you interviewed. Remember: if you want the job, *ask for it*! We always half-jokingly tell candidates not to let their hands touch that doorknob to leave until they have an invitation to come back.

Have an effective follow-up plan. If you do not get the offer, be sure to write follow-up thank-you letters, thanking everyone who interviewed you for their time and restating your interest in the company. It is a classy thing to do and something that will definitely separate you from the rest of the interviewees. If they give you specific reasons why you were not chosen, work to correct those.

Visualize it, and it *will* materialize! If you are a long-range goal planner, I encourage you to go onto one of the job sites, such as http://www.indeed.com/, that compiles all the job postings everywhere on the Web and look up your literal dream job. Look at the requirements and go out there and start building a resume that reflects those requirements. Also, make a follow-up folder and check in with companies with which you interviewed on a monthly basis. It's always a good idea to create Google alerts for specific companies alerting you to job openings, changes in the company, and so on. When you are alerted to new positions opening up, news in the industry that may affect the company, and so on, you will have a terrific reason to contact the company again. You would be surprised at the number of people who end up in their dream jobs after being turned down initially; however, through perseverance and determination, they end up in just that job.

Wishing you success in *all* your endeavors.

BIO

A recruiter since 1996, Ann Zaslow-Rethaber is the president of International Search Consultants (ISC), a global recruiting firm launched in 1999. Headquartered in Tempe, Arizona, ISC has become one of the country's most reputable search firms, working with companies both in the United States and on an international basis. With a team of 15 talented recruiters and utilizing the very best high-tech tools available, ISC can easily handle multiple searches that can produce highly qualified candidates in a short amount of time for companies with high-volume recruiting needs. For more information, check out ISC's website at http://www.iscjobs.com/, or call (888) 866-7276.

34

EFFECTIVE COMMUNICATION

Achieving Effective Communication

≈⌒≈

Sarah James

Effective communication in the workplace is a key element to forward movement for personal career growth and achievement of company goals. You must be able to communicate well if you want to optimize your potential in a company. Poor communicators may have the education and ideas that are useful in the workforce but may struggle developing their careers to meet their levels of expertise. To communicate productively, you must maintain excellent skills in all aspects of communication. This means that your listening skills need to be as strong as your speaking skills.

Effective Listening

One of the largest mistakes people make when they are listening to someone else's words is that they are too busy formulating a response rather than actually hearing what the other person is expressing. Following are some fundamental strategies to utilize to become an effective listener and, in turn, a better communicator.

1. **Filtering the information.** As you listen to the speaker, how are you experiencing the information? Are you feeling stress, because this is yet another thing your boss wants you to do? Perhaps you are feeling inadequate because you have had several failed attempts at the same project. As a message reaches you, your filter can keep your from hearing the intended message. What place are you in when you receive the information? You may have had an argument with your spouse that morning that is hindering your ability to hear what you are being told. Be mindful of how your filters may distort what is being said.

2. **Remember that you are engaged in listening.** While listening to most topics, your job is to understand the message the speaker is intending to send. It is not to pose your ideas or disagree. You are not to react emotionally if your filter tells you to do so. Learn to manage your personal responses

to the message. Your only job is to remain present and to understand what the speaker is saying. You will get your time to speak and send your message to the speaker.

3. **Focus on the speaker.** Nod your head, position your body to engage, and make eye contact with the speaker. Actively monitor what the speaker is saying by summarizing the message in your head or out loud to the speaker. Ask the speaker to clarify any points that you may question to crystallize your understanding of what he or she is expressing. Make sure you have a complete understanding of what the speaker is trying to communicate and his or her motivation for doing so.

Effective Speaking

To thrive in your speaking skills, the message you are intending to send needs to be received by the listener. Many of the following skills pertain to written communication as well. Maintaining a positive tone of voice, eye contact, and body position are important characteristics of effective speaking. Listeners will hear your nonverbal language as well as your verbal language.

1. **Think about your audience.** Consider to whom you are sending a message and how he or she is likely going to perceive it. This is being an aware and considerate speaker. You want to reduce the emotional charges the listener's filtration system may experience and make it easier for your message to be received clearly. Remain honest in your communication at all times. Dishonesty will nearly always discredit you in the future.

2. **Make a plan and be clear.** What is your objective? What would you like to have happen as a result of your interaction? Create purposeful action to streamline your message. The clearer the picture you sustain of what you want the outcome of your conversation to be, the better chance you have of obtaining it. Be certain about what you need to communicate. This means focusing on pertinent information to the issue at hand and not wasting time on extraneous details or conflicting motives (e.g., proving how smart you are) that may weaken your message or undermine the willingness of your audience to hear what you are saying.

3. **Make your point and be assertive.** Your goal is to stay on task and communicate one message at a time, while checking in with your listener to ascertain his or her level of understanding of your message. You may also summarize at the end of each message to enhance the listener's comprehension. Maintain an assertive presence. This does not mean that you should become aggressive in your communication; rather maintain respect of your rights and views as well as those of the listener's.

4. **No assumptions.** Do not assume the listener has gained complete understanding of your message even though you have said it, and remain engaged with your listener by checking in with him or her. If the listener reflects back to you what he or she heard and that is not what you intended to say, simply remain patient and clarify. Being clear at this time will help alleviate confusion that could occur later and take more time to resolve.

5. **Validate and remain positive.** You will optimize your results in communication if your goal is for both the speaker and the listener to feel heard, validated, and valued. In both the speaker and listener roles, you should remember that people are motivated by positive feelings of self-worth. Therefore you will be more likely to achieve your communication goals if you engage people with respect for their values, opinions, and capabilities.

The goal of enhancing your listening and speaking skills is to eliminate ineffective and mindless reactions to messages sent in the workplace. Too often, individuals are highly reactive to one another, which is both unnecessary and ineffective. The preceding approaches to communication must be used on a regular basis for them to become habits. As you exercise these skills, notice how you experience conversations with others and how others appear to be experiencing you. Strong communicators who lend feelings of worth to those around them tend to experience greater long-term success in their careers than those who do not. By continually improving your listening and speaking skills, you are likely to find a corresponding increase in your job satisfaction and career opportunities.

BIO

Sarah James is a psychotherapist with a private practice in Lone Tree, Colorado. Her practice specialties include life transition, self-growth, depression, anxiety, and posttraumatic stress disorder. Sarah was a collegiate All-American athlete and utilizes her leadership skills, drive, and passion as an athlete in her work. To learn more about Sarah, you can visit her website at http://www.thecoloradocounselor.com/.

35

EMPLOYABILITY

Go from Underemployed to Superemployed in Three Steps

Sunny Klein Lurie

Tough times can shake people's faith in their ability to make a career change to something better. In the midst of a sluggish economy, many people are staying in unsatisfying jobs where they are unhappy and underemployed. To pull free of the wrong job fit or find a rewarding career after a job loss, it's time to rethink your approach so you can go from underemployed to superemployed.

What Is Underemployed?

When you believe your work is unsatisfying, you are not using your strengths or passions. Following are some signs of being underemployed:

- On most days, you don't enjoy going to work and would rather be doing something else.
- You are underpaid, overskilled, and often not challenged to your potential.
- You do not regularly use your strengths or talents in your work.
- You often lack energy and enthusiasm for your work.
- You feel your work is not particularly interesting or meaningful.
- You often hear yourself say, "I need a new job."

We do not have to remain in a draining, unfulfilling job. Most of us would prefer to be superemployed.

What Is Superemployed?

Following are some signs of being superemployed:

- You look forward to doing your work.
- You feel natural and confident in your work role.
- You usually have good concentration doing your work.
- You are paid a competitive wage for your skills and ideas.

- You often lose all sense of time when involved in your work.
- You are curious to learn new information and enjoy new challenges.

To make the switch from being underemployed to superemployed, here is a crash course of three essential steps.

1. Discover *you*—your strengths and passions. Often individuals who thrive consistently have high self-awareness about their strengths and passions. Many successful people, including Oprah and Richard Branson of Virgin Air, have said that a condition for great achievement is *passion*. When your strengths and passions are applied in your work, your potential and enthusiasm will be limitless. People who use their strengths and talents are more than three times as likely to report an overall excellent quality of life.

Once you clarify your authentic strengths and interests, you'll be a powerful force when interviewing and striving toward your career goals. Do not look for a new job before you identify your strengths because you are likely to become underemployed and mismatched in the wrong position.

So how do you determine strengths to select a path that is right for you? Begin by brainstorming what triggers your enthusiasm and what motivates you. Sit down in a quiet place to list twenty things you like to do, then look for patterns. Do you prefer working with data, people, things, or ideas? You may discover, for example, that it's more important than you realized to be physically active and that your work should not be behind a desk all day. Or you may discover that you want to be around busy and loud environments, which might rule out a secluded, one-person office. You'll know a particular career is right when you are curious and enthusiastic about getting started.

Get clear about yourself by answering the following questions:

- What is one skill or strength you do well that you would like to use in your work?
- Which of your previous work results are you proud of—what were you doing?
- What tasks and topics get your heart racing?
- If you could do one thing in your professional life that would have the most positive impact, what would it be?

After completing the questions, it helps to talk through your answers with someone. Talking about yourself with a peer will help to uncover patterns and shine a brighter light on your skills and interests. Often creative ideas are born during discussions with people who hold a different perspective. Many times, all it takes is an encouraging word or new idea from a friend to move forward. But a career change is not easy, and step 2 will help you handle change.

2. Learn to navigate change. When you feel it's unbearable going into work or your job has been eliminated, changing your career may be the only choice. Change is like fire—it will burn you or it will warm you. People who embrace change as an opportunity for growth are often at an advantage to be warmed by change. These individuals are flexible enough to respond quickly and tackle the process of career change.

Going through a job change can make your stomach tighten up, but it's important to shift your view and loosen up by having more tolerance for uncertainty and ambiguity. If you freeze and become paralyzed by the unknown, you will remain stuck and unable to move your career forward. If you focus on trying to adapt, you will navigate more smoothly through the blur of change.

To maneuver change, write clear career goals to target which industries, organizations, and jobs to pursue that match your strengths and interests. Put an emphasis on action. Track down the information you need. Be open to learning new information, and focus your energy on reaching beyond your comfort zone. If you adjust your mind-set to being optimistic about new challenges and resilient to change, you are ready to make connections with step 3.

3. Adopt a master connector, or become one. We've heard that "together we can move mountains." It is true that your best strategy to reach your destination involves connections. This means you must become a great relationship builder, or if you are not savvy at connecting, you have to find people who are.

To grow your network, go outside the confines of your inner circle. Look around your life at religious affiliations, neighbors, school alumni relationships, and community and sports groups. Difficult economic times motivate people to support one another. We have learned that banding together provides more security for our survival, so seek out others and connect. Use your network to get your foot in the door, assist in identifying interesting opportunities, determine ways to brand and market yourself, keep you on track, and introduce you to people in a variety of fields.

If you are uncomfortable with relationship building, two other options exist: connect with someone who is a master connector to help you, or use social networks, such as LinkedIn or Facebook, that make online communication easy. To adopt a master connector, make a list of individuals with large networks in a range of industries who make it their business to know people, organizations, and events taking place and who enjoy staying in touch. Reach out by explaining that you are changing careers. Don't make a career change alone. Remaining isolated is a fate bound to failure.

There are innate strengths and passions within all of us. When these are tapped and properly used, you will greatly increase your chance of finding a satisfying career. A career change is an opportunity to adapt to new challenges and stretch your imagination to interesting possibilities. You cannot get there alone. It is essential to build a solid network and use your contacts to help you successfully go from underemployed to superemployed.

BIO

Sunny Klein Lurie, PhD, is founder and CEO of Fast Focus Careers, http://www.fastfocuscareers.com or email: info at fastfocuscareers.com. Her firm helps people go from underemployed to superemployed. Lurie's doctoral research and twenty years of experience in organizational behavior and career development taught her that using talents on the job greatly increases job satisfaction and performance. Lurie is the author of *Build Your Career to Thrive Consistently: 6 Rules for Breakthrough Success to be released late 2011*. She has served on the boards of the National Association of Women Business Owners and the American Society for Training and Development. She has been a speaker for many business associations and has written articles for publications such as *Small Business News*.

36

Getting Started for Recent College Graduates

❧

Natalie Menendez

"The Next Step"

I wish that I could have spoken to you four or six years ago and told you how important it is to plan for graduation day. I would have told you that it's time to grow up because by comparison, four years of college go by so quickly and easily compared to working in a position that you don't love. But since we're here at this point now, I hope I can tell you a few things that I've learned that can help you make provisions for the next step. It might seem at first that everything I'm suggesting is done solely for the purpose of filling a résumé with data designed to land a dream job. Though this may be somewhat truthful, my goal is to prepare you as a professional so that when you have to make a decision, it will be the right one.

If you are reading this and you have just received your diploma, you are probably looking for a way to pay for your student loans. Unfortunately, the current economic atmosphere does not offer comfort or security for recent graduates; however, this is something that one always needs to be prepared for. As a recent college graduate, I would like to share some personal experiences that I hope will make this transition as painless as possible.

The importance of forming a network and the continual broadening of that network is one of the most valuable tools to have. It is a source of shared information from fellow students, colleagues, and educators on which each of us can rely. You have now become a member of my network, and I offer you some of my secrets to making this journey a success.

Talk and Inquire!

Casual conversation led to my internship, my mentor, and even to writing this short article. I had no possible idea that someone I met briefly at a craft fair would become so instrumental in my decision to pursue industrial psychology. I mention this because I want to stress the importance of showing the world who you are, what you have to offer, and where you are going. I often think of what I would be involved in had that chance meeting not taken place.

Be Resourceful about Ways to Find Out More

It is so important for students to make use of every resource that a college provides. Investigate the many services that your school offers such as career services, résumé writing seminars, and perhaps even training programs such as programs in diversity awareness and leadership skills.

These programs are invaluable and will be of assistance when it is time to formulate a résumé. It is never too early to think about all the facts that should be incorporated into a résumé. To a prospective employer, your résumé is the sum total of who you are and the accomplishments you have acquired during the course of your education. It is critical that this document be filled with all personal endeavors, so it is therefore your responsibility to make intelligent decisions about which activities would best suit your career choice.

Volunteer

Volunteering is a wonderful way to become acquainted with your profession and, at the same time, perform an act of goodwill, which is always positive. This is also an excellent opportunity to meet prospective employers. It is through volunteering that I have formed some of my most valuable relationships, where I was guided and mentored. It was as a volunteer that I discovered my sincere passions and charted the way toward a career about which I felt enthusiastic.

Clubs and Professional Organizations

As a psychology major, I joined the psychology club and was made president in my junior year. This was a total immersion into my field. As volunteers, our group worked hands-on with organizations requiring mental health assistance, career guidance, and lessons in life skills. This was an opportunity to work in my future profession and become involved. Contacts were built as we shared ideas and experiences during meetings. Faculty advisors offered friendship, guidance, and the benefit of their knowledge to aid our journey from students to professionals. It was during this period that I began to think and function as a professional by taking initiative, motivating others, and working in a group of my peers.

Résumé

It is important to consider every club and organizational affiliation, each volunteer experience, and every social act as something that can be incorporated into a résumé that relates to someone what you are about. You are handing someone a piece of paper that describes your actions over the last four to six years. It is important to plan for this event and have enough material to make this document stand out for future employers. There are books that can teach you how to do this, but it may be best to contact a professional résumé writer. Believe it or not, it is easy to distinguish a fill-in-the-blank form and a professionally written résumé that highlights and sells your skill set. It shows an employer that you're willing to spend the extra money and present yourself in the best possible way.

Last, it's important to look and feel like a professional. There are so many opportunities that will make you more valuable to your employer, and it's your responsibility to find out what they are.

After so much money, time, hard work, and devotion spent toward the completion of your degree, you owe yourself the opportunity to demonstrate to a corporation that you will be a valued employee. I hope these things that I have learned and done for myself are lessons that you can apply to your current situation.

Bio

Natalie Menendez is known among her colleagues as an ambitious young professional with a passion for the discipline of psychology and its application within social and workplace environments. While completing her graduate degree in psychological counseling, she is a certified professional resume writer, she has worked closely with predominant industrial psychology and consulting firms. She has been a member of Psi-Chi National Honor Society for Psychology, Eastern Psychological Association, Society of I-O Psychology, and Chi Sigma Iota Graduate Honor Society and has served as the president of Monmouth University's Psychology Club. Natalie has been nominated for numerous community service awards and has been hand-selected to participate in elite campus-leader programs. Contact her at nataliemenendez@gmail.com or online at http://www.loebconsultinggroup.com/.

37

Transitioning from Student to Professional

What They Don't Teach You in School

❦

Pongo Resumes

The move from school to the workplace is one of the most profound transitions life throws at you. All your life, you've been asked, "What do you want to be when you grow up?" Well, now you are grown up. But if you're like many recent grads, you still don't have a clear answer to the question.

And that's OK. Most people entering the workforce today will start with a two- or three-year series of less-than-ideal jobs. This is the real-world education that will teach you the survival skills you'll need to excel in the professional world and help you clarify where you want your career to go.

Following are five tips for making the transition from student to professional go as smoothly as possible.

1. Adjust Your Focus

In school, the focus was on meeting your needs and preferences. You chose your classes, your instructors, your schedule, and the people with whom you spent time.

At work, you no longer have that level of control. But on the upside, you get a paycheck. And to get a job and succeed in the workplace, you'll need to turn your focus toward the people who sign those paychecks.

Think like an employer, and figure out how you can contribute to the organization's business needs. After years of thinking about your own needs, your focus must shift—at least at work—to putting the organization's needs above yours.

2. Work on Your People Skills

"Drama" is often part of the fabric of school life. Tempers flare, competitions arise, and people take sides. That stuff doesn't cut it at work.

Personality clashes among employees are a huge drain on a business because any time spent resolving conflicts cuts into productivity and detracts from the bottom line. Regardless of who's right or wrong, drama in the office reflects poorly on all parties involved.

Any hiring manager will tell you that a person who is likable and pleasant to work with is a more valuable employee than an equally skilled—or even more skilled—individual with a bad attitude. If you're not a natural people person, you'll need to build up those skills. A quick Web search for "improving your people skills" is a good place to start.

3. Watch and Learn

Learning is what school is all about. But learning is really what your first couple of jobs should be about as well. Since you're a newcomer to the working world, it's always wise to observe and learn from the more experienced workers. In any workplace, it will soon become apparent who the most respected players are. Model your behavior on those people. Seek their advice. Maybe ask one of them to act as your mentor, one who can help you do your job better and navigate the sometimes treacherous waters of workplace or office politics.

4. Network, Network, Network

As a student, your networking may have been limited to social networking on sites such as MySpace or Facebook. It's time to expand your thinking. A strong network will help you at every step of your career, but especially at the entry level. A good word from someone who can vouch for your character and work ethic is a lot stronger than a résumé that says you excelled in English literature and were the leading scorer on the lacrosse team.

When you're looking for a job, talk to anyone and everyone: family, friends, neighbors, the gas station attendant, your old boss at the pizza shop. You never know who knows someone who knows someone who has a job opening. Tell them what kind of job you're seeking, and make sure they know how to get in touch with you.

5. Keep Updating Your Résumé

Even if you're quite comfortable with your job, it's always good practice to keep your résumé up to date. When you land a job, add it to your résumé. Then, each time a significant accomplishment or promotion comes your way, you can update it.

A new opportunity can come along at any time, and being prepared with an updated résumé could put you a step ahead of other qualified candidates. So be sure to keep a record of all the contributions you make and the compliments you earn, saving copies of those that were e-mailed or handwritten. As your accomplishments and accolades build, they will help vault you to your next career challenge.

Conclusion

With your diploma or degree fresh in hand and a head full of knowledge, you probably thought your education was complete. But a successful transition from school to work is a learning process all its own.

You're learning what you're good at, where you must improve, and how the real pros operate. And you're starting to build a professional network that could serve you throughout your career. Experience in the real world is what helps you decide "what you want to be," whether that means staying on the path you chose in school or taking another route.

BIO

Pongo Resumes' content-writing team—Julie O'Malley, Rick Saia, and Brianna Raymond—collaborated on this chapter. All three are Certified Professional Resume Writers, with diverse professional backgrounds that include writing, editing, journalism, and marketing communications roles. They cover a wide range of job search topics in articles, e-newsletters, blog posts, and Web content for Pongo Resume (http://www.pongoresume.com/), an online service that features a résumé and cover letter builder, along with comprehensive tools and support to help job seekers land interviews and job offers.

38

EXCLUSIVITY

Put Your Exclusivity to Work

※〜∞

JoAnn DePolo

Get the Edge

Redirecting your focus toward others immediately sets you apart, placing your career on the path to excellence with an unrivaled competitive edge. Ask yourself these important questions throughout your career: Why am I doing this? What is my motive? Answering these questions will set the stage for you to approach and achieve your goals. Be honest with yourself and what you are searching for. Truly the outcome is for the benefit of others. A selfless attitude will open the door of success and fulfillment, keeping you grounded while others take notice of your talents and abilities.

Each of us is created with a unique personality that cannot be duplicated; put that exclusivity to work in your favor. Originality is the basis for gaining an unrivaled competitive advantage that will separate you from the rest, as a truly inspired innovative approach cannot be duplicated. In addition to having a distinct personality, every person has definite talents and abilities that match specific occupations. Passionately pursue a career best suited to accommodating your talents, and success will follow seemingly without effort. Allow time for your career to develop into the vision you have set forth.

Esteem every person you meet with a sense of value and significance because they are as unique as you are. Be aware of those around you, and treat them with respect—regard for others, placing others' needs above your own—is the mark of a true professional. Keep in mind that you are dealing with consumers who make quick observations and want to work with a confident professional. Become an exceptional salesperson because a successful salesperson knows the importance of finding the common ground with each individual client. Finding a common ground will open the channel of communication, which will help to win consumers' confidence.

Maintain a Teachable Mind-set

Although preparation is ongoing, be ready to work with what you know and what you have. Do not fool yourself into believing that you will be better prepared at some other time in the future—you are prepared right now. Training continues throughout your career. Maintain a teachable mind-set that keeps you prepared to advance and in the position for increase. Real preparedness is a sense of confident contentment, enabling you to apply what you already know. Immediately, this contentment platform will allow you to operate at your present potential, providing the stability you need to springboard toward the next phase of your career. Each level of success you attain will prepare you to advance. By applying this type of mind-set, you will find yourself in the position to enjoy each stage in your career, living to your potential daily and using the knowledge you have gained from yesterday. Taking a slow and steady approach will allow your personal growth to develop, along with increased responsibility. Through the course of time, this solid personal foundation will enable you to withstand and overcome any pressure that would otherwise intimidate you and confine career advancement and growth.

Go the Extra Mile

Do you view yourself as a professional? What is that, anyway? By definition, a professional is one who receives a financial return for an activity or for a field of endeavor often engaged in by amateurs. It may also be defined as meeting the standard in a particular line of work, but really it is the revealing of your inner self. It is the passion or core of your career. You do not have to work at it because it is who you really are. It is a part of your design. You may need to adjust your habits but not the character or professional essence of who you are. You care about your clients because you care about people. Professionalism is not a checklist or a neatly composed system; rather it is an approach. Having the proper attire, maintaining neatly ordered papers, or sending a correct e-mail is not all that is involved in being a professional. A true professional is someone who goes the extra mile to accomplish that which others cannot see or sometimes cannot comprehend. It involves standing alone, if you have to, because it is the right thing to do. There is no one specific thing, situation, or series of steps to use that will make you into a professional because being a professional comes from within. You must believe in yourself and put your expertise to work.

Your career rests with you. Be determined to change, modify, and reorganize everything that has not worked in your career up to this point. Develop a distinct approach centered on your individuality. Discipline yourself to maintain the course as you continue and press on through to greater success.

A good number of artists find that they are short on time when it comes to merchandising and promotions, only to become frustrated because they are not consistently moving forward, gaining public recognition, and achieving financial gain. *Making It as an Artist* is a resource to help skilled and emerging artists handle these issues as they proceed in the art profession. *Making It as an Artist* is available everywhere books and e-books are sold.

BIO

JoAnn DePolo is a visual artist with a contemporary focus and is author of *Making It as an Artist*. She is a teaching artist, the founder of Come & Create™ Fine Arts & Community Murals, and a contributing artist for *Extreme Makeover: Home Edition*. Regarded as a visionary, her audience extends internationally amid several celebrities. JoAnn presently serves as Secretary on the Executive Board of Directors for the Artists Archives of the Western Reserve. *Making It as an Artist* reveals the inside workings of the business of art and has been endorsed by artists, galleries, and art collectors. Visit http://joanndepolo.com/ and http://joanndepolo.blogspot.com/ for updates and events.

39

Why Are You Treating Me Like a Two-Year-Old?

3 Strategies for Turning Employee Excuses into Everyday Accountability

⚜⁓⁓⁓

Ray Perry

Are you tired of employees who offer excuses instead of results—who commit to one thing but do another? How do you hold these nonperformers accountable? Your answer reveals much about how well you are harnessing the power of accountability to enhance team performance—as well as your career.

Patrick the Pushover

It's 2:30 in the afternoon, and Patrick is furious that Jennifer, his HR manager, did not complete next year's operational budget, as promised. He storms into her office, roaring, "Where the heck are the budgets you promised me?" Jennifer casually responds, "I've been so swamped with this relocation project. I just haven't had a chance to finish crunching the numbers."

With an accusatory tone, Patrick replies, "But you said you would do it by this morning and . . . " Before Patrick can finish, Jennifer defensively shoots back, "Why are you treating me like a two-year-old? You let Marcus slide on that proposal just yesterday!"Suddenly finding himself in a defensive role reversal after his employee's artful dodging, Patrick guiltily responds, "I'm sorry, I didn't realize how busy you are—when do you think you could get it done?"

What happened in this situation? Patrick folded like a house of cards and taught Jennifer that if she pushes back with a little emotion, she won't be held accountable. More important, this management approach simply encourages nonperformance in the future. And if it happens consistently, and with others, it creates a team in which dysfunctional accountability becomes the norm.

So how could Patrick transform his team from a culture of dysfunction to one of everyday accountability? Like any one of us in this situation, Patrick simply could use an accountability MAP to get to his preferred destination. MAP is an acronym representing three transformational strategies that can be leveraged to create a strong accountability culture in even the most dysfunctional of workplaces:

1. *Model* the expectations.
2. *Announce* the policy.
3. *Proactively* hold the team accountable.

Accountability Expectations

At the heart of the accountability MAP are two expectations that apply whenever a team member commits to an interim and/or final deliverable deadline:

Communicate to the manager that the deliverable is completed by the due date *and* has met quality expectations;

OR

Provide an advance warning to the manager that it can't be done by the deadline, why the problem exists, and the new, adjusted deadline.

Think about it—is this really a lot to ask of our employees? Quite the contrary! One could make a compelling case that this is the essence of professionalism, responsibility, and initiative.

Model the Expectations

How effective would you be insisting that your staff arrive on time to meetings, if you are typically late yourself? Just as true, how effective would you be in creating a stronger accountability culture if you weren't able or willing to consistently meet the expectations yourself?

Action strategy. *Before* announcing the accountability policy, spend one month holding yourself accountable to both expectations. It's absolutely critical that you "walk the talk" before announcing the expectation policy.

Why important? Announcing the policy will set the performance expectations for the team—not just through words but through actions. The payoff? You gain tremendous leverage in persuading both habitual and occasional nonperformers to change future behavior. Based on Pygmalion effect research, you simply will have a significantly greater chance that your actions will become a self-fulfilling prophecy.

Announce the Policy

Does stuff happen? You bet. Do priorities change? Often hourly. Do problems arise? Is the earth round? Did Jennifer have a good reason for not completing the budgets when promised? Absolutely—*a competing priority moved to the front of the pile.* Sound familiar? So what was the problem? Jennifer didn't take the professional and responsible action of letting Patrick know ahead of time.

How can we expect employees to do the right thing, though, if they don't know what the right thing is? It's great to assume that they should do it, but unless they clearly understand the expectations, they cannot—and should not—be held accountable. It's rather unfair, wouldn't you agree?

Action strategy. After spending a month modeling the accountability expectations, announce the expectation policy. In preparation for the announcement, create and memorize a "why sentence" that succinctly explains why the policy is important for the team, and also identify and commit to memory three benefits from implementing it. When announcing the policy, discuss both the why and the benefits, and then gain agreement on the policy. Leverage the time you spent modeling the expectations to morally persuade any team member who pushes back on the policy.

Why important? As managers, we can't hold our employees accountable if they don't clearly understand the ground rules. And if we can't hold employees accountable, we can't change accountability behavior. Most important, if they clearly know the expectations, it will be easier to hold them accountable because they can't hide behind excuses.

Proactively Hold the Team Accountable

If Patrick's team were *always* to meet both accountability expectations, when would he have to follow up and actively hold team members accountable? Never. Why? Because team members would either come to him with a finished, on-time deliverable that met quality expectations *or* take the initiative and let him know ahead of time if there were a problem. The policy allows Patrick to take a proactive—instead of a reactive—accountability approach.

Now, let's rewind and assume that Patrick has *not* fostered a prevailing culture of accountability in his office. When would Patrick have to follow up and actively hold team members accountable? The answer is simple—only when a team member didn't meet a deadline and failed to provide advance warning. More important, what does Patrick say when holding an employee accountable for nonperformance? (And let's face it: a lot of us are conflict averse.) Instead of using reactive language, he would use proactive language.

Action strategy. Follow up immediately after a missed deadline. Calmly customize the following five-part proactive language format when holding an employee accountable:

1. Reiterate the expectation agreement.

2. State the facts.

3. Ask, "What happened?" Stop talking, and respectfully listen.

4. Hold the employee accountable for not providing an early warning.

5. Gain a new commitment.

For additional accountability strategies, including how to deal with employees who refuse to be held accountable, see: http://www.SkillTrack.org/accountability.html.

Why important? Actions speak louder than words. When we aren't proactive, our actions scream, "The accountability expectations to which we agreed were meaningless, and in the future, just ignore the policy." On the other hand, by taking the right accountability approach, we teach employees and operationalize that "on our team, when we say we're going to do something, we do it—or we let the person know ahead of time if there's a problem."

By using a MAP approach to reach your accountability destination, you will gain more confidence, control, and collaboration. You'll be able to transform employee excuses into everyday accountability. The inevitable result of all this is that team performance, morale, and retention (PMR™) will climb to peak levels. It's a perfect way to set yourself apart as a manager, and of course, it's a great way to enhance your career.

BIO

The founder and president of Skill Track Inc., Ray Perry is a trusted adviser, coach, and speaker on proactive accountability, strategic planning implementation, and continuous employee development. For more than twenty-five years, his results-driven approach has inspired clients to take action and realize the type of lasting change that unlocks greater performance, morale, and retention (PMR™). Among the clients with whom Ray has worked are Johns Hopkins University, Dartmouth College, the Association of American Medical Colleges, the U.S. Department of Commerce, Accenture, Black and Decker, IBM, American Express, Federal Express, Disney Imagineering, and Northrop Grumman. For more information, please visit http://www.SkillTrack.org/rayperrybio.html.

40

Your Face Is as Important as Your Résumé

❧

Cynthia Rowland

Seeking employment can be daunting, especially if you have been out of the workplace for a while or if the previous company for which you worked downsized and you were caught in the fray. You may be concerned that your skill levels may not be what they were, and you may feel that you have lost confidence in your appearance.

Your face is your calling card—your power suit—and you want to portray the very best you. If you are involved with a job search, you will absolutely want to put your best face forward so that you can nail that job with ease.

You may or may not know that wearing a younger-looking face is a huge asset. No matter if you are forty, fifty, or sixty, your face speaks volumes about you. A lined, haggard face wearing a down-turned mouth might say to the world, "I am depressed!" If you are wearing a smiling face with an attraction-getting, happy-go-lucky attitude, it probably means that you are an innately happy person. That smiling face can go a long way toward creating success.

Psychologists tell us that an old-looking face might portray old ideas, so if you're contemplating dusting off your résumé, you might want to look in the mirror and do something very proactive to enhance the shape and contour of your face. After all, a droopy face with jowls, pouches, hooded eyes, and a double chin can make you appear older than your years.

Wearing a younger-looking face can assure you that your income can be higher than that of a person with the same credentials. According to economist Daniel Hamermest, a drop-dead gorgeous man can earn $250,000 more than his least attractive counterpart over his career, and these findings go for women, too.

In a *Newsweek* article, it was disclosed that 57 percent of hiring managers said that qualified but unattractive candidates are likely to have a harder time landing a job, and the managers advised the applicants to spend their money on "making sure they look attractive" rather than on perfecting their résumés.

This is startling news! What really counts is your face because hiring managers are looking at more than just your résumé. Hiring smart, attractive-looking people with a passion for success is the mission, and you have to wear a high-caliber look.

So how do you make certain you look attractive? Do you take pride in your appearance and wear an aura of confidence? For your confidence to soar, you have to get more than just your résumé, suit, and shoes ready—you will want to spiff up your face, too.

One simple, inexpensive way to make certain that your face looks its very best is to learn a facial exercise routine. Using facial exercise rather than resorting to costly facial surgeries and injections that plump and paralyze means that your face will look younger and fresher without spending much money; you won't run the risk of ruining your good looks with modalities that may or may not provide long-term benefits or spend hundreds or thousands of dollars needlessly.

What makes facial exercise so enticing is that the routine only takes a few minutes each day to execute, and once you have learned the movements, you can thoroughly exercise your face in less time than it takes to pack a gym bag, back the car out of the garage, drive to your workout place, and find a parking spot.

Facial exercise is a very reliable method of keeping your face toned, lifted, and tightened. When you see hooded eyes, a double chin, or cheeks that are elongating and pooling into your jaw line, you have very few choices to easily rectify sagging facial muscles. Yes, cutting is one way to address this type of aging, but that can involve complications that you do not want. Surgery requires recuperative time, and you want to earn money, not spend it.

Exercise is natural. Just as you exercise your arms, legs, buttocks, waist, tummy, hips, and thighs, you can successfully exercise your face using the very same resistance techniques that trim those bulging areas that make you look fat, old, and tired.

Without spending a lot of money, going under anesthesia, taking myriad drugs, or spending time away from your family and friends, you can systematically begin an exercise regimen that will de-age your facial features five, ten, even fifteen years.

Simple isometric resistance exercises will target every area of the face and strengthen those tiny, underlying muscles. By firming and lifting these muscles, the youthful contours of your face will return so that your skin looks younger, healthier, and fresher. As you learn how to anchor the muscles and muscle groups, you will see and feel your face respond to these natural, proven exercise movements; your face, like your body, receives great benefit from exercise, and your confidence level will improve because you will see and feel your face lifting and responding to the specialized exercises.

Without spending a lot of money; going through pain; or having sutures, injections, surgery, or anything harmful, you can enjoy a more youthful-looking face. Your friends and family will recognize you, and your self-assurance will soar.

With your skills, experience, and abilities at the ready, you can be assured that your face is as powerful as your résumé.

Bio:

Cynthia Rowland is a widely recognized expert in all natural facial fitness. She has appeared on several popular television shows including The View, The Today Show, Rachael Ray and The Doctors. Cynthia is co-host of The Ageless Sisters on blogtalkradio.com and author of The Magic of facial Exercise. Cynthia is leading the crusade to keep men and women looking vibrantly younger through natural techniques without spending their children's inheritance. To learn more about her anti-aging techniques, visit her website at http://www.rejenuve.com/FacialMagicSL.htm

8 Fatal Mistakes Most Executives and Up-and-Coming Business Professionals Make—and How to Avoid Them

≈≈≈

Rita Hyland

Mistake 1: Not loving what you do. Many people find themselves in a career they think they should be in rather than one they want to be in. When individuals are experiencing a supreme case of being stuck, it's most often because they aren't following their heart's desire and inner ambition. When you don't follow your passion, your creative spirit won't assist in making your career successful because you're going against what you really want. You'll wind up frustrated by limiting your career and financial potential, and your relationships and personal well-being will be negatively affected. If your work is costing you mentally, physically, or emotionally, it's time to find a job or business you love and pursue it.

> **Remedy.** Commit to designing a future that rewards you in all ways. It's possible to get paid to do what you love—and be wildly successful!

Mistake 2: Suffering from an "upper limit." This idea comes from Gay Hendricks's fabulous book *The Big Leap*. Each of us has an internal thermometer for how much career success, wealth, happiness, love, and intimacy we'll let ourselves experience. That's our upper limit, setting, or our success comfort zone. When we exceed this limit and our career, business, or life gets a fabulous result (land a big client, develop a new product, get a long-awaited promotion, have an influx of money, get healthy and thin, find a great relationship), we unconsciously sabotage ourselves and drop back to the old, familiar place where we feel in control.

> **Remedy.** Become aware of your upper limit during or even before it manifests. You'll notice it when something you want always remains at arm's distance or you can't maintain it. Get comfortable with the new reality you desire by acknowledging what is great and rich in your life already. Tell your clients how much you love working with them; tell your

family how you're grateful for them; appreciate and respect today's bank account. Prepare yourself mentally and emotionally to accept the wins you want and are creating. *How good you can stand it is how good it gets!*

Mistake 3: Not practicing the 80:20 rule. Most of us know that if we spend 20 percent of our time on the highest ROI tasks, we'll get 80 percent of our results. Yet many fall prey to not doing this. How often do you find yourself immersed in the unimportant, mind-numbing minutiae that your work seems to require?

> **Remedy.** Clarity of intention and prioritization of tasks and projects make it easy to know what to do. However, you must possess the structure or systems and boldness to follow through. Processes provide the organization you need, while boldness is the key ingredient for effective time management. Ultimately, boldness is the willingness to follow through on your priorities and use your systems and structures, regardless of what chaos, interruptions, or distractions you encounter during your day. Leverage the first two hours of your day to do the top 20 percent of action items. *You'll enjoy the feeling of achieving 80 percent of your results—without getting burned out!*

Mistake 4: Waiting until you're confident to take the next step. Confidence is overrated. Every rung of the corporate ladder is filled with individuals who (when they get honest with themselves) wish they were more confident and less afraid. The difference between those who truly thrive and those who merely survive is that the successful ones don't allow the fear to run them, and they don't wait to get confident. Instead, they do what the classic Susan Jeffers book states: "Feel the fear and do it anyway."

> **Remedy.** Acknowledge when you're afraid, and allow the mental theater to have its fright fest movie going on in theater B while you remain focused as the star of the main attraction on the center screen. As the actor of your own show, you can "fake it 'til you make it"! *Confidence arrives while doing, not while preparing!*

Mistake 5: Not investing in your greatest asset—*you*. Jim Rohn stated, "If you want to have more, you first have to *become* more." In essence, *you*—not your career—is what needs to be invested in. Your career and success will only be as great as you are. Continue working on making yourself more skilled, knowledgeable, and attractive—both inside and out.

> **Remedy.** The best investment you can make is in you—your greatest asset. Purchase opportunities and experiences rather than material things. Create your own university by listening to audios, reading books, and attending

workshops, lectures, and classes. Read, study, grow, expand, travel, reflect, provide value, give more—become a better you. Additionally, get support, collaboration, and feedback from a good mentor or strong coach. Working with someone to reach your professional and personal goals gets you where you're going faster, with less pain and more fun than doing it alone. *You're worth it!*

Mistake 6: Having a lack of clarity. Possessing crystal-clear focus on what you *don't* want guarantees that you'll never land or develop the career you want. Lack of clarity will destroy a goal every time. Many have more clarity around what they want to avoid (another down revenue year, a manager like that one) than around what they want to achieve. Reasons you may lose clarity include forgetting your purpose, not connecting to a compelling reason to do what you do, and not mastering giving high value, among other things.

> **Remedy.** Get laser-focused on your goal. It is very unlikely you will ever hit a target you don't see. Clarify the results you desire in your career and life. Make decisions from what you want rather than from what you want to avoid. What do you need to take your career to the next level? What do you want to do, be, or have that would make you look back at your career and life and say "wow!" On a daily basis, never leave your office without already seeing what you want to achieve and experience the following day. As you go to your office each day, you're visualizing and stepping into what's already laid out. *You can do almost anything when you're crystal-clear and your why is big enough!*

Mistake 7: Not understanding that you're in the business of relationships. Regardless of what business you're in (financial consulting, consumer products, manufacturing light bulbs, or your own photography business), you're *really* in the business of relationships, in other words, people. Your relationships with people will either catapult you to the top or be the anchor impeding your career progress.

> **Remedy.** If you're within an organization, know the teams and the direct reports you serve—their needs, their fears—and work to support them. Be more interested than interesting. Listen and care. Be a steady giver of high-value content, information, tools, and insights. Few people make it to the top without other people wanting them to get there. People don't care how much you know until they know how much you care. *Love and care for people—it always comes back to you!*

Mistake 8: Not realizing that taking others to the top is essential to making it to the top. Individuals who have individual success, and may even be intellectually brilliant, but never contribute to others' growth and improvement have limited careers.

>**Remedy.** The job for every existing and up-and-coming, career-driven professional is to develop organizational talent. Dedicate time weekly, and even daily, to being able to replace yourself so your boss can advance you and be confident your shoes will be well filled. *Teaching others is the best way to learn, and sharing your success increases the success of everyone around you!*

BIO

Rita Hyland's coaching company serves Fortune 500 corporations, small businesses, and individuals, helping them set and reach their professional and personal goals. Rita is a no-nonsense life and career coach dedicated to helping entrepreneurs, corporate executives, up-and-coming professionals, and stay-at-home moms who are seeking professional excellence and personal well-being through business, entrepreneurship, and spiritual transformation. She powerfully combines practical, creative, and intuitive solutions to assist clients in taking consistent action to achieve success. Her brand Bold, Rich, and Fulfilled is designed to provide the tools, inspiration, and accountability to turn one's passion into profit and achieve emotional, spiritual, and financial wealth. For more information, visit http://www.ritahyland.com/, or contact Rita at breakthrough@ritahyland.com.

42

The Unfortunate Career Phenomenon

❧〜❧

Susan Crampton Davis

You've probably heard the statistics—it's estimated that less than 80 percent of today's workforce shows up for work on Monday morning excited and fully engaged. Throughout my corporate career, I had an unrelenting sense of curiosity about why happiness could elude so many. I even had the same thoughts about myself.

There were too many times I had all the right ingredients in my career and yet was living in a reoccurring cycle of disenchantment. The outward signs of success were there—nice title, good income, great companies. At some point, this was no longer enough, and I embarked on a journey of self-discovery to define how to bring more meaning into my career. Half a dozen years later, I was a living testimony to what all the experts espouse creates deep career fulfillment, and yet I found myself succumbing to those familiar feelings of disenchantment. It didn't make sense. I was working for the largest philanthropic foundation, my strengths were being leveraged, and I felt impassioned by the work. And yet somehow I felt like an imposter because I still knew I wasn't living my deepest professional and personal dreams. While looking at the promotion of a lifetime in the eyes, I decided to leave and continue my quest to find the real answers to loving work.

Today my clarity about what stands in the way of happiness, engagement, and success at work couldn't be clearer. I'm even bold enough to say that we are going about career fulfillment all wrong. We don't need a louder declaration to bring our strengths and passions to work as a way to solve today's biggest business dilemma. Happiness at work can't be solved with more money, flex hours, on-site gyms, or even the next big promotion. These are analogous to putting lipstick on a pig, because none addresses the real reasons we can't love work. *We are afraid.*

I'm not talking about the kind of fear that causes us to lock our car doors and bedroom windows but rather the type that closes our hearts and puts us in self-preservation mode. We fear this isn't the right career, or we're nervous it is. Internal self-doubt tells us to ignore our own intuition and keeps us from going after what we really want. In the backs of our minds, we wrestle with the anxiety that we're not good enough, smart enough, or deserving enough and play defense to prove our worth. We become cynical and find fault in the most ideal circumstances.

Unfortunately, too many find it easier to blame the establishment, circumstances, or a poor manager or to declare that this is just *the way I am* to avoid looking inward. In fact, our mind constructs the ego so we don't have to look too hard at ourselves. It keeps score of our disappointments, insecurities, and wounds and erects an invisible fence in our psyches as a way to help us avoid similar circumstances and feelings in the future. It conveniently points out disparaging things about others so that we can feel better about ourselves. Most dangerously, it is the gathering place for the culprits that block our pathways to greater happiness and success in the workplace: our *self-limiting beliefs.*

I want to be clear that I am not just talking about unproductive thoughts. These are *beliefs*—deeply held definitions of right or wrong that send direct neurological commands to the body. In the same automatic way we breathe, drive a car, or sing the words to our favorite songs without any conscious thought, we have disempowering programs that tell us what to see and how to think, feel, and behave. If we believe *we're not good enough,* we might unconsciously give up on the notion of applying for the big promotion at the moment of contemplation. A striving for perfection and control is born from the belief *I am not perfect or capable.* If we believe *I don't deserve prosperity,* we will not see or realize our opportunities or abundance.

Once I uncovered that I held a belief that *I don't deserve success,* my career themes started to make sense. In fact, my whole life made sense. I had an internal program that said *I'm not capable or smart enough.* It gave birth to this notion that *I didn't belong* every time success moved too close. My beliefs generated the unconscious interference that would self-sabotage whenever things seemed too good to be true. My mind could always manufacture a reason to bolt.

The unfortunate phenomenon is that many of our disempowering programs keep us from moving toward what we want and deserve. I was so afraid of success and wasn't even aware of it. What I was experiencing wasn't an anomaly; everyone has avoidance messages that are a natural consequence of childhood. It could be easy to blame the *can't* or *shouldn't* messages we receive when we are very young, but the bigger problem is a natural design flaw of the brain that is exacerbated in our youth.

In the simplest terms, we have a fully functional *old brain* at birth. This part of our brain is responsible for storing the automatic programs so we can effortlessly ride a bike or get ready in the morning without any mental gymnastics. Also, this part of our brain runs and preserves the body, houses the emotional epicenter, and is wired first and foremost for our safety. In other words, it is on constant lookout for threats.

Whereas the old brain comes functional, the logical and cognitive reasoning housed in the *new brain* will take over twenty years to mature fully. In the absence of the logical counterbalance in our formative years, we lack the full faculties to make rational sense of information and experiences that happen early in our lives. Therefore, without consciously realizing it, many of us move into adulthood still carrying a storehouse of automatic programming born from self-limiting beliefs that are meant to keep us safe—but from what?

Unfortunately, our minds are attempting to protect us from repeating a misinterpreted past. Our memories of the past are held in an enormous inventory of internal representations—*collages of pictures, sounds, and feelings*—that storehouses experiences misconstrued by fear. For example, someone with arachnophobia can see a small spider and lose himself or herself in a sea of anxiety. It is not the spider that scares the person but the internal representation of spiders installed through the lens of fear. In the same way, our beliefs are also tied to a set of collages in our minds. What most people don't understand is that we can change the internal representations and, in return, uninstall the patterns of fear and avoidance that plague our lives.

In fact, with 100 percent certainty, I can say that there is always a bridge between the themes of disappointment and the self-fulfilling prophecy of someone's self-limiting beliefs. For this reason, today's biggest business epidemic doesn't call for another newfangled career engagement or fulfillment strategy; it doesn't even require us to change jobs. Instead, it requires an understanding that while fear-based programming is internalized early in our lives, we are fully capable of unlearning these patterns and rewiring our minds. This is where we find the real secrets to loving work—and life.

BIO

Susan Crampton Davis is the founder of the Positive Change Network (www.awakeningexcellence.com), a Seattle-based consultancy and coaching practice that helps people remove the self-imposed mental barriers blocking greater success. Prior to starting PCN, Susan held senior leadership roles at the Bill & Melinda Gates Foundation, Getty Images, Staples, Amazon, and W. L. Gore & Associates, Inc, where she was responsible for coaching and guiding individuals to success for over twenty-five years. Today Susan has a thriving practice where she uses the simple and powerful coaching techniques that helped her to change her life. She is a master-level NLP practitioner, a hypnotherapist, and a practitioner of Belief Reconditioning Therapy™, which is a client-centered therapy that involves several healing modalities.

43

Obstacles to Manifestation

Fear of Success

⚜⟋⟍⚜

Laura B. Young

Man can only receive what he sees himself receiving.
—Shinn, *The Game of Life*

Many of us, at a deep level, are afraid of success. On the surface, we declare that we are going for the gold, earning a PhD, running a business, . . being the best! That which actually manifests in our life may be something entirely different. What is certain is that our core beliefs will express themselves in our lives regardless of what we say. Core beliefs are ingrained early in life when we are indeed helpless, powerless, and unable to make conscious or intelligent choices. Although core beliefs can enhance the quality of our lives, they can also severely limit manifestation. It is those limiting beliefs that have wide-ranging consequences that not only determine our level of self-esteem and self-worth but also influence happiness and satisfaction in life. When there is conflict between conscious wants and unconscious beliefs, guess which wins. Our unconscious beliefs have the most powerful influence on the level of success we can achieve in our lives.

During the 1960s, thousands of young people rebelled against their parents' definition of success. They declared the roles parents and society imposed as "suffocating," lacking in creative personal choice. The males denigrated their fathers' choice of work, the "gray flannel suits" they wore as well as their leisure time activities. The females were against the traditional marital housewife roles, which included submissiveness to the husband, the "head of household." Subsequently, many were against the status quo, the roles and the rules; however, that is only half the story. Many were not free enough to be for something else: an individual model of success. This rebellion cracked many glass ceilings; however, a new identity of sameness evolved. To be identified as a "free" person, one more or less donned a new uniform. This conformity consisted of long hair, beads, free-flowing clothing, and usually, drugs and alcohol. Some young people went the required distance to create their own success.

Over the years, I have seen clinically many who gave up the search and returned home, to the bosom of safety of the familial way. One such client—I'll call him Mike—had angrily left his father's house right after high school graduation. Owing to the likelihood of being drafted to go to Vietnam, he considered going to Canada, but after drifting for a while, he ended up attending Woodstock in 1969. Being a self-described chameleon, he was unable to avoid peer pressure and joined a group of heavy drug users. He also "merged" with a girl who ignited a freedom and passion within him that he never dreamt possible.

After more wandering with the group, he found himself lacking resources and weakened from drug abuse. He called home requesting money and was urged to return. He was welcomed home as the biblical prodigal son. He attended college, studied business, and received a Vietnam deferment. After joining his father in the banking business, the inner gnawing started. He realized there was a steep price to pay for safety and security. He married another banker's daughter, had children, and joined all the right clubs.

Mike was in his fifties when I saw him. He said he had never lived for himself and had pushed down his hopes and dreams. He remembers his good times on the road with a yearning. There were moments then when he could have created a life for himself but had not. He said those moments of exuberance and freedom left a poignancy within him that had never ceased.

Mike's hobby, photography, became his passion. He was not only creative, he was also in great demand. It was when he started receiving opportunities to do photo shoots for a major magazine that he considered leaving the banking business and becoming a photojournalist. This time, his immediate family balked, not willing to change their lifestyle. His children were grown but continued to be dependent. His wife threatened divorce if he followed through with his desires. Mike gave up the country club and the mansion, and there was a divorce.

Do not expect family and friends to be supportive when you venture out to become successful on your own terms. They are more likely to be supportive when you are down and discouraged. When one member of a family seems to be getting ahead of the tribe, other tribal members may experience anxiety, anger, or even jealousy because his or her gains create discomfort within them. Maybe they have not progressed in life as far as they had hoped. The situation creates enough uneasiness that support, and sometimes acceptance and love, is withheld from the successful member. The covert message is "conform, be like us, or be ostracized."

Loyalty to the family's social status, beliefs, and acceptable behavior is so strong that success beyond one's "place in society" as nothing is impossible. When one ventures beyond, to a different level of success, feelings of disloyalty and guilt often prevent enjoyment.

More than a few of my clients, after achieving success, felt they had very little in common with their roots. Some reveled in the gains and were emotionally independent enough to push on, letting the process of adjustment with their families and friends take place. Others sabotaged their gains to feel once again "at home" because they could not handle the inner conflict their success had caused with family and friends.

Creating one's own paradigm of success may mean discarding some family expectations. There are both positive and negative consequences to all changes. If things go wrong, we have to assume full responsibility for how we manifest success in our lives. Acceptance of consequences is quite difficult for many because the expectation that there will be someone to blame, or to bail us out, is deeply rooted.

After having made the decision to live life your way, you will be able to manifest success. Use the power of vision and imagination to see your success as already having occurred.

My last correspondence with Mike was a postcard I received from Alaska. On it, Mike scribbled a postscript: "Much less money, but an overwhelming sense of peace and happiness—at last!"

Bio

Laura B. Young is a Licensed Marriage and Family Therapist, a Licensed Professional Counselor, and a Certified Clinical Hypnotherapist specializing in relationships, life transitions, grief resolution, and stress management. Laura is devoted to helping people achieve more of their potential. Laura is the author of the book *The Nature of Change,* which is a dialogue to encourage, uplift, and inform readers facing life's changes. Laura is the manifestation expert and a contributing author on the SelfGrowth.com website. All her articles may be found on her website LifeResourceCenter.net.

44

Succeeding as a Woman without Selling Your Soul: How to Be Authentically and Successfully *You* in the Workplace

Helen Kerrison

This is one of the best times in history to be a woman. As women today, we are liberated, we are educated, we have equal opportunity, we have freedom of choice, and we have the capability to fully realize our potential—so why do so many of us still feel that something is missing, that we haven't got what we're really looking for?

What Is It We Are Looking For?

What are we trying to prove, to ourselves and to others? Why do we strive day after day to achieve Wonder Woman status to feel successful? These are interesting questions, especially as what we ultimately achieve tends to be frustration, stress, and a feeling of being overwhelmed!

Does all this sound familiar to you?

What we have lost sight of as women in today's world is the amazing energy and power of our true, feminine nature. In our struggle to succeed in a male-dominated arena, we've adopted the values and power of masculine energy as our own. That's not to say that there's no place for masculine energy in our lives—there most certainly is. However, in embracing it so completely, we have become separated from the essence of who we really are, our feminine energy—the source of our true feminine power.

What Is Feminine Power?

Feminine power is recognizing, acknowledging, embracing, and celebrating the true value of female energy. More often than not, we devalue our uniquely feminine way of being. It is regarded as a limiting weakness to be controlled and suppressed rather than celebrated and expressed.

This is especially true in the workplace. There logic is valued over intuition, competition over cooperation, "head knowledge" and qualifications over wisdom and experience, and hierarchy over sociality. More value is placed on controlling feelings and emotions than on expressing them; on speaking than on listening; and on creating fear, tension, and conflict than on nurturing support, sharing, and agreement.

Given that women spend much of their working days in male energy, playing the "successful career woman" role, is it surprising that many of us end up feeling stressed and inadequate?

How Do We Reclaim Our Feminine Energy?

I believe the first step is to become aware of Your True Self as a woman. Over thousands of years, we have become accustomed to the cultural conditioning of male energy. Its male values that are accepted as the way of life, the norm, the "way things are done."

Of course, challenging this can be painful. On the flip side, challenge represents the path to self-discovery and can result in an uplifting, liberating, and truly enlightening experience.

As we step out on this path, the first hurdle and biggest challenge for many us comes not from the outside but from deep within ourselves—from feelings and beliefs about ourselves and our self-worth and the value we place on our personal contribution.

This is where the journey to reclaim feminine power must start. This is where we need to look under our metaphoric stones, explore the hidden, and uncover the myriad ideas, habits, values, and beliefs held subconsciously that drive our behaviors and through which we create our lives.

This is where we need to question and challenge ourselves:

- How do my subconscious beliefs prevent me from accepting, acknowledging, and expressing my feminine power?
- Where have these beliefs come from, and who gave them to me?
- What are they creating for me, today?
- What might my life look like if I were to remove the beliefs that are blocking the expression of my true feminine energy?
- What fears and insecurities do I have to address to do this?

As we open up and shine a light on our inner selves, it becomes easier and easier to access, accept, and validate the feminine qualities that, until now, we had chosen to hide.

What Happens When We Acknowledge, Express, and Embrace Our Feminine Qualities?

First of all, we let go of the need to be Wonder Woman, the Bionic Woman, and Charlie's Angels all in one. How good that would be!

We stop striving to be the perfect mother, partner, lover, sister, daughter, boss, employee, and friend. We understand that by trying to be everything to everyone, we end up being nothing to ourselves. We let go of juggling the different roles in our lives and become one integrated and complete person. And as we become more deeply associated with our feminine qualities, we learn to value and appreciate what comes from within us, to believe in ourselves, to trust and use our intuition, to express ourselves from within with clarity and honesty, to share and create opportunities for growth and expansion, to connect energetically with all our senses and allow our creativity to flow and create the magic of endless possibility.

How Can You Start Acknowledging Your Feminine Power in the Workplace?

I invite you to take a few moments for yourself, to relax and take a few deep, cleansing breaths. As you relax and unwind, allow yourself to reflect on You. As you answer the following questions, take the time to deeply consider and connect with yourself and who you are, both in and outside of work.

- How do you in the workplace differ from you outside of work?
- How do you feel, act, and behave in the workplace?
- How do you feel, act, and behave outside of work?
- How do you interact with others and express yourself in the workplace?
- How do you interact with others and express yourself outside of work?
- Which feminine qualities do you suppress when you are at work?
- What compromises do you make?

- Which male qualities do you adopt at work, even though they are not "you"?
- What small, easy changes could you make right now to be more aligned with your feminine power?

All Great Journeys Start with a Single Step

The journey of women as they reclaim their feminine power is no exception! To all women out there, I encourage you to delve into Yourselves, become aware of all your amazing qualities, acknowledge and celebrate them day after day, and step up to the life that is truly yours.

BIO

Helen Kerrison is an intuitive, inspirational healer.

Helen uses her gifts to enable women to recognize and connect with their true selves and live authentic, fulfilled lives. She empowers those she works with to step out of the shadows of limit, doubt and restriction and step into the light of their true purpose, passion and infinite potential.

Helen lives her own purpose every day as she inspires and supports women to uncover and embrace their powerful and uniquely feminine selves and claim the happiness and success they truly desire.

Helen is British and has lived and worked in a number of countries around the world. She is currently based in Brussels, Belgium. Helen is a certified corporate and executive coach, a personal development coach and NLP and EFT practitioner.

http://www.insightinbusiness.com
helen.kerrison@insightinbusiness.com

45

FIRST EXPRESSIONS

You Never Get a Second Chance to Make a First *Expression*

⁂

Tiger Todd

If I Could Go Back to High School, Knowing What I Know *Now* . . .

There are two things I wish I had known in high school that would have removed many of the barriers to my personal and business success. The first would be to know why I was in school. Though most students—and many teachers—believe students are in school to get an education, to make friends, because it's the law, because parents make them, and because adults hate them, the truth is that we send human children to school *to change,* first from first graders into second and third graders, and later, from freshmen into engineers and accountants, and from grad students into doctors and lawyers.

You Never Get a Second Chance to Make a First Impression

The second thing I wish I had known was that the people who would be the most effective adults beyond high school were not those who were the hottest but rather were those with the greatest *expression.* Whether they expressed themselves through their effort, their talent, or their faces, these were the people who would come to rule the future.

This leads me to the following truth: we never get a second chance to make a first *expression.* Let me explain what I mean. Have you ever tried giving instructions to a teen, a student, or an employee who you just knew wanted to be anywhere but in that room, listening to you? How did you know? That's right, by the person's expression. In fact, the majority of our communication cues and messages come not through printed or spoken words but through our faces and tones. According to the work of Dr. Albert Mehrabian, there are three elements to all face-to-face communication: words, tone of voice, and nonverbal behavior—or *facial expressions.*

What's Your Face Saying?

Dr. Mehrabian's work led to the discovery of the 7–38–55 rule, which quantified the relative value of each of these communication elements. The interesting conclusion was that the words we speak only account for 7 percent of effective communication! Tone of voice is over five times as important as the words we speak, at 38 percent. But the most telling elements—at a whopping 55 percent—are our nonverbal messages,namely, our facial expressions!Nonverbal elements are particularly important for communicating feelings and attitude, so if our facesdo not match our words,people will believe the face and not believe what we say.

Applying this principle to effective communication with a prospective, current, or future employer means that we should spend more time practicing what our faces say than how our résumés are formatted. Most important, we should invest at least as much type aligning our faces to the words we want people to believe as we do lining up interviews.

The Power to Alter Human Behavior

We've learned that we can become more believable and less misunderstood by aligning our facial expressions to the words we speak. But what if I told you that you could also make people want to hire and help you using this rule of facial communication on purpose? Welcome to what I call Goal-Directed Communication (GDC).

And where did I learn this brilliant, all-powerful communication method? Through wisdom gleaned from a Dale Carnegie or Wharton workshop, or from my experience teaching tens of thousands of homeless men, women, and youths how to become responsible, employable community members? Nope. I learned it from a baby in a shopping cart, while waiting in line at Walmart.

While in line waiting to check out, I noticed a baby in a shopping cart in the checkout line next to mine. Now, when I see a baby in a shopping cart, I am tempted, just like you, to make the baby smile. Within moments of employing my world-class baby skills, this baby was beaming. That's when it hit me—I had just altered human behavior... with my *face* ... and *on purpose*! This baby didn't know Persuasion 101, PowerPoint, or Portuguese, and still, it responded *exactly how I wanted it to*! You've had this power in you all along.

How to Make People Want to Hire You

Let's break this process down and then see if we can apply it to getting what we want from adults, particularly from those who have the jobs, promotions, and opportunities we want.

First, begin every communication opportunity with a *goal.* Do you begin the job interview process by declaring a goal? "Yeah, my goal is to get hired." Unfortunately, that goal is outside your control, like Miss America's goal of world peace. But what is in your control is making the interviewer want to hire you! Look, if you can achieve your goal of making an illiterate, unemployed, and unproductive baby respond favorably to you, you should easily be able to make a literate, employed, productive adult respond favorably to you, too.

Next, align your face to your goal, just like you do intrinsically when you want to make a baby smile. Use this thought: "What does this interviewer need to see to make him or her want to hire me?" You might consider making this your new mantra.

Last, practice connecting your facial expressions to the words you speak. Make a list of adjectives like *excited, perplexed, engaged,* and *confident,* and then read them while looking in the mirror to connect what your face is saying to the words you are speaking.

After many failed interviews, a student in one of my HeroSchool seminars used this approach for a job for which he was significantly unqualified. His goal was not to get the job but to make the interviewer want to hire him. As it turned out, his face was so welcoming that he unwittingly made the receptionist want to refer him to the executive assistant, who likewise wanted the CEO to meet with him. The next thing he knew, my student was interviewing with the CEO and making the CEO want to hire him, even though there was not a position that fit his qualifications. So do you know what happened next? The CEO picked up the phone and called a friend—another CEO in a similar industry—and recommended hiring my student that day.

In Summary

Desire is the key to motivation, but it's determination and commitment
to an unrelenting pursuit of your goal—a commitment to excellence—
that will enable you to attain the success you seek.
—Mario Andretti

If you want to be heard, begin by asking, "What do *I* want?" What do you want from the next job, the next opportunity, or from life? Knowing what you want is the key to having what you want. With GDC, knowing what you want tells your face which message to communicate. Each of us has the power to effectively communicate our goals directly into the emotional center of those human beings who have the jobs, resources, and opportunities we seek. In challenging economic times, everyone is going through something. Those who will succeed are those whose faces show not what they are going through but what they want and who they want to be.

BIO

Tiger Todd is chief strategist at Heroes Incorporated. Heroes works with business owners to quickly identify causes for repeated history and limited growth, develop strategies to overcome both, and then employ solutions that will ensure effective operation and future success. You can follow Tiger Todd and HeroSchool on Facebook and Twitter via http://www.HeroSchool.us/. We invite you to sign up for Hero School Life Leadership seminars, or even partner with any of our many HeroSchool nonprofit community initiatives, by calling (702) 795-7000.

Fuel Your Success

The New Trend Business Owners Overlook to Increase Their Bottom Line and Six Simple Strategies to Get Started

᙮᙮᙮

Stacey Weckstein

You summon the energy to get yourself out of bed, and your body feels heavy and tired. While getting ready for your day ahead, your mind feels heavy and foggy. You are incredibly sluggish, and when you wake up enough to realize what time it is, once again, you are running behind schedule. As result, you decide to forgo breakfast at home and drive through a fast-food joint, where you grab breakfast on the way. The only choices on the menu are unhealthy, but your appetite is more important that your conscious food choices at this point, so you pick what you think won't upset your stomach as much as the other choices on the menu.

At your office, you hope your first cup of coffee is finally going to give you the edge you need to get the rest of your day on track. You drink one cup, two cups, and even your colleague runs to the coffee store, bringing you back a third cup. Before you know it, you drink a whole pot of coffee, and it doesn't help. Instead, you are feeling sluggish, wired, unfocused, and extremely stressed out.

By the time 3:00 p.m. rolls around, you are feeling even more disorganized and extremely exhausted. You have tried to fix this problem with a boatload of coffee and all the junk food you could eat in one day. Nothing is working.

Finally, your day ends, and as you head home, you recall your day in your mind and think about how it unfolded. It occurs to you that if you had had better energy, the day may have turned out quite differently. If you had taken the time to make better food choices that would fuel your energy, you might have had better mood and improved focus.

Does this sound like you? Although this scenario can be an exaggeration, there are many parts of this story to which business owners can relate based on their hectic lifestyles and lack of time to really impart healthy habits into their day-to-day activities. The result of incorporating easy, healthy, tasty, fast, new techniques will improve your sleep, stress level, energy level, weight, and clarity of mind. When you make simple changes to turn this all around for yourself, you will have more energy and focus for your business that will ultimately affect your bottom line.

Would a few simple things, done in a slightly different way, give you the business edge you need, while adding value to your life? Healthy habits are the most overlooked business strategy, as too often, business owners don't take the time to make the correlation between good lifestyle choices and the effect these choices ultimately have on the bottom line.

1. Eating on the run. Business owners need to eat on the go, so they run out and pick up the easiest meal they can find. You may think you are eating nutritious proteins, carbohydrates, and dairy; however, this meal is usually packed with calories, fats, and chemicals. The meal fills you up but does not fuel your body, leaving you full, bloated, sluggish, and foggy minded.

The solution to this is a five-minute, power-packed, healthy, and energizing smoothie. A smoothie station is so easy to set up in your office. All you need is a blender, your favorite fruits and greens, some water, and maybe a knife. This will take you less time to prepare, eat, and clean up than leaving the office for an unhealthy alternative.

A smoothie has all the nutrients you would need to feed your cells to reenergize you to stay focused and finish out your day. By adding mild-tasting greens, such as Swiss chard, spinach, or romaine, you will add extra nutrition and support to aid in digestion, balance your blood sugar for increased and consistent energy, clear the fog from your mind, decrease food cravings, clean out some toxins and cholesterol from your blood, and, as a bonus, perhaps also lose some weight.

2. Wet your whistle. Proper hydration is key. One of the biggest challenges my clients have is that they do not know how much to drink. The rule of thumb is half your body weight in ounces of water. An example is that a two-hundred-pound person should drink one hundred ounces of water per day.

Another issue that comes up with my clients is how to get all that water in during the day. The first thing you need to do is have a water source. Bring a large bottle with you to work, order water with the supplies, or have the office offer water service. To get in all the water you need to drink in one day, drink 8 ounces upon rising then drink 8 ounces every 3 hours until dinner time. You can set a reminder in your PDA or outlook so you stay properly hydrated.

3. Move it or loosen it. Feeding your body all the greens and fruits you can handle is great, but if you are not being aware, taking care of your stress and focus throughout the day, you are not working at your full capacity. It is important to take mini breaks as you work. Take a moment to stop, look away from what you are doing, and get yourself in a calmer, more focused state.

Many people spend a majority of their lives living in their minds. By practicing living in the moment, we free our creativity and can operate far more effectively in all areas of our lives, from driving a car more safely to paying more attention to our loved ones to making clearer decisions. We can also eliminate suffering by remaining present, as you cannot suffer and be present at the same time!

4. Stocking your office for success. Snacks are a really great way to stay fueled and focused throughout your day. An important factor to energy management and good health is to maintain consistent blood sugar levels throughout the day. An easy way to do this is to eat a small, nutritious bite between meals. We all stock up on paper and staples; it's just as important to stock up on healthy snacks that you can grab.

5. Ask for help. What do you do to mainstream your time so you can focus on providing your clients with the best parts of you and your service? I don't know about you, but I ask for help (I know asking for help is a touchy subject, so if that term is daunting to you, call it *delegating authority*). For me, tasks like bookkeeping, gardening, and cleaning my house are some of the things in my life I would rather not do; they take away from my time to help my clients and family, so I ask for help.

Your time is valuable. If you were to calculate how much each minute is worth based on your salary and then ask yourself if you can afford to lose this money on tasks that you're not great at, don't like to do, or can have someone assist you in doing, I'll bet you'd be able to come up with a great list of things for which you can ask for help. That's why you hire people: to assist you in getting to the next level. That's why I am here talking about these tips: I know that energy management and fueling your success from the inside out are going to affect your bottom line. Do you get that?

I hope you have learned that subtle choices in food and focus throughout the day can make an extreme impact on your health and vitality. This new vitality will contribute to an increase in your bottom line.

BIO

Stacey Weckstein knows that the real secret to a successful business lies in energy management. She's helped businesspeople achieve dramatic improvements in their health—in turn, making them more motivated, capable, and productive. With her keen ability to sense what works at the individual level, Stacey helps her clients upgrade their energy management skills and transform their health. She's a certified health counselor, having trained at the Institute for Integrative Nutrition in New York (accredited by Columbia Teachers College), and has spent a decade in management with some of the most successful food businesses in the country. She has a Bachelor of Science from Boston University and an Associates Degree in Culinary Arts from Johnson and Wales University. Visit her at http://www.NutritionForBusinessOwners.com/.

47

Passion, Purpose, and Proportion: The Landmarks on the Road to a Fulfilling Career

Colleen Georges

What does it feel like to truly love what you do for a living? Whereas some people wake up each morning excited to get to work doing what they love, others would rather just stay in bed! Maybe this lack of energy comes from doing a job in which you don't feel invested—a job that just doesn't fit with who you are. Perhaps you feel frustrated from long hours, challenging coworkers, or inadequate pay, or maybe you are experiencing a layoff and don't know where to begin to get back on track. Whatever your unique reasons are for feeling unfulfilled in your career, you can decide right now not to accept this as your destiny. You deserve to love what you do and can make your career dreams a reality. It begins with a little self-exploration.

Consider the process toward discovering and achieving your ideal career to be a journey. Each of us takes different roads to reach our ultimate career destinations. The people and situations we encounter along the way serve as our road maps. They teach us more about what we excel at and what we enjoy, thus providing direction during our travels. Even when we make a wrong turn and feel lost, we learn which roads will lead us astray and will know not to take those roads in the future. We often learn more about what we want to do after we discover what we don't want to do!

You have been on a career journey from the day you were born. Your family, friends, schooling, jobs, and hobbies have been helping you navigate and alter your course when necessary. Now, as you continue your travels, you'll need some landmarks. Landmarks are key elements in ensuring that you are headed in the right direction. On your career journey, you should be on the lookout for the three *P*s: *passion*, *purpose*, and *proportion.* When you find the three *P*s, you will know you are close to reaching your dream career destination.

Make a Right at Passion

Think about the times in your life when you are most happy. What are you doing? Where are you? Who are you with? The answers to these questions are clues to your dream career. Perhaps you are currently working in a nine-to-five desk job with the same ten colleagues every day and hating it. When you think about the times you are happiest, you are traveling, seeing new things, and meeting new people. This could indicate that your career needs more variety, more action.

Perhaps you've discovered that you've been really happy at work when you're developing new ideas, projects, or services, and maybe such activities compose just 10 percent of your current responsibilities. This creativity might need to be a much greater aspect of your career.

As you ask yourself these questions to identify your passions, write down the answers you discover.

Make Another Right at Purpose

What do people always come to you for? What does everyone say you are great at? What roles do you often find yourself in with family, friends, or colleagues? Everyone has a purpose. Your purpose is the thing or things at which you excel naturally—what you were meant to give to the world.

Maybe you have an uncanny understanding of health and medicine and everyone you know comes to you when he or she doesn't feel well but doesn't know what's wrong. Or perhaps you are a wiz with numbers and always find yourself doing your friends' taxes during tax season.

Write down everything you find. Seeing any themes arising yet?

Continue Straight Ahead to Proportion

What's important to you? What do you value and need to feel fulfilled? What careers will enable you to incorporate each of these things into your life? Now, write down your answers. We are not one-sided; we are multifaceted. We need a life with proportion—a life that allows us to spend adequate time engaging in all of the things we value. If you value spending quality time with your family but are working at a job that has you maintaining seventy hours a week, you are lacking proportion.

Passion, purpose, and proportion are equally critical for a fulfilling career. We can love to do something at which we aren't great. For example, I love bowling, but I have a seventy-four average. Hence I probably won't be considering a career as a pro bowler! We can also be naturally gifted at something that wouldn't allow us adequate time to do other things that are incredibly important to us. You could have a knack for investing but feel that the crazy hours of a Wall Street career would make it challenging to maintain the exercise and sleep regimen that are invaluable to you. You'll know you are close to reaching your ideal career destination when you have found *all* your landmarks—passion, purpose, and proportion.

The landmarks get you close, but you must also be able to effectively get past roadblocks. The roadblocks are the people, situations, and personal belief systems that get in your way. It's your friend that says you're crazy to leave your lucrative sales position to manage a nonprofit. It's that you'll need to go back to school to become a nurse. It's the voice in your head that tells you that you're not savvy enough to start and manage your own business.

Just like the unpredictable roadwork and detours you encounter in your general travels, metaphorical roadblocks will appear on your career journey, and just as you would listen to traffic reports to plan ahead, you'll need to develop an action plan for your career journey. Know where your roadblocks will be and plan your alternate route. What will you say to your doubting friend? What nursing schools are close and affordable? How can you educate yourself on business start-ups? And what will you do with the answers to these questions? Write them down—writing leads to doing.

Pursuing a career that will express your passions and purpose and allow you to live a well-proportioned life will take work. It will present challenges. But it will be worth every minute, for a lifetime. What does it feel like to truly love what you do for a living? You are about to find out.

<u>Bio</u>

Dr. Colleen Georges is a Certified Professional Résumé Writer, Certified Professional Career Coach, and NJ Licensed Professional Counselor and received her doctorate in counseling psychology from RutgersUniversity. She is owner of Colleen's Career Creations (http://www.ColleensCareerCreations.com/) and Concentric Life Coaching(http://www.ConcentricLifeCoaching.com/). For the last thirteen years, Colleen has been coaching and writing résumés for clients across the spectrum of career fields. Colleen's professional background has included work as a psychotherapist, a career counselor, a university department director and hiring manager, and a college instructor. Colleen's two greatest passions have always been writing and helping others achieve their personal and professional goals. Contact her by e-mail at Dr.ColleenG@gmail.com.

48

Necessary Goals That Will Lead You to the Career of Your Dreams

JoAnn Youngblood King

Having the career of your dreams takes a certain amount of technical skill in your area of expertise. However, there are plenty of people who have the skills to do what they do and still are not happy and satisfied with their jobs. Having the skill set is great; however, having the right mind-set to go along with it would be even better!

To experience the successful career you desire, you must start within. You must create the energy of what you want within yourself before you can have it on the outside. I'm sure you have no problem saying what it is you want in your life. However, you must get rid of any doubts you may have deep inside about being able to accomplish your goals and dreams. Regardless of what we say, we usually get what we expect.

It was always a dream of mine to have my own business. I always sold other people's products and made a little extra money on the side. I wanted to create my own company and sell my own products and services. Years ago, a friend of mine said to me, "You should treat your current position as your own business." So I acted as if my position were my business. "Executive secretary" became my business instead of my title. I started organizing files in a better way, created new forms for the staff to use, and implemented new procedures to follow. My coworkers started asking me to create forms and signs for them, and before I knew it, I was getting paid to do personal jobs for them (flyers, brochures, résumés, letters, business cards, etc.). This was how my first company, Youngblood Multigraphics, was born.

If you feel that it's taking too long to achieve the career success you desire, one way to get there a little more quickly is to act as if your goal were already achieved. This action may seem foolish when you try it, but it's actually fun once you get used to it. Acting-as-if alone obviously won't help you obtain results; however, when you act as if, you are putting yourself in the future state of where you want to be, which fuels your desire to get there. This is a very effective tool. If you want to become a writer, take on the mind-set of a writer and start writing. Acting-as-if will strengthen your belief that your goal will be achieved because you will be physically doing it, not just thinking about what it would be like. I would like to offer you some goals that will help you accomplish your current career goals. I believe these goals, along with some affirmations, are absolutely necessary and will help to support the goals you already have. (Affirmations are statements that declare a situation to be true. Basically, everything you say is an affirmation. When you repeat affirmations, you are sending energy out into the universe to bring into existence all that you need and want. Affirmations are also helpful in replacing any limiting beliefs you may have.)

Goal 1:To be constantly aware of your greatness. You can do whatever it is you set out to do! You may not be aware of what you can do at this moment; however, know that anything is possible. You don't have to be perfect or know exactly how to do a particular thing before you start; you just have to get started. I didn't know how to write a book until I did it—all it took was first realizing that I had the potential to do it. You have the same potential!

Affirmation: I realize that I am the one who makes the choices to live the way I do. Greatness is a choice. I choose to let my greatness shine through!

Goal 2:To have strong determination. Once you realize your potential for success and make the choice to succeed, you have to have a very strong determination to see it through. The strength of your determination is what will move you to your intended result, regardless of time and money. There are many stories of successful people who started out with very little time and money. However, because of their strong determination, they didn't let anything stop them from accomplishing their goals.

Affirmation: I am determined to have the successful life and career I desire!

Goal 3: To be flexible. You must be willing to be flexible and make changes when necessary. Begin to consciously make specific changes that will contribute to your career success. Be mindful that the most significant changes you make will be the changes you make on yourself. The state of your career, as well as your life, is a reflection of what is going on inside you. One little change in your attitude can make a world of difference. Start making a few small changes.

Affirmation: I am open and willing to make changes when necessary.

Goal 4:To be grateful. To attract the success you would like into your life, you need to appreciate and be grateful for the success you already possess. You may easily spend time thinking of things you want and things you don't have. At those times, you should remember to give thanks and be grateful for what you have already. The more grateful you are for the things you have in your life, the more things you will have to be grateful for.

> **Affirmation:** I am grateful for every experience in my life. When I am grateful, I will be able to move to a higher level of consciousness, and things will turn around for the better.

Goal 5:To be courageous. I love the acronym FEAR; it stands for *false evidence appearing real*. Basically, it says that what we fear is not real—it has not happened. In essence, we really fear nothing. This may sound funny, but think about it—if you have a fear that you won't be able to make your business sales quota by the end of the week, not only are you focusing on what you don't want but you are fearful of something that may not even happen.

> **Affirmation:** I have all the courage I need to be successful. I know that fear is just false evidence appearing real. I will knock down all fear!

Goal 6:To pray daily and have absolute faith. I'm sure there are times when you may not realize or may often forget how powerful you are. A lot of us go through our daily lives hoping, wishing, and praying for things to be better than they are. The fact is that they can be better than they are. It's all up to you! You are the one who has to make the decision about how you want things to go. When you pray and ask for guidance and wisdom, you must have strong faith and know that the answer will come. It's up to you to remain open to receiving the answer.

> **Affirmation:** My form of prayer gives me hope and allows me to let go of any worries or concerns while I am on the road to fulfilling my dreams.

BIO

JoAnn Youngblood King is a CTA-Certified Success Coach, author, and owner of Live Your Potential. Live Your Potential helps entrepreneurs and small business owners discover, tap into, and live their inherent potential for success. As your success coach, JoAnn will support you in staying on track with your dreams and goals and will be committed to your success and happiness. JoAnn has a diploma in small business management and is a member of the Coach Training Alliance and the International Association of Coaches. To contact JoAnn, e-mail JoAnn@liveyourpotential.com, or visit http://www.liveyourpotential.com/.

49

How to Be a Good Employee

❧

William S. Cottringer

Being a good employee is something that is expected by all employers. I suspect most employers would be extremely happy if all employees were to comply with a dozen basic expectations. These simple requirements are a prescription for being a good employee. If you practice these suggestions, you are likely to get recognized and rewarded and be much more successful in your career development efforts.

1. Show up on time. No job can run efficiently without all employees being present and showing up on time. Absences and lateness are very disruptive and put an undue burden on other employees. Poor attendance always puts a company's business at risk. There is nothing more admirable than an employee having a perfect attendance record, and that standard is bound to get the employee noticed in a positive way.

2. Be neat in appearance. No matter what job you are doing, there is no reason *not* to be neat in appearance. Your appearance reflects on both you and your employer: a good appearance speaks well, while an unkempt appearance speaks poorly. A good appearance is a good advertisement for the company and can mean more business and more opportunities for all employees. Another good reason for being neat and clean is that you often feel the way you look. Look good, feel good, and do good!

3. Demonstrate a positive attitude. All business is founded on positive attitudes by employees. Businesses can't succeed in giving customers quality service without positive attitudes. There is no room for negativity. Negativity will interfere with other employees' productivity, make for an unhappy workplace, and keep the company from meeting its business goals. Having a positive attitude makes work more enjoyable and passes the time more quickly. Being positive is being upbeat, optimistic, and enthusiastic and showing a refreshing willingness to go the extra mile with a smile.

4. Give the job your best effort. Employers only ask that you give the job your very best effort. This means doing the quality and quantity of work that is expected in a conscientious, diligent, efficient, and effective manner. There is no reading between the lines here. Just do your best, and most employers are going to be happy with you. Make sure you know what is expected and that you can and will do those things. Every employee has it in himself or herself to give his or her best effort. Besides, you really can't feel good about yourself if you are goofing off, doing the bare minimum, or performing poorly.

5. Respect your supervisor. Supervisors are in the position they are because of their experience and abilities. The least you can do is approach them with courtesy and respect. If they tell you to do something, it is for legitimate reasons. Do it without giving any lip. If a supervisor does something inappropriate or wrong, you don't need to be rude, abusive, or insubordinate. There is always a management staff member in the chain of command who will listen to you. Getting along with your supervisor is a sure way to win his or her respect and attention.

6. Follow the rules. Policies, work rules, and safety guidelines are all developed with your, others,' and the entire organization's welfare in mind. These rules aren't silly; they are there to help you help the company stay legal, remain safe, and be prosperous. Always know what the rules are and follow them. It can't get any simpler than that. Rule breakers cause employers heartburn, and so that is not the way to get on the right side of your employer. You can't go wrong by following the rules.

7. Be honest. All businesses have to be honest, and the only way they can do that is if all their employees are honest. Do not do anything that will even be misperceived as being dishonest. Tell the truth, don't go places that are off limits, and don't take things that aren't yours. Also, most gossip and rumors are dishonest, so avoid those things, too. When you are honest and tell the truth, you never have to remember anything. Being dishonest is very confusing and will always catch up to you sooner or later. Lies beget more lies and take too much time to unravel, which is very annoying and disruptive.

8. Take care of equipment. Equipment misuse and abuse can be costly for a company. This extra cost can take away pay raises for employees. Don't misuse equipment, and don't operate any equipment on which you are not trained and about which you are not knowledgeable. Always ask if you are not sure. Take care of all supplies and equipment as if they were your own. Always report faulty or broken equipment promptly.

9. Ask questions. You never have to feel stupid about asking dumb questions. Actually, the only dumb question may be the one you don't ask. Whenever you don't understand something fully, ask questions. The best way to learn how to be an excellent employee and succeed in your job is to ask a lot of questions. You can learn much valuable information from asking good questions. Don't allow employers to assume you understand the job and what is expected of you when you don't. If you don't ask questions, you will be the loser.

10. Speak up. If you don't agree with something or if you think you have a better way of doing something, speak up! But do so assertively and politely, not loudly or disrespectfully. If you speak up about something in a rational, unemotional way, you will be listened to. When you whine, complain, or threaten, you are wasting your words and certainly not being a good employee who will be recognized and rewarded.

11. Learn more. One of the easiest and best ways to get ahead in a company is to show the initiative and motivation to learn more about the job. By seeking more training and improving your skills, you will be grooming yourself for a promotion. Employees who do this are sure to get recognized and rewarded. Employees who just do their jobs and nothing more are telling the employer that is all they want. And most likely, that is all they'll get. There are always managers in your company who have important skills and knowledge. Find them and ask them to be your teachers.

12. Get along with everybody. All jobs require good teamwork. Employees should make an effort to get along with each other by being friendly, cooperative, and helpful and by working as a team to get the job done better than any individual could do alone. Many of the company's goals can be met with good teamwork. Without good teamwork, the quality of service a company is trying to deliver will be in serious jeopardy. When you get along with your fellow workers and are a good team player, you will enjoy your job much more than if you were to go off on your own and make trouble with other workers.

All company presidents began as employees. They got to where they are by starting out as good employees. Such a management vacancy might not exist where you work, but my guess is that if you follow these dozen suggestions, you will be climbing the ladder in your own career. If you are not looking for more responsibility and are happy just being a good employee, following these twelve suggestions will be rewarding in itself.

<u>BIO</u>

William Cottringer, PhD, is president of Puget Sound Security Inc. in Bellevue, Washington, along with being a sport psychologist, business success coach, photographer, and writer living in the mountains of North Bend. He is the author of several business and self-development books, including *You Can Have Your Cheese & Eat It Too* (Executive Excellence), *The Bow-Wow Secrets* (Wisdom Tree), *Do What Matters Most* and *"P" Point Management* (Atlantic Book Publishers), *Reality Repair Rx* (PublishAmerica), and *Reality Repair* (Global Vision Press). Bill can be reached for comments or questions at (425) 454-5011 or via e-mail at ckuretdoc@comcast.net.

50

Success Is Where the Heart Is

❦

Mega R. Mease

Heart is the central, vital part, the real meaning, the essence, the core. Seeking, finding, and accessing the heart of the matter is essential to the enhancement and success of any endeavor. It is a solid truth in career and the only valid pathway to simplicity, honor, and integrity in the arena of business.

Heart-based equations for success include an equal marriage of vision, feeling, thought, and action. This powerful combination provides personalized instruction to redesign your life one moment, one breath, one step at a time. Usage of these four components together encourages the enhancement of one focused area while allowing other areas to grow simultaneously. Thus one area of life need not suffer while another is learning to thrive.

The nontraditional wisdom of the heart easily guides an individual to connect with his or her natural gifts and build on that skill set to support peak performance. The result is a perfect balance of heart, head, and hand that creates fulfillment, happiness, and success on many levels.

In comparison, the average linear equation for success offers a play-by-play map of details designed to get from point A to point B within an established time frame. Traveling this route can definitely get a person to his or her desired destination, but there may be a high price for the ride. This frequently used roadway may include seventy-hour workweeks, sleepless nights, and minimal time for family, friends, and pleasure. Temporary financial lack, unmanageable anxiety, and damaging stress are often prevalent when choosing this conventional path. As one gets closer to achieving a much sought after goal, the absence of heart may promote fatigue, a compromised immune system, loss of passion, frustration, and a lessened sense of accomplishment. The desire for further improvement diminishes, causing lower levels of creativity, decreased momentum, boredom, and eventually, even failure.

This comparison clearly indicates that the most efficient and enjoyable way to enhance career and gain success is to seek, find, and access the heart of the matter. Please don't stop at career as this formula works for health, relationships, and life in general. When access to heart is achieved, all the benefits of the conventional linear equation will be present, but without any of the adverse side effects. It is a win-win, best-of-both-worlds scenario. The challenge is getting started, staying focused, and recognizing the target when you actually find it.

Humor is the quality that brings breath into everything, so wrap yourself in it as you begin your travels on the road to seeking heart. Seeking begins with willingness, desire, and determination to be and do. Even the most sincere intention to seek, however, may fall short. To be truly successful, seeking must be accompanied by the ability to see with wonder and beyond what appears to be impossible in the now. It is this vision that allows us to marvel at life and invite the unknown, unexpected pleasures of success and life into reality.

A strong commitment is necessary to accomplish what you seek. You must make a pledge, a promise that melds you to your purpose of mindfully listening and tenaciously following heart-based directions once you find them. It is this rare form of 100 percent commitment that opens up and secures the energetic pathways to your natural flow of being. Some may refer to this as being in the zone. This is the place where answers to the unconscious, unasked questions live. Ask yourself the following:

- What am I doing?
- Why am I doing it?
- Is this helping me to achieve my goal?
- What am I willing to change to accomplish this?

When you arrive at the home of the heart of the matter, you will find yourself surrounded by acknowledgment of truth, deeper awareness, and pureness of integrity. You will feel forgiveness of self, honesty, and appreciation. The answers will be soft and come with ease. Seek, find, and access. The result is that your desired enhanced and successful future is now your present-day reality.

Bio

Mega R. Mease, founder of the Center for Advanced Energy Therapeutics in Tucson, Arizona, is an Energy Diagnostic, Vibrational Healer, and Empowerment Facilitator. She is the creator of HeartRay™ Energetic Therapy and Bone Energy Re-patterning™ modalities. Known as the Everyday Ordinary Healer, Mega provides a vehicle through which others learn to live a healthier, happier, more abundant existence through health, business, relationship, and life mentoring. She supports people internationally via phone, e-mail, and Skype consultations. Mega gives back to her community by sourcing, funding, and directing the CAET Reiki Volunteer Program at University-MedicalCenter.

Visit http://www.AdvancedEnergyTherapeutics.com/, http://www.HospitalReiki.com/, and http://www.Facebook.com/AdvancedEnergyTherapeutics/.

51

HOME BASED BUSINESS

Plan B

Geometric Gains in Your Home-Based Business:
5 Differences That Make a Difference

❧

Cesar Viana Teague

> You can't ask for what you want unless you know what it is.
> A lot of people don't know what they want, or they want much less than they
> deserve. First you have to figure out what you want. Second, you have to
> decide that you deserve it. Third, you have to believe you can get it.
> And, fourth, you have to have the guts to ask for it.
> —Barbara de Angelis

Having a Plan B to protect yourself, while providing more overall security in your life, is critical in times of change and uncertainty. The objective of this chapter is to explore a shift in thinking and action, moving away from being stuck in a full-time job and a part-time life to having a full-time life and a part-time job—*living life on your own terms*. Having a Plan B fundamentally means having your own home-based business to generate cash flow.

In the e-book titled *Plan B*, I share with you what has worked for me, putting the lessons learned along my journey of trial and error into a clear format that you can use to create your own Plan B. Each chapter targets a particular area in which positive changes must be made:

1. "The Differences That Make a Difference" helps you to identify the key risk and reward activities responsible for creating multiple, exponential results—not just incremental gains.

2. "Success vs. Struggle" explores your mind-set and examines what subconscious thought patterns may have created obstacles for you in achieving your goals.

3. "Focus and Flow" moves you through a succession of concepts, each one building on the previous one to create a stronger foundation.

4. "Aligning Opportunities and Goals" takes these two elements, which are often considered separately, and integrates them to help you achieve better results.

5. "Action Steps for Geometric Gains" provides hands-on exercises to propel you toward your goal and dreams. It examines your daily method of operation, income-producing activities, and sales and marketing plan.

The benefits of a home-based business are undeniable for those who choose this course. They include flexible working hours, no commuting hassles, more personal or family time, and the likelihood of financial freedom, which all fulfill living life with *passion*.

However, for those caught up in working-hard routines and not manifesting their truly desired results, the entrepreneurial dream of self-actualization can quickly vanish. In the face of these challenges, it's easy to retreat into your comfort zone while grabbing hold of excuses such as "the economy is bad" or "maybe next month or next year." But remember that though you could retreat into your comfort zone because it feels more secure and familiar, doing so is ultimately unfulfilling and stressful (and sometimes boring).

Hard work is not the only important ingredient to creating your success. Whether in your career or in your own business, knowing and applying the Plan B strategies will enable you to realize better lifelong results—*if you give yourself permission to do so*.

I've worked with many entrepreneurs and have faced the challenges of self-employment myself. As I've watched people struggle, a number of key questions came up over and over:

- Why do they work such long hours every day, every week, without gaining results?
- Why do they repeatedly attend workshops without achieving their true goals?
- Why do they get fired up applying what they have learned only to attain the same unsatisfactory results?

The answers to these mysteries lie in the mind.

Your mind is the most powerful tool at your disposal. Some call it your "blueprint." Subconscious thought patterns and beliefs can sabotage your best conscious efforts toward success. It's what happens on the inside that determines what happens on the outside, and grasping this truth is key to unlocking your potential, both personally and professionally.

Success at entrepreneurship, or at any other challenge, requires a dramatic change from within. You've most likely heard the popular definition of *insanity*: doing the same thing in the same way, while expecting different results. I'd like to express this notion in a slightly different way:

Whatever got you here will not get you to the next level.

It got you *here*; it can't get you *there*.

So what now? How do you change the beliefs and thought patterns that have brought you *here*? *Plan B* is a road map to guide you through the personal growth necessary to achieve your goals.

My own journey began seven years ago, at a low point in my life. I was stuck and had to reevaluate my life's circumstances. As I regrouped, I modified my thinking and started identifying personal strategies that began to make a difference. In the process of honestly assessing my situation, I was able to create a prosperous home-based business and began to attract good people and projects into my life. Mind you, it hasn't been easy, but along with the love and support of my family, I have made it happen!

Yes, this process involved change. However, I prefer to call it progress.

Change is inevitable; progress is not.

The first and most important step is to acknowledge that you may need to make changes in the way you think. Without this realization, no real progress can be made. Why is that? Because if you're not ready to admit that you need to make changes, you'll find plenty of excuses not to do so. Again, you'll fall into your comfort zone. You'll find many external factors to blame for your current lack of success.

The old adage remains absolutely true: *we avoid change until the pain of not changing becomes greater than the pain of changing*! However, when we avoid change and stay in our comfort zones, we have only endless repetition of similar results—which we begin to see as "normal." But go a little deeper and ask yourself, are these the results I *want*? Are these the results I *deserve*? You will then begin to think of it in a new way.

Everything you really want is outside your current comfort zone; otherwise, you would already have it!

I understand that making any kind of change can be extremely intimidating, but like any journey, change occurs one step at a time. As you begin to move through the chapters of *Plan B*, you will learn more about specific steps you can take to get from here to there.

Much of the information and philosophy outlined in the e-book comprise the secrets that successful people have used throughout history. However, even the most powerful, effective book available is still limited by your willingness to absorb its information and put its methods into action for yourself.

This book is a guide, but only you *can take action.*

I wish you all the best, and remember: *you* are the creator of your own destiny!

> We must be willing to get rid of the life we've planned,
> so as to have the life that is waiting for us.
> —Joseph Campbell

BIO

Cesar Viana Teague, MBA, CSL, has experience encompassing international sales, marketing, and management. Starting at Merrill Lynch International, he moved into sales management, building distributor networks in North America. He continues to help develop new businesses and coach entrepreneurs and independent distributors. His training includes an MBA from Golden Gate University, a BSc in economics from the University of San Francisco, plus training from Speaking Circles International, MethodSpeaking, NLP Coaching, Leadership Training, and Landmark Forum. He is also a Certified Seminar Leader. He volunteers as a business coach at the San Francisco Renaissance Entrepreneurship Center, helping small business owners reach the next level. Contact him at cesar@nextlevelup.org, or visit him online at http://nextlevelup.org/homebusiness.html.

52

IMAGE

Dress, Impress, and Succeed!

✖〰✖

Monica de Liz

Dress to Impress!

"You never have a second chance to make a first impression." If your clothes could talk, what would they be saying? Stand in front of a mirror and evaluate yourself—be brutally honest! Do you look professional or sloppy? Credible or unreliable? Organized or messy?

Dressing is a nonverbal language. According to the pioneering research of Professor Albert Mehrabian at UCLA, effective communication has a simple formula: 7 percent is what we say (words), 38 percent is what we hear (tone of voice), and 55 percent is what we see (image). This means if your visual expression does not match your talk, you are being incongruent; therefore you are not able to communicate clearly what you want—there is a glitch in your message.

Whether you like it or not, we live in a judgmental society. Regardless of your knowledge and expertise, it takes less than five seconds for people to make positive or negative assumptions about you—that's human nature! If you want to be successful, you need to consider your wardrobe as part of the process. It's time to stop dressing for comfort and start wearing clothes that will help you get ahead. Here is how you can stand out at work:

1. Dress for where you want to be. What position do you aspire to in three years? When you dress like you've made it, people will perceive you as successful and be naturally drawn to you. Think as if you were Ali Brown or Donald Trump. Like any product on the market today, *you* are a brand, and your clothes are the packaging. How are people going to buy you? Before saying a word, they first buy what they see. Is your packaging attracting or repelling others? It's almost like dating: if someone catches your eye, you get curious; if not, you just ignore him or her. You are more likely to command respect and get what you want if you are put together. Start now: fake it until you make it!

2. Wear shoes that wow. Your feet have seen better days. You look great . . . from the ankles up. Imagine you are making the lineup of an exclusive VIP event: what is the first thing the doorman will look at to let you in? Your shoes! If they are worn out or inappropriate, you are out! The same applies to the business world: if your footwear style is not relevant, the doors of professional advancement and prestige will be closed to you. The reality is that people will look at your shoes when they meet you. Why? They can tell a lot about your effectiveness, hygiene, and personality. It's sad but true, so make sure your shoes are not holding you back in any way.

3. Choose flattering colors and shapes. We associate colors and shapes with many things: age (young or old), mood (happy or sad), and temperature (hot or cold). They stimulate our senses. We come in different bodies and skin tones, and not all clothing styles and colors will enhance your appearance. If it doesn't fit, don't wear it. Be aware of garments that are too big, too small, too long, or too short. That bright red dress or tie may look great on your colleague and horrible on you. Your best outfits will attract compliments, and the least favorable ones will make you look outdated. Study your shape and learn what enhances your natural features.

4. Pay attention to grooming. Small details can compromise your overall image: the hem on your pants coming down, underarm shirt stains, visible bra or panty lines, clothes with holes. Develop a constant routine to care for your hair, nails, and teeth that will help you always look polished.

5. Maintain a healthy posture. How many times have you seen people sitting, walking, or standing strangely and felt bad for them? Cultivating a good posture instantly improves your appearance and makes you look more appealing and confident. It also facilitates your breathing and increases concentration.

6. Speak to inspire. Opportunity always finds those who focus on possibilities, not limitations. Differentiate yourself from the complaining crowd by choosing words and actions that motivate your team to be more. Lead without a title, and you will be regarded as a valuable asset. Negativity in any shape or form will stop you from connecting with new people, job opportunities, and profitable ideas.

7. Create a positive online image. Keep in mind that in today's social media reality, first impressions have already been made through Google, LinkedIn, Facebook, and Twitter, even before you meet someone. What you publish on the Internet for the world to see can build or kill your reputation. Avoid posting words or pictures that will raise questions about your professionalism. It's important to understand that knowledge will get you far, but making the right first impression will get you even farther.

A successful appearance will not save you from a lousy job performance, but a poor first impression can get in the way of an excellent promotion, raise, or project. Before getting dressed tomorrow, think about what you have been wearing to work. Is it the best you can do? Dress with intention. Express your personality. Smile. Make it your ultimate career goal for the next 30 days.

BIO

Monica de Liz is a passionate Brazilian-style coach and speaker. She has positively inspired thousands of people to look and feel fabulous. Through her courses, events and retreats, Monica helps women identify and overcome negative-body-image-beliefs that limit their self-expression and prevent them from being happy in their clothes and their own skin. Want to look younger and slimmer? Go to www.image4success.com and sign up to receive your free style tricks report.

53

INTERVIEW SUCCESS

Knock Their Socks Off and Get the Job You Want!

❧

Anna Aparicio

Times are changing at lightning speed. Whether we like it or not, we either keep up or are left behind. We have massively evolved through time and history, but never this rapidly! Trends, be it in fashion, food, or technology, that we swore by a mere few months ago are now obsolete.

In the current economic climate, we find ourselves with millions of highly intelligent, overqualified job seekers around the world fighting for the same jobs. Millions of curricula vitae are emailed every day, followed by millions of phone calls and interviews, followed by rejection and disappointment.

In today's competitive job market, it seems that intelligence, great qualifications, or even a burning desire are not enough to get you the job you want. At any given time, thousands of people just as clever as you, just as experienced and hardworking as you, are applying for the same position—so, how are you going to stand out from the rest?

If you've made it to the interview room, then you have done something right. You have got something: a final chance to impress, influence, and persuade. Following are my proven tips on how to knock the socks off your interviewers and get that job offer, fast.

Believe in yourself. *Believe that you are the best candidate for the job.* Hoping for it, wishing for it, or even badly wanting it is not enough and may even go against you. Giving out a vibe of neediness may put your interviewers off. They are not going to offer you the job because you need it or hope to get it. The job will be offered to the person who gets to them, the person who makes the best, most impactful and lasting impression—that person with whom they can vividly imagine working, that person with whom they can see themselves dealing day in and day out.

Remember that there are lots of other jobs out there for you and that it may take some time to find your ideal job. However, it is up to you to walk into that interview with a sense of self-belief and confidence that will simply knock your interviewers' socks off.

Know what you are selling. You are not selling your CV, your new suit, or how nice a person you are. *You are selling feelings.* Remember that your interviewer is only human, and most decisions we make as humans are not based on logic but on feelings. You have to realize that the interview is not really about you; rather it's about your interviewer. In addition to how well you match your talents, experience, and skills to the job, the company, and people in it, you also have to focus on making your interviewer feel good. When people feel good around you, they are more likely to like you and promote you.

What simple things can you do to help your interviewer be at ease and feel good around you? Look your very best on the day. Dress professionally. Smile, give a firm handshake—without squeezing!—and keep eye contact with your interviewer throughout the interview. Also, be aware of your body language. Learn some NLP (Neuro-linguistic Programming) to know how to create rapport with your interviewer through mirroring, pacing and leading.

Do your research. I am always surprised to hear human resources staff at the companies I work with complain about interviewees' lack of preparation. Knowing the name of the company to which you are applying and kind of liking what they are about is not going to cut it!

Many years ago, I applied for a job as project manager for an international engineering company. I had no qualifications specific to that position, had no clue about engineering, and had never done that job before. I found out about the mission statement of the company, the working ethos, the different people and their roles in the office where I was potentially going to be working, the role I was going to undertake, and what would be expected of me. At the interview, I didn't necessarily mention all of this, but I was able to confidently and naturally answer all questions I was asked and show genuine interest by asking specific questions. Against other applicants who had the qualifications and experience, I got the job.

Research the company. Become curious and genuinely interested in what they do, how they do it, the company mission, the people who run it, and the people you will have to work with—learn as much as you can about what is most important to them. If you are applying for a position in which you have no previous experience, it may be a good idea to speak to someone who is already doing that job or has done it before. Spend some time with that person, ask some good questions, and learn!

Also, *know yourself*: know your strengths and weaknesses and how they'll affect that particular job. Remember, for every weakness you mention, buffer it up with two strengths!

Rehearse! I am stunned when I speak to personal customers who have job interviews coming up and they tell me they haven't rehearsed. Imagine being an actor and showing up to film without knowing your lines. No matter how good you think you are, you are bound to mess up.

Certain questions are to be expected at your interview, for example, the infamous "where do you see yourself in five years' time?" or "what are your strengths and weaknesses?" or "do you have any questions?" Know your answers to these and other potential questions, give specific examples, and avoid going off subject. Answer questions confidently and in a way that presupposes you are the right person for the job.

Be in top form on the day. You may be thinking this is easier said than done, especially if your upcoming interview is your fiftieth so far. Well, this may be your fiftieth lucky interview! *The more confident and relaxed you are, the better you will perform.*

It helps to run through the interview in your mind before it happens. Imagine being already there. Imagine things going perfectly, exactly the way you want them to go. See what you'll see, hear what you'll hear, and feel how good it feels to do your very best and make a great impression.

Make sure you eat healthily the day before your interview, and sleep well. Avoid simple carbohydrates, sugary foods, and caffeine as they play havoc with energy levels and mental clarity. Drink plenty of water and do a few breathing exercises. Doing so will help you relax and be more aware and in control.

Ask questions. Many companies are looking for more than just someone who can do the job. They are looking for proactive people with a personality and vision. Show the type of person you are and how interested you are in the job by asking questions regarding growth and opportunities. Think about what you would be looking for if this was your company or you were the interviewer. By imagining what you would expect, you can put yourself in a more resourceful mindset.

After the interview, wait a week or so, and if you haven't heard from your interviewer, contact him or her and get some feedback. This is a way of reminding them of you and also of finding out useful information you can use to get that job or an even better one!

<u>BIO</u>

Anna Aparicio is regarded as Ireland's top female IINLP/NHR Coach. She uses Neuro-linguistic Programming, Neuro-hypnotic Repatterning, and cutting-edge personal development tools to develop profound and lasting changes in your life. As a self-image and confidence expert, Anna is regularly featured on Irish TV, radio, and in top lifestyle publications. She is the author of the controversial e-book *Why You'll Never Get What You Want Unless You Do This*, which is available for free download at http://www.delite.ie

54

How to Have the Right Job Find You

Lisa Rangel

Make no mistake. Being found by the right job is not a passive job search tactic. Eliminate from your mind the vision of a job seeker sipping margaritas on the deck waiting for recruiters to call. There is a lot of work and thought that the job seeker must do to ensure that he or she is part of communities where hiring managers source for viable candidates.

There is much written about how to find the right job. One of the most overlooked items in a strategic job search plan is how to ensure the job seeker is searchable—or how to have the right job find you. With the prolific rise of the Internet to source candidates by corporate and search firm recruiters, it is paramount that job seekers take steps to ensure that they can be located and sourced for the positions they seek.

Posting an ad to recruit for an open position is one of the last tactics a recruiter wants to utilize. They result in too many résumés of ill-qualified candidates to sort through, and many other time management inefficiencies arise. This is why it is often not most effective for job seekers. Recruiters source and recruit. Candidates who are present and active in those pools get attention. Be one of these candidates. Following are things you can do to be found by the right job.

- **LinkedIn title.** Ensure that your LinkedIn profile title states your situation and what you are looking for in your next role. It helps your network help you. For example, do not have your title be simply "SVP—Strategic Marketing." Instead, have it read "Versatile Marketing Professional seeking new, strategic marketing opportunity in consumer products."

- **Social media status updates.** Regularly update your social media status offering pertinent industry information, attendance at virtual and live trade-shows, participation in industry learning events, volunteer activities, or athletic and hobby achievements. Stay present in the information stream. This is important for two reasons:

o You stay in the minds of your connections. Out of sight is out of mind. To be thought of for particular roles, you need to be top of mind. To stay top of mind, you need to be branded effectively to your audience.

o You are demonstrating that you are a lifelong learner and active-in-the-world type of person. This is highly desirable to prospective employers.

- **Be search term rich.** Hiring managers use search terms to locate candidates for the positions they are looking to fill. Ensure that your online résumé, social media profiles, status updates, user group discussions, blogs, and so on, all have relevant keywords peppered throughout the text. The more search terms you have that are well placed, the more you increase your chances of being discovered in a recruiter's search.

- **You can never have too many friends.** Ensure that you qualitatively maximize your connections, friends, and tweets. This is not to have impressive numbers but to expand your reach within each of their networks. Specifically on LinkedIn, the larger your connection base, the exponentially larger your third-degree reach to search for prospective hiring managers within your target company list.

- **Join relevant social media groups.** If you have exhausted your connections for the moment, you can increase your reach through joining relevant social media groups. You can join groups in your discipline, in previous industries, in industries you have interest in pursuing, with geographical relevance, and so on. This will optimize your search results by expanding the pool in which to search.

- **Join like-minded user/industry groups.** This can be done both virtually and physically. Financial recruiters often recruit executives through groups like Financial Executives International or Financial Executive Networking Groups. IT recruiters source candidates in online user groups on gaming, specific programming languages, products, shareware, and so on. Become an active participant in the in-person events and virtual discussions, and see how you get noticed for your knowledge and generosity. Follow up with new and previously known contacts after the group's get-togethers. Contribute to online publications and newsletters. Stay visible so you can remain top of mind.

- **Answer questions and inquiries.** Offer insight to specific questions posed by individuals inside and outside your network. Often it can be awkward to just introduce yourself to someone, but if a person you would like to engage poses a question in an online forum, feel free to offer your expertise or insight to break the ice. You never know what recruiter is reading your answer and seeing what you may have to offer.

- **Give to get.** This is a universal networking mantra. All the previous tips have this underlying philosophy as their basis. When applied to job seeking, give job leads to fellow job seekers that are not fully suited for you. Offer candidate referrals to corporate and search recruiters. Post resources that can be helpful to those in your industry or discipline. You can be helping people within your network. Then, in turn, when positions applicable to you arise, your network will keep you in mind. Metaphysically speaking, if you are giving to the world, somehow the world will give back. So it may not come back to you reciprocally from sources to which you gave, but it will come back.

BIO

Lisa Rangel, PHR is the Managing Director of Chameleon Resumes (http://www.chameleonresumes.com) and a graduate of Cornell University. As a search firm recruitment leader for over 13 years, Lisa has partnered with Fortune 500 and boutique firms to source top talent for their organizations. She has written resumes, prepared candidates for interviews and performed job search coaching for professionals ranging from executive to entry-level spanning across a multitude of disciplines, industries and corporate cultures. She has been featured on Good Morning America, Fox Business News and niche job blogs. Lisa is the Career Services Partner for eCornell.com, the online division of Cornell University.

55

Breaking Up Is Hard to Do

❧

Vikki Loving

Why is it that so many of us become fixed and rooted in a career that does not feed and nourish our souls? A counselor friend of mine once told me that the process of leaving a committed relationship, whether it's a marriage or a job, takes, on average, five years. When she mentioned this, I was shocked that so many people take such a long time to make a decision to end something that is obviously painful. But of course, people who are wholeheartedly invested find it more difficult to let go of the potential of their dream of how things should be rather than the actual loss of the relationship itself. The pain that comes with ending any committed relationship causes us to experience some of the grief associated with death.

Elisabeth Kubler-Ross (1993), author of the book *On Death and Dying,* describes the five stages of grief as denial, anger, bargaining, depression, and acceptance. Others agree that with *any* loss—whether it be your job, income, freedom, a life, or even a divorce—an individual will go through at least two of these five stages. If we can understand that grief is an inevitable part of being human and recognize these stages of grief a little more clearly, perhaps we can be more gentle with ourselves as we work through the process—in, I hope, much fewer than five years!

Not dealing with our grief in a healthy way is what keeps us paralyzed. When we lose touch with our purpose—when we forget that passion is real and attainable and when we fail to plan—we often quit believing in our own strengths and talents. When that happens, it's easy to see how people can get stuck between the proverbial rock and a hard place and just resign themselves to living in that uncomfortable position.

Let's look at where over 50 percent of the workforce is right now. According to a survey from Adecco Group North America in a recent *CNN Money* article, "fifty-four percent of employed Americans plan to look for a new job once the economy rebounds" (Dickler 2009). The sentiment is even stronger among younger workers. Of those ages eighteen to twenty-nine, 71 percent say they are likely to look for new jobs once the economy turns around. Another recent survey uncovered the following statistics on American job satisfaction when it reported that across America,

- 45 percent of workers say they are either satisfied or extremely satisfied with their jobs
- only 20 percent feel very passionate about their jobs
- 33 percent believe they have reached a dead end in their career
- 21 percent are eager to change careers

Unbelievable! Only 20 percent of workers feel passionate about their jobs. And over half of those surveyed believe they are in a dead-end job or are eager to change careers!

Let's go back to Ross's five stages of grief for a moment and discuss how each of those stages might appear in someone dealing with job loss:

1. **Denial.** This can't be happening. I can't be losing my job. They can't be serious. They can't run a business this way.

2. **Anger.** Why me? Who else can I blame? I don't want to leave. I don't like what they are doing or how they are doing it!

3. **Bargaining.** If only such-and-such would occur, then maybe . . . or if I can just hang on long enough.

4. **Depression.** I will just disconnect, ignore, and resign myself to the uselessness of the fight.

5. **Acceptance.** I acknowledge the truth. I understand this way does not work for me. I am beginning to comprehend that there might be other possibilities for me.

Personally, I would like to add another stage to this list:

6. Hope.

Hope arrives after you've experienced some, if not all, these steps and realize that there is another path for you—one that is not so rocky and painful. Hope has been living as a tiny seed in you from the beginning and has been begging for your recognition. It was hope that started you down this uncomfortable journey of self-awareness by telling you that something, *anything,* had to change!

In my twenty-five years as an executive recruiter and career counselor, I have come to believe that this fear of letting go and taking a leap of faith is the main obstacle in our way toward a greater purpose, a greater passion, and a greater plan.

Find your purpose. Simply put, purpose is what adds greater meaning to your life when you attach it to your personal expertise, experience, and talents. (I highly recommend that you read a very small, wonderful book about purpose written in 1899 by Elbert Hubbard called *A Message to Garcia.*)

Find your passion. Find something you believe in so strongly that you will commit your energy and time to it. What has been whispering in your ear wanting your attention, but you've kept putting it off? (If you want to read about passion, pick up *Three Cups of Tea* by Mortensen and Relin [2006]. Mortensen was bit hardby the passion bug.)

Know what you value. The number one reason relationships fail is because of a difference in values. Get in touch with the purpose behind your values. Reconnect with the passion your values give you. Then create your plan.

Build your plan. What are the things that you feel you *must* do? Who might benefit from being part of your plan? How can you develop a road map to confidently get there? (For a compelling plan of action, read Harriet Jacobs's [2000] *Incidents in the Life of a Slave Girl.* Few of us would dare to risk as much as she did to enact her plan.)

There is an old saying that "you cannot read the label when you are sitting inside the jar," so don't be afraid to find a friend or two and ask them for their insights about you or to help you research possibilities by which you can utilize your key ingredients: your passion, purpose, and values. Another option is to contact a professional career coach whose specialty is to help you identify your strengths and aptitudes and get you pointed in the right direction.

When we connect hope together with purpose, we create a new plan and start moving energetically forward. Life is an incredible journey filled with many exciting opportunities! Enjoy the ride and the constant surprise of its capacity to give you much more than you could wildly imagine.

References

Dickler, Jessica. 2009. Stuck in a crappy job—tough. *CNN Money*, July 8. http://money.cnn.com/2009/07/08/news/economy/unhappy_at_work/index.htm?cnn= yes.

Hubbard, Elbert. 1899. *A message to Garcia: Being a preachment.* Repr. East Aurora, NY: Roycrofters.

Jacobs, Harriet A. 2000. *Incidents in the life of a slave girl.* Repr. New York: New American Library.

Kubler-Ross, Elisabeth. 1993. *On death and dying.*New York: Collier.

Mortensen, Greg, and David Oliver Relin. 2006. *Three cups of tea: One man's mission to fight terrorism and build nations—one school at a time.* New York: Viking.

BIO

Vikki Loving has been an executive recruiter and professional career coach for more than twenty-five years. Her passion is helping individuals overcome fear and discover their hidden talents so they can embrace life and achieve their greatest potential. She lives in Austin, Texas, with her husband and daughter. Vikki's company is InterSource Recruiting (http://www.InterSourceRecruiting.com/).

56

Secrets to Being the Complete Employable Package

~~~

Laura DeCarlo

Congratulations! You've assembled an outstanding résumé that emphasizes your unique selling propositions, and you've mastered the art of job searching, interviewing, and salary negotiation. Whether you've landed your dream job, your success, happiness, and satisfaction will hinge on one key factor: your attitude.

Don't roll your eyes. I'm not going to go all self-help on you or be a bouncy cheerleader. But please understand that while you need to be prepared with the tools to win in your job search and career, the bedrock of success, the enduring foundation of a champion, is a positive attitude.

Attitude Really *Is* Everything

Self-belief truly is a self-fulfilling prophecy and will be the number one advantage or disadvantage you bring into your career and life. So if you decide that you are too old, too fat, over- or undereducated, unskilled, or unqualified, or if you let yourself get caught up in any other negative belief, you will hold yourself back every time.

It's a destructive loop that your negative thoughts will create for you: first, you won't give your job or career goal your all because you will be too busy in your head already giving yourself reasons and excuses to fail. Then you won't ever sell yourself above your competition for the job, the promotion, or the raise because there will always be someone who blindly or boldly stands out above you simply because that person believes that he or she can. Finally, you will fulfill your own prophecy of defeat, never getting what you really want, what you really deserve.

Thoughts Are the Gatekeepers to Success

The stories you tell yourself, the voice in your head that drives you to go forward or give up, rarely seems like something of your own creation. That's probably because you've been living with it as long as you can remember, so you think it's your own wisdom there to keep you safe with its warnings and commentary. But it's really just a tape you helped program and decided to name Your Reality.

The good news is that this is a cycle that can be broken! You can program a new reality!

Thoughts are just thoughts! They are not reality. They represent rules you have created to live by based on what other people have told you or based on chances you have taken that didn't work out so well the first time. You think you are protecting yourself by listening to those self-limiting thoughts, but in reality, they are so heavy that they are smothering you and holding you back from discovering what you could really have if you were to remove them from your life.

Change Your Thoughts, Change Your World

Sometimes just knowing that it is your own thoughts, and not something real and concrete, that have been holding you back is enough to allow you to make a powerful shift. But, as we could be talking about decades of living with this automatic handicap, it is rarely that easy and would seem to be just a little frustrating.

You don't really get to say "today I'll be happy" until you learn to be happy. If you do and it works, bless you, because you must be sitting on a pot of gold and already living the life of your dreams. For most of us, old habits die hard, so we must make room for change, and then we must do things that elicit the change! Following are my favorite steps toward this end.

Step 1: Start each day with a powerful gratitude exercise.

First, let me say that it does get easier. If your head is filled with negative thoughts, you won't find yourself having many things to list aloud in your next morning shower for which you are grateful. Keep doing it each and every morning. It takes 120 days to establish a new habit, but it won't take that long to feel positive results. As you continue to find things for which to be grateful, you will begin to open up and notice the wonders in your world that you were taking for granted.

Opportunity is all around us, it's just that we either see it or we don't!

You can take this process to the next level by infusing your gratitude list with emotion. As you become more comfortable finding things for which to be grateful, ask yourself what about them makes you feel grateful and how that makes you feel.

It's OK to be skeptical, but it will put a bounce in your step when you begin to see everything you do have to be positive about.

Step 2: Interrupt your thoughts and put them on trial.

You've lived with your thoughts a very long time, and so they are going to continue to pop into your head. Your goal is to become active with your thoughts and decide what you want to think moment to moment. To do that, you will find yourself initially acting like a traffic cop—you will always want to be ready to bring them in and put them on trial for sentencing.

How?

First, again, know that you think, and your thoughts are just thoughts that you've tied up in not-so-pretty emotional packages that you've been pushing or pulling along with you.

Stop and take the time to examine the package. Ask yourself, "Is this really true?"

For instance, if your thought is "I won't get a promotion because I am fat," then ask yourself, "Do I know that this is really true?"

Your first thought will probably be yes because you believe it is so. However, you need to challenge that thought with more rational exploration. A powerful activity is to pretend you are watching a movie with actors (not you) going through the situation about which you are thinking. Now you are looking at another person you see as fat on the screen, and perhaps you expand your thinking to realize that in this movie could be any person who ever was fat or considered fat or thought he or she was fat in the history of the world.

So is it true that no fat person ever got promoted in the history of the world?

No, it is not true. Job promotion is not an exclusive club for thin people. Lots of fat people, whether they really are so-called fat, have climbed the corporate ladder.

Furthermore, you might challenge your thought that you are fat by asking yourself, "Would everyone in the world say that I was too fat to promote?" or "Would everyone say I am fat?" You might not even be fat! That could be a story you've been telling yourself since you were a child that's not even true.

When you really start putting your thoughts on trial, the dominoes are going to start tumbling as you realize one thought after another that just cannot be proven true. All kinds of positive outcomes are going to be in store for you when you unload the heavy weight of these negative, attitude-crushing beliefs.

Interrupt your pattern again and again and again. Through repetition, it will get easier, and it will be automatic to decide whether a thought serves you or needs to go to jail, never again to see the light of day.

Step 3: Take ten minutes a day to change your destiny.

By changing your thoughts, you will find that you suddenly have more energy and time, which you will find many ways to use to your advantage. Be sure to use some of that time for keeping up the momentum and carrying it forward—commit to reading, listening to, or learning one positive new thing each day that will help you continue to grow.

There is so much inspirational literature available from leaders such as Louise Hay, Jack Canfield, Jim Rohn, ZigZiglar, Les Brown, and hundreds of others; you need only look on the Internet to find their quotes, newsletters, and inspirational messages.

If you were to spend just ten minutes each day on something positive and new, at the end of the month, that would be five hours of positive juice for your happy attitude battery!

By the end of the year, that would add up to over sixty hours of new inspiration and knowledge. People have changed their lives in less time than that, but you'll barely feel it at just ten minutes each day!

**Step 4: Let each day provide a lesson for positive
growth and attitude nurturing.**

Your old thinking will interpret the day's activities in black and white—they are either good or bad. Left unexamined, these perceptions will weigh you down if they sneak past your questioning cop. You can interrupt this process and end the day on a positive note just by taking the time to learn from it.

Make a list of what you are proud of today. Ask yourself, "What about this makes me feel proud?" Make a list of areas with which you aren't as happy. Ask yourself,

"What could I have done differently?" "What is another way to look at this?" and, of course, "Do I know that what I am thinking about this is really true?" You will find that these situations or actions that were disappointments are really nothing more than lessons learned, something to laugh about or something to try differently tomorrow. This exercise will give you a different perspective on the weight you were carrying around and, it is hoped, will allow you to set it down and drift into a peaceful sleep with positive visions of how your great attitude is going to take you wherever you want to go.

Each of these steps has one thing in common—each requires action. Learning is an active process. Changing is an active process. Just as your body will go soft and return to its old shape if you stop exercising, so will your mind.

To continue moving forward and embracing a positive and fulfilling career, you must commit to feeding yourself an emotional diet high in inspiration, positive thinking, gratitude, and giving. You reap what you sow, so planting a little more each day will give you momentum to move toward being the kind of person inside and out who can overcome any challenge to reach his or her goals. Take that finely honed strategy you've gained from this book, couple it with your winning attitude, and no goal will be beyond your reach!

BIO

Laura DeCarlo has developed a reputation as the "career hero" for the efforts she has pioneered in the career services industry for both job seekers and career professionals as the founder of the global professional association Career Directors International (CDI). An industry leader, she has earned two degrees and eleven industry certifications and designations. Furthermore, she has received the industry's most prestigious awards for career coaches and resume writers. Laura is the author of *Interviewing: The Gold Standard* and *Interview Pocket RX* as well as coauthor of *Job Search Bloopers*. Laura is a former two-year employment guest columnist for the *Florida Today* newspaper and has been quoted in *Forbes (IMPRESS), Working Mother*, and the *Wall Street Journal*.

57

JOB SEARCH SECRETS

Straight Talk from a Recruiter

Job Search Strategies

～

Cori Swidorsky

There have been many changes with job-searching strategies throughout my eleven-year recruiting career. When mentoring job seekers, I suggest experimenting with several strategies, and I give advice from a recruiting point of view. Here I discuss a few favorite strategies that can enhance your career search.

Résumé Strategies

Opening Statement

Also referred to as an *objective* or *personal branding statement*, an opening statement should make the reader want to find out more about you and should include three parts:

1. **Who you are.** This is similar to a job target or the title of the position for which you are applying. It tells the employer about your specializations. For example, you could write C# Software Developer, Human Resources Manager, VP of Marketing, or Account Manager.

2. **Your biggest strength.** Highlight your biggest strength that would benefit an employer. Employers want to know what you can do for them and how you will be able to do it. For example, can you develop new business, solve complex problems, improve processes, or create marketing campaigns?

3. **The benefit you offer a company.** The last part of the opening statement tells the employer what benefit you can offer the company by being who you are, and it also highlights your biggest strength. It tells the employer why you would be an asset to the company and how the employer will benefit by hiring you. For example, you could emphasize that you will reduce

downtime, increase profits, improve production, reduce turnover, or save the company money.

Following is an example of an opening statement after you put it all together: Human Resources Manager establishing new personnel programs for hiring, training, and motivating new employees, which reduces turnover by 50 percent.

Accomplishment Section

Grab an employer's attention with an accomplishment section on your résumé. Competition is tight in today's job market. There are more job seekers than job opportunities, so it's an employer's market. Selling skills is just not enough these days. Focusing on specific accomplishments will improve your chances of being interviewed and separate you from other candidates.

Following are four results-oriented accomplishments that may show how you helped past organizations:

1.   how you made a company money

2.   how you saved a company money

3.   what goals you met or exceeded

4.   how you improved a company's work life

Job-Searching Strategies

The Hidden Job Market

The hidden job market is any position that isn't advertised or posted anywhere. For example, when I was between recruiting projects, I walked into a recruiting company down the road from me to see if they were hiring recruiters. I asked to speak to the recruiting manager and ended up having a twenty-minute interview with him. It ended up that they did have a recruiting opportunity that was going to be available the first of the year, but it wasn't advertised yet. This would be considered a hidden job opportunity because there was an opportunity available that wasn't advertised yet, and I just happened to stumble across it by walking into the company.

Recruiters do get access to the hidden job market as well. If a company has a confidential job opening, it usually won't advertise it. The company will utilize recruiters to assist with filling the position. Also, companies don't want to be overwhelmed with job applications from job postings, or they may not have the budget to advertise jobs where they need to.

Following are examples of how you can tap into the hidden job market:

- Work with recruiters and staffing agencies.
- Walk into companies and hand deliver your résumé.
- Attend job fairs and networking events.
- Get involved within your community and with volunteering.
- Let friends, family, and acquaintances know you are on the job market.

LinkedIn Groups

LinkedIn groups are a great way for recruiters, hiring managers, and job seekers to connect. The groups benefit recruiters because we can send members of the group messages directly. The only other way to send someone a message is to request a connection or upgrade to a paid subscription. The strategy for job seekers is to join groups that recruiters and managers would most likely join to find someone like you such as groups covering geographic areas, industry experience levels, and skill sets. Once you are in the group, you can search for managers, team leads, and project managers and contact them directly.

Seven Strategies to Get Your Résumé Noticed Online

Don't miss out on being found online! Use as many resources as you can to make sure that your résumé is getting noticed online:

1. **Create a career blog.** Start a blog that focuses on your career industry and include tips, articles, news, and industry-related topics. You don't have to be a writer to create a blog. You can link to other articles and news about that industry topic and add comments showing your industry knowledge. Also, set up a page on the blog for your résumé and highlight your industry knowledge, experience, and expertise. You can easily set up a blog for free using programs such as Blogger.com or WordPress.com.

2. **Join free document-sharing websites.** There are a number of free file-sharing websites that can help you gain more résumé exposure online. Save your document in different forms, such as DOC and PDF, so that your résumé shows up under those search terms. Recruiters search for résumés using words such as PDF, RTF, DOC, and CV. Here are few free sites to check out: KeepandShare.com, SlideShare.net, and http://docs.google.com.

3. **Set up a résumé Web page.** A one-page website for your résumé gives great exposure and is a wonderful way to link others to your résumé. You can add your website URL to your résumé, to other online profiles, and at the end of your signature in e-mails and forum posts. You can find free résumé website builders such as Emurse.com and VisualCV.com.

4. **Use social and professional networking websites.** It's no secret that social and professional networking websites are becoming hubs for job seekers and recruiters. If you aren't using networking websites, you are missing out on a ton of exposure. You can utilize these websites by putting in your professional profile or résumé and links to your résumé website and blog. The majority of recruiters utilize LinkedIn, Twitter, and Facebook.

5. **Use keywords.** Recruiters are searching for résumés using keywords. If your résumé doesn't include the keywords that are being searched for, most likely, it won't show up in the search results. Make sure you include technology and terminology that's common in your industry.

6. **Join online groups.** There are a ton of online groups that can help get you exposure online, and recruiters are going into online groups to source for candidates. You can join industry-specific groups, association groups, and groups based on location. I highly recommend joining LinkedIn groups. Other groups you can look into are Google groups, Yahoo! groups, and Meetup.com groups.

7. **Check out job boards.** Many recruiters still use job boards as their primary sourcing tool. Get your résumé posted to popular job boards such as Monster.com, CareerBuilder.com, Dice.com, and TheLadders.com. Search for local area job boards as well.

BIO

Cori Swidorsky has over eleven years of experience in the recruiting industry. Her experience includes professional résumé writing, job search training and mentoring, and teaching creative job-searching strategies. She has been writing advice articles since 2007 on topics such as job-searching strategies, résumé tips, networking, and interviewing. She is a contributing writer to Examiner.com and Ehow.com. Cori is the owner of http://www.1on1careerhelp.com/, http://www.jobsearchingstrategies.com/, and http://www.SeeWhosHiring.com/. Cori earned her bachelor's degree in business administration management and resides in Pittsburgh, Pennsylvania. Contact Cori at cori.recruiter@gmail.com.

The Four Most Effective Job Search Strategies Out There!

Charlotte Weeks

There are numerous ways to go about finding a job, but they almost always fall into four categories: applying to open positions, working with recruiters, sending your résumé to companies that don't have advertised openings, and networking. Though some of these strategies have higher rates of success than others, it's a good idea to diversify and use them all. The key is to spend more time in the areas that have the greatest likelihood of getting you an interview.

Let's start with the first one. Applying to open jobs (usually online) is by far the most used method by job seekers. It's because of this reason that it's also the *least* effective way to get an interview. When a company advertises an opening, they'll likely get hundreds (sometimes thousands) of résumés sent to them. Even if you're a great fit for the job, and have the world's greatest résumé, the odds against you are very high. Still, people obviously find work this way, or these sites would not exist. Just be sure to maximize your use by having a first-rate résumé and cover letter with plenty of relevant keywords. From a time management perspective, spend no more than an hour each day applying to positions online (and when you do, be even more efficient by using a search aggregator like Indeed.com, which gathers job advertisements from a variety of sites).

Working with recruiters is statistically more effective, with approximately 15 to 20 percent of candidates finding a job this way. Most people aren't familiar with how these headhunters work. They are hired by a company to find the perfect candidate, not the other way around. Though you may have been contacted by a recruiter in the past, there are some proactive ways you can get in touch with those that hire for your industry.

First, try a *proactive passive* method and post a strong LinkedIn profile. Recruiters overwhelmingly look at LinkedIn first when sourcing for candidates. Increase your chances of coming up in a search by having your profile highly targeted and filled with keywords.

Another method overlaps with networking. Seek out recruiters via LinkedIn, networking events, or introductions from your contacts. When you do get called, make an effort to stay in touch; refer leads, follow up regularly to see if any new positions have become available—build an ongoing relationship, even if you're not the right person for the job at hand, they'll remember you for future roles and possibly refer you to someone else. Increase the effectiveness of networking with recruiters by targeting those in your industry.

The final method is the easiest: use a recruiter distribution service. Your résumé is blasted to hundreds or thousands of recruiters across the country. From a strictly numbers perspective, it has a very high return on investment. The key is finding a *reputable* service—there are many on the market that are a waste of time and money. Make sure the distribution list to which your résumé is sent is targeted according to your experience level, income, and/or industry.

My clients are always shocked when I tell them to send their résumés cold to a company that doesn't have any advertised openings. The fun thing is that *you* get to choose your target companies (instead of waiting to see what pops up online) and then work on getting an interview there. Even though this sounds like a long shot, this is actually more effective than applying to open positions. At this point, you're only competing with yourself, so if any open jobs do come up, you'll likely be considered for an interview.

One way of going about it is to identify a certain number of companies (say, twenty-five) that meet your criteria for location, industry, and so on. Research these places, especially the names of key decision makers in your department of interest and staff in human resources.

Once you have gathered this information, give yourself an extra edge with *how* you apply. Try sending your résumé and cover letter by mail or fax, which will certainly make them stand out among all those sent through e-mail. If you have any contacts at the company, mention their names in the cover letter. Be sure to follow up after doing this (which *significantly* increases your chances of getting an interview). If you don't get in touch with anyone, try back. In general, follow the three-strikes rule—this is the number of times you can reach out before taking this company off of your radar.

The final method is the number one way people find a job: networking. Basically, in the job search, this comes down to getting to know the company's decision makers or the people who can connect you with them. Rarely a quick method, it works best when you've built and maintained a network *before* you need it.

If you're starting from scratch, or you'd like to expand your network, make the most of your time by targeting those people who can help you the most. Seek out people in your industry, especially those in a position to make hiring decisions. Next, establish and build relationships with these contacts. This means offering tips, leads, articles of interest, and so on. Networking givers are most likely to receive in the end.

Networking can be done online (through LinkedIn, Twitter, etc.) or in person. Most cities have networking events at which people can get together to mingle. Another effective option is to get involved in an industry association to meet some of the movers and shakers in the organization. Oftentimes, people use both methods—they meet people in person and then keep up online.

There you have it: the four most effective job search strategies, with tips on how best to use them. These methods *do* work, and they've been proven time and time again. The key is to remember not to focus on any one to the exclusion of others. Diversify and persevere, and you won't go wrong!

BIO

Charlotte Weeks, Certified Career Management Coach, Nationally Certified Résumé Writer, and Certified Professional Résumé Writer, owns Weeks Career Services Inc., based in Chicago, Illinois. She specializes in helping association executives find their passion and land at the top! Prior to beginning her business, Ms. Weeks had a career in human resources and experienced the hiring process from the employer's point of view. She has since worked with clients located across the globe. Ms. Weeks provides services of the highest quality by assessing each client's needs and customizing individual solutions. Whether he or she needs effective career marketing documents (such as a résumé, cover letter, or LinkedIn profile), help figuring out what type of work they want to pursue, assistance uncovering open positions, or interview preparation, each client receives outstanding value and individual attention. Ms. Weeks has served as a featured expert for various media outlets, including the *Wall Street Journal*, NBC-Chicago, WGN-TV, Fox-TV/My50 Chicago, and Yahoo! Hotjobs. She is president of the National Résumé Writers' Association and a member of Career Directors International (CDI), Career Management Alliance (CMA), and the Professional Association of Résumé Writers and Career Coaches (PARW/CC). She also serves as the career and résumé expert for ConnectWork Chicago. For more information, visit http://www.weekscareerservices.com or e-mail charlotte@weekscareerservices.com.

59

How to Create a Killer Résumé

*8 Insider Secrets to Land Interviews
and Stand Out from the Competition*

⚜

Robert Mandelberg

In this chapter, I provide eight great tips to help you create an interview-generating, competition-smashing, Pulitzer Prize–winning résumé. But before I get to that, we need to come to an understanding.

Commit to a Specific Job Target: No Generic Résumés!

The only way to succeed in today's ultracompetitive job market is by focusing your efforts on a single type of position. Employers are seeking specialists, not generalists. They want candidates who are perfect fits to solve their challenges and achieve their goals. And with the volume of résumés submitted for each position, employers can afford to be picky. If your résumé is not pinpoint focused to address the needs and objectives of a specific position, then there is little chance you will stand out among hundreds—or thousands—of other candidates, many of whom have created targeted résumés.

The benefits of committing to a specific job target are substantial. Once you commit, you are able to focus 100 percent of your job-search plan, networking strategy, online presence (LinkedIn), *and* résumé on your *value* as it relates to the target position. You are also able to portray "expert status" and position yourself as an exceptional candidate.

Many job seekers are afraid to commit to a single focus for fear of limiting their opportunities. And while it is true that a generic résumé may allow you to *apply* for many types of jobs, it is unlikely that you will ever be *selected* for an interview— especially when you are competing against people with targeted résumés. *Don't try to be all things to all people.* Be a specialist to increase your chances of success.

If you take this advice and commit to a single job target, then you will find these tips quite useful.

Use a headline. This is a perfect device to demonstrate your commitment to the target position. The headline clearly states your goal and is much more effective than an ordinary objective. It is placed directly below your name and contact information and is written like a category header (same font and size as other category headers such as "Professional Experience" and "Education"). Example:

Senior Health Care Sales Professional

Include a branding statement. This is a phrase written directly below the headline, highlighting your most important value point. If you had just one sentence to capture an employer's attention, what would it be? Example:

Senior Health Care Sales Professional

*President's Club Winner and #1-Ranked Sales Specialist with
12 Years of Experience in the Pharmaceutical Industry*

Craft a summary. Following your headline and branding statement, include a brief section that highlights the value you bring to your target position. What results can an employer expect if you are hired? What track record have you established? Use these few lines to succinctly explain why you are a perfect fit. Avoid soft skills such as "strong organizational abilities" and focus instead on what you have been able to accomplish in your career. You do not need to label this category, as it will be a part of the initial section with your headline.

List areas of expertise. An essential component of your résumé (usually included just below your summary), this listing of keywords and searchable phrases shows the breadth of your experience and reinforces your commitment to your target position. It also helps your résumé get noticed by scanning software that many companies use to search for specific keywords. For our previous sales example, some keywords may include "Business Development," "National Account Management," and "Relationship Management." These keywords are generally listed in columns or separated by bullets.

Highlight results—not responsibilities. To make your résumé sizzle, focus on achievements and avoid generic job descriptions. There is no benefit to cluttering your résumé with listings of day-to-day duties. Most employers already know your responsibilities—especially if you are seeking a similar position to the ones you are describing. What they don't know is *how well you have performed these responsibilities.*

Employers want to see how you've met your goals and solved challenges. In the example of the salesperson, the goal, quite clearly, is to increase sales. Period. There is no point in writing about prospecting clients or conducting sales presentations; employers know this already. Instead, highlight your successes. The next few tips provide more insight on how to accomplish this.

Be specific. It's one thing for you to say that you increased sales, but it's quite another to offer quantifiable results. By how much did you increase sales? Did you reach your goals? Did you outperform your peers? Here is a great way to express your achievement:

Increased territorial sales volume from $1.2 million in 2010 to $1.64 million in 2011, exceeding sales quota by 11%. Ranked #1 in region (out of 14) and #4 in nation (out of 142) in goal attainment and territorial growth.

And this does not only apply to salespeople. Think of your own achievements. Did you save money for the company? (*How much?*) Did you increase productivity? (*How many hours did you save?*) Did you lead a departmental restructuring? (*How did you improve operations?*) Listing quantifiable results is as close as you can get on your résumé to "proving" that you are the right fit for the job you are seeking.

Demonstrate impact. Showing results is a terrific way to exhibit your value, but demonstrating *impact* to the company is even better. How have your achievements benefited the company? Try to find the "*so what?*" behind the result. Here is an example:

Reduced supply costs 22% by renegotiating vendor contracts, centralizing the ordering process, and instituting tighter inventory controls. *Cost reduction enabled the company to replace aging order processing software and maintain a competitive advantage in the marketplace.*

Not only did you reduce expenses by 22 percent but your efforts provided the company with the resources for necessary upgrades. That's impact! How have your efforts helped to achieve your employers' short- or long-range goals?

CAR achievements. Exhibit your problem-solving acumen by using a CAR (challenge–action–result) approach. Provide the reader with the context of the problem, the actions you took, and the outcome. Here is an abbreviated example of this powerful technique:

Assumed leadership of a branch with a high rate of employee turnover. Identified and resolved long-standing internal issues, instituted weekly staff meetings, and designed performance incentive programs. *Increased retention rate from 64% to 99% within first year.*

CAR is effective at all levels of an organization, not just at the management level. This is a perfect way to show initiative, capability, innovation, and problem-solving talent. What problems have you resolved, and what were the results?

The preceding techniques are great examples of how you can demonstrate your value to hiring managers. It is up to you to provide the information employers need to make an intelligent decision on your candidacy. If you fail to present your value in a genuine and compelling way, then you have done a tremendous disservice to yourself and may have missed some great opportunities.

By committing to a specific target, focusing on achievements, and highlighting your value, your chances of success and career happiness increase exponentially. I wish you the best of luck in your job search!

BIO

Robert Mandelberg is a Certified Professional Résumé Writer, published author, and owner of The Creative Edge Resume & Writing Service LLC. Since 1987, he has helped thousands of job seekers achieve their career goals. He is also the producer of the Job-Search Summit, a groundbreaking event featuring national leaders in the career-services industry. Would you like Robert to write your résumé? For résumé samples, job-search tips, and information on professional résumé-writing services, visit http://www.CreativeEdgeResumes.com/.

60

Rock-Solid Leadership

A 5-Step Leadership Self-Development Plan

Randy Goruk

A leadership self-development plan is essential for all leaders to continue to grow professionally and make advancements in their careers. Leadership development is an ongoing process and is critical to the short- and long-term success of the leader and his or her organization. However, with busy schedules, crucial deadlines, and tight budgets, formal leadership development training is often minimized.

When training budgets are cut, or don't exist, individuals are often left to their own resources to continue their education or grow professionally. In this challenging environment, many put their professional growth aside and wait for a different or better time.

When it comes to professional growth and development, waiting is not an acceptable strategy; however, a leadership self-development plan is a viable solution. To enhance your career, you can implement this simple and affordable five-step leadership self-development plan. You can also share the concept with others.

Step 1

You must make a commitment to allocate a minimum of 10 percent of your time to your professional growth and development. For most people, this equates to anywhere between four and six hours per week, or a staggering twenty-six to thirty-nine eight-hour days per year.

This becomes your goal, and with any goal, you need to work hard at achieving it. It may not seem practical at first, and you may not be able to immediately jump into four to six hours per week. However, you can start by getting rid of the things that are wasting your time, then begin to dedicate thirty minutes in your calendar to self-development, then sixty minutes twice per week, then three times a week, and then before you know it, you will be easily achieving your goal.

Like any goal, keep it visible by tracking your progress. You will have taken a positive step toward achieving professional growth and career advancement.

Step 2

Determine what specific skills, characteristics, qualities, or attributes on which you need to work in your plan. There are a number of ways you can do this. Here are five very realistic approaches to identifying opportunities for improvement:

- Ask your boss what areas he or she would like to see you improve.
- Ask your coworkers for feedback.
- Ask your mentor for feedback.
- Complete a formal 360 degree feedback survey.
- Complete an online self-assessment form.

You've now identified the areas to concentrate on developing. We call them *opportunities for improvement.*

Step 3

Determine which methodologies or tools are best for you. Everyone learns a little differently, so evaluate the best way for you to learn. Here are seven valuable ways you can learn:

- Attend workshops and seminars.
- Listen to educational CDs (or MP3s).
- Watch educational DVDs.
- Find a professional coach with whom to work.
- Find and attend free webinars.
- Find and read books and online blogs.
- Role-play situations.

You can see with the number of learning options available to you that there is no way you can fall short of your goal. You also don't need to spend a ton of money.

Step 4

Proper and complete execution of your plan means you will need to prioritize and stay focused and disciplined in achieving your goal and desired outcomes. Whether you have two or twenty opportunities for improvement identified in step 2, you will need to decide which to work on first. To do this, take a full sheet of paper and create a matrix with three columns and three rows. When you complete this, you will have nine boxes.

Let's identify the columns as "Effort Required." Now label the column on the left "Hard," the column in the middle "Medium," and the column on the right "Easy."

Let's identify the rows as "Time Required." Now label the top row "Short," the middle row "Medium," and the bottom row "Long."

Inside the matrix, or the boxes that have been created from the columns and rows, simply write the opportunities for improvement in the appropriate quadrant. As an example, if becoming a better listener is an opportunity for you, and you think it requires the least amount of work and is the quickest fix, it will be in the top right-hand box. Once all your opportunities have been positioned within the matrix, I recommend you start with opportunity that will take the least amount of effort and the shortest amount of time.

Prioritize the other opportunities for improvement that make most sense to you and your career. Then go to work on them in the time you've allocated in step 1, utilizing the methodology you've identified in step 2.

Step 5

Hold ninety-day reviews. Evaluate and adjust your plan.

In summary, I've asked you to make a commitment to grow professionally and prepare for career advancement by creating a five-step leadership self-development plan:

1. Set a goal of allocating time to self-development.
2. Identify relevant competencies or opportunities for improvement.
3. Determine the best tools to leverage your development.
4. Prioritize and focus.
5. Evaluate and adjust your plan.

I wish you the best of luck in the creation of your personalized self-development plan and in your career advancement.

BIO

Randy Goruk is known for two things: real experience and real results. Randy Goruk is a seasoned corporate executive who started his career on the ground floor and successfully climbed the corporate ladder to become senior vice president of a multi-million-dollar organization at the age of thirty-one. He contributed to and lead change initiatives that resulted in company growth from $60 million to $1 billion annual revenue over a twenty-six-year career. Today he is a leadership coach, professional speaker, and author. His website contains information on professional coaching, 360 degree feedback surveys, and a complimentary leadership self-assessment. Visit http://www.LeadersEdge360.com/, or e-mail randy@LeadersEdge360.com.

61

Developing Leaders: Conscious Leadership

❦

Jennifer Howard

Many of us think about leaders as those *other* people who are highly visible, maybe famous, or possibly CEOs or politicians we see on TV or about whom we read. We often think they must be far more qualified than we are, or they wouldn't be in such a powerful position. Or maybe there are people we know of who are less visible in the public eye, such as bosses, clergy, or other authority figures, but still characterize how we define a leader.

Leadership and leading have been described in many ways. According to the book *Business* (Pride, Hughes, and Kapoor 2009, 179), "leading is the process of influencing people to work toward a common goal." According to Answers.com, another way to think about leading and leadership is "persons of authority; the capacity to guide or inspire others."

Seeing leaders as those *other* people places us at a distance from being leaders ourselves and might put us in the one-down position. From this way of thinking, it is hard to see and embody our own power. The result of this could even encourage our avoidance of exploring our stuck places that impede us from reaching our greatness.

Or could it be that you already see yourself as a leader? What does that mean to you? Do you feel calmly empowered on a daily basis or more like an imposter just waiting to be found out? Maybe you're somewhere in between these two.

Whether we know it or not, from the largest perspective, everyone is a leader. Everyday we are the president of our own lives and our own destinies. We are always setting an example and influencing others in every interaction.

Developing leadership by being awake and deciding to lead consciously moves us toward living from our highest choices. If we choose to listen to the wise voice inside that expresses those deeper possibilities, we can live from our greatness and

228

inspire others to do so as well. Innately, we have the ability to connect with this fundamental level of ourselves and live out our life's purpose.

There are ways that might help us to think about our own leadership and foster the coming forth of our very best. Living and leading from this voice of a deeper connection, which we could call *conscious leadership*, includes high authenticity, integrity, maturity, and humility. Action taken from conscious leadership will honor the truth of everyone involved.

The old leadership paradigm has often encouraged winning friends and influencing people with subtle and not-so-subtle manipulation and coercion. It is based on the "power-over" model. The leader is often unquestioned and dominating. The atmosphere is fear based and competitive, reinforcing scarcity, demanding one to always have the right answers and enforcing unreasonable expectations. From their unintegrated ego challenges, this kind of leader attempts to present infallibility and often seeks adoration and glorification.

However, there is another kind of conscious enlightening leadership that shows a different promise. It supports cooperation, empowerment, and collaboration and inspires others to do *their* best and grow *their* talents. It encourages an atmosphere of the highest vision, passion, and aspiration and demonstrates win-win. These kinds of leaders can see how all may profit; all may be challenged to their razor's edge, and all may be fulfilled. This mutuality helps everyone develop as a person in his or her daily life and work as a leader.

True conscious enlightening leadership requires the leaders to continually walk the rigorous path of self-discovery and true empowerment. It takes courage, dedication, a committed level of self-reflection, and intimacy with oneself. This leader shows compassion beyond his or her own self-interest, together with skillfulness in navigating his or her own thoughts and feelings, and demonstrates the ability to be vulnerable. This leader is curious and open to the ideas and comments of others, allowing creativity to flourish.

As conscious enlightening leaders, we continue growing and learning so as not to fall prey to our own unhealed egos. Otherwise, we run the risk of riding the emotional roller coaster of people's opinions, being seduced into believing the projections and fantasies of peers, employees, students, and even bosses. If we choose to live a conscious life and be a conscious enlightening leader, we must hold our toes to the fire by challenging our self-distortions. This can include our lack of knowledge, playing on the weaknesses of others, our greed, and our never fulfilled hungry ghost of wanting more and more, sometimes at the expense of others.

This kind of guidance and leadership allows for an enthusiastic, creative, and innovative atmosphere that will inspire everyone to be and do their best. Trail blazing from authenticity, integrity, maturity, and humility unearths and liberates everyone's pent-up magnificence.

A synergistic combination of setting the intention and holding a cohesive vision creates unbounded possibilities. Congruence within the leader becomes foundational and sets the tone for everyone and every connection. Self-responsibility is viscerally mentored with clarity and integrity. You can then imagine how outrageously effective any business, company, or organization can be when it's being led consciously.

And what does that mean for us? Conscious leadership is a path that leads to living a powerful, mature, genuine, compassionate, humble, and happy life.

Reference

Pride, William M., Robert J. Hughes, and Jack R. Kapoor. 2009. *Business.* Mason, OH: Cengage South-Western.

BIO

Dr. Jennifer Howard teaches the art of conscious living. She is equally at home sharing ancient spiritual wisdom, the latest scientific understanding, and proven and practical life-changing techniques culled from over twenty years as an internationally acclaimed coach, licensed psychotherapist, teacher, and energy healer. She leads a variety of teleseminars and is a leading thought leader on spirituality and psychology. Having appeared as an expert on numerous national network television shows, she is also the host of the popular radio show "A Conscious Life." Twitter: @DrJennifer; Facebook: Dr. Jennifer Howard; website: http://www.DrJenniferHoward.com/.

62

Learn to Lead

The Rest Will Follow

❧⟶☙

Natalie Loeb & Scott Cohen

You've exceeded expectations consistently for years as an analyst. You have demonstrated diligence and excellent customer service as a project coordinator. You have been recognized as a competent and reliable supervisor. And at this year's performance review, your boss gives you the best news of all. Congratulations! You've just been promoted to manager. Now what? This scenario is too familiar to many new managers. Promotions frequently come with seniority or exemplary project performance instead of as key milestones in a continuous process of training and development. The environment in today's business world is fast paced and demanding. Shrinking budgets, enormous workloads, long hours, and the pressures of numerous competing priorities are common in all departments. To succeed under these conditions requires more than good managerial skills, job knowledge, and seniority. It takes leadership. But what is leadership, and how does it differ from management?

The Characteristics of Leadership

We define leadership as the ability to inspire others to act toward the achievement of a commonly held vision. Although descriptions and definitions of leadership vary widely among the experts, an astute observer will notice a common factor demonstrated by successful leaders. These seasoned professionals have mastered skills identified as emotional intelligence (EI) by Daniel Goleman in his 1995 book *Primal Leadership: Learning to Lead with Emotional Intelligence.* He describes the following emotionally intelligent qualities:

- self-awareness (self-assessment and self-confidence)
- self-management (self-control, transparency, adaptability, achievement, initiative, and optimism)

- social awareness (empathy, organizational awareness, and service)
- relationship management (inspiration, influence, developing others, change catalyst, conflict management, teamwork, and collaboration)

EI enables a leader to foster a set of skills that are useful in dealing with the everyday challenges found in today's challenging business environment. These skills range from managing the team to managing the expectations of demanding executives. Emotionally intelligent leaders are always mindful of these qualities and choose to apply them skillfully as they inspire others and move them toward action. Daniel Goleman and other researchers concluded that emotionally intelligent qualities and leadership skills can be developed, giving individuals the opportunity to transform themselves from great managers to great leaders.

Leaders Have a Vision of the Future

One quality consistently found in effective leadership is the leader's ability to create and communicate a clear vision of the future. A vision can be intensely inspirational when shared by all members of an organization. People will start to reflect and ask themselves what they can do to help move the department toward its goal. It is important to remember that having a clearly defined vision is just the first step. Highly effective leaders must gain buy-in by flexing their EI as well as skillfully and relentlessly communicating their vision to others.

Leaders Inspire Others to Act Toward the Achievement of Their Visions

If you look around your own organization, you are bound to notice at least one team with members who are highly engaged in what they're doing and working collaboratively toward clearly communicated goals. They are providing feedback to one another willingly and comfortably and sharing information and ideas openly. You might also notice a certain kind of respect between the staff members and their manager. This is a high-performing team that is consistently delivering results to its customers. How did this happen? The odds are strong that this team has an emotionally intelligent leader—one who chooses to apply the four qualities of self-awareness, self-management, social awareness, and relationship management to inspire the team continuously to reach its highest potential. This is a leader who demonstrates personal integrity, humility, commitment, character, drive, encouragement, and respect for team members. He or she is a person whose behaviors include influencing, challenging, persuading, or simply engendering enthusiasm and optimism about the organization, its work, and its objectives.

The Relationship between Leading and Managing

There is a profound difference between management and leadership, and both are important. To *manage* means to bring about, to accomplish, to have charge of or responsibility for, to conduct. *Leading* is influencing, guiding in a direction, course, action or opinion. Simply providing a team with good management is not sufficient if consistently high performance is the goal. Management focuses on the mechanics of keeping an organization functioning such as planning, budgeting, policy making, and other forms of organizational control. In the absence of leadership, maintaining this control becomes more difficult, and team performance almost inevitably deteriorates. Sound management and effective leadership are complementary capabilities that must be present for the team to be continuously successful. New managers are well advised to pay attention to both their management responsibilities and the development of their leadership qualities.

Practical Steps to Becoming a Leader

The following steps can be taken immediately to begin developing and applying emotionally intelligent leadership qualities as you begin your transformation into a leader.

Link performance expectations to your vision. Leadership is the ability to inspire others to act toward the achievement of a commonly held vision. Some leaders face significant challenges in influencing team members to buy-in to their vision. One way to overcome these challenges is to link performance expectations to the vision. For instance, if your vision is to be the best litigation support department in the industry, think of specific ways in which each team member can help bring this about, and use those as performance objectives. Performance management discussions provide a regular and highly effective opportunity to reinforce commitment to the vision.

Flex your EI skills when coaching and mentoring. Coaching and mentoring are activities in which good leaders engage regularly. Leveraging EI skills during these one-on-one discussions will dramatically enhance their effectiveness. For example, listen actively and consider your approach and tone when providing guidance and feedback. Check frequently to see that your message is being received in the way that you intended. Use these discussions as an opportunity to build trust, mutual respect, and the skills and confidence of your team members.

Develop talent for the future. It is truly amazing to see the transformation in team performance when the team sees its leader actively supporting the growth and development of each team member. When you engage in this behavior, you are making an investment that pays large dividends to individual team members, to yourself, and to the firm. There are many ways to do this. Provide training opportunities to learn new skills. Provide challenging and interesting work assignments. Succession planning helps to prepare future leaders. Mentoring high-potential individuals allows you to continuously challenge them while developing and building on their strengths.

Now Get Out There and Lead!

Whether you are starting your first day as a new manager or your tenth year as a department head, it's never too late to begin to lead. The road to leadership begins by learning to believe in yourself and proceeds with the continuous process of developing and enhancing the qualities that help to gain the respect and trust of your team. You can expect many challenges along the way, but there are also many rewards. Effective leadership leads to improved team performance, staff retention, and higher customer satisfaction. Learn to lead—the rest will follow.

Bio

Natalie Loeb is the founder and lead consultant of Loeb Consulting Group LLC. She is an executive coach and facilitator with over twenty years of experience in employee relations, training program design and facilitation, and executive coaching. Clients include top tier legal services firms and other large and mid-sized organizations placing a priority on leadership development and using respectful and skillful communication to enhance diverse work cultures and inspire collaboration. Natalie's experience as a member of the human resources team at the international law firm of Skadden, Arps, Slate, Meagher & Flom LLP and Affiliates in New York City, provided the foundation for launching her consulting business in 1997. As the lead coach and facilitator, Natalie offers unique and creative coaching and training methods to her clients to support the development of skills and strategies to manage change, transition to management roles, and transform into effective leaders. More information about Natalie and her team can be found at http://www.loebconsultinggroup.com/.

63

If You Want to Enhance Your Career, Focus on Your Own Leadership Performance

❦

Talent Development team™ (TDt)

Is It Time for a Leadership Tune-up?

Even the finest automobiles need an occasional tune-up. It's not that they're running badly—in fact, they may be running quite well. The critical question is whether they will continue to perform at a high level in the future. Without periodic road tests and diagnostic evaluations that analyze the current performance level of the vehicle—and appropriate servicing—there is no assurance that high performance levels will continue.

As a leader, you are in the driver's seat for your organization. Your team, your employees, and your processes and technology comprise the complex engine that runs the organization. To ensure that you are leading in a manner that will guarantee superior performance in your current organization and enhance the likelihood of future success, how often do you calibrate your performance? Ongoing superior performance cannot be taken for granted—maybe it's time to run some diagnostics and find out if your performance needs a tune-up!

You may question that a personal leadership tune-up is necessary. Consider the facts! Our research indicates that approximately 40 percent of the workforce is disengaged. Organizations routinely abandon 50 to 70 percent of key initiatives and strategies— they don't take hold or they fail to attain the desired results (Davis, Frechette, and Boswell 2010)! Odds are that even though you are an effective leader, your organization is experiencing these same issues.

As a leader, you would be wise not to assume a smooth road ahead. Develop a clear understanding of what is running optimally as well as what you can and should do to enhance organizational performance by pursuing your own leadership excellence.

Four Steps to Leadership Excellence

Diagnose Needs

You probably know the saying that "the minute you become a leader is the last minute you hear the truth." But as a leader, you set the pace. You drive your organization, and you influence how your team and your employees—the engine of your organization—achieve optimal performance.

So how do you determine what needs fine-tuning? The first step is to self-diagnose. To begin, dedicate some thoughtful time to candidly ranking your current performance on these ten key traits in our LEADERSHIP Index™:

RESPONSE SCALE for LEADERSHIP Index

1. Strongly Disagree
2. Mostly Disagree
3. Disagree

4. Agree
5. Mostly Agree
6. Strongly Agree

---

1. I actively build collaborative relationships throughout the organization. _____

2. I discuss issues openly and candidly. _____

3. I welcome creative ideas. _____

4. I am open to constructive feedback, I admit my own mistakes, and I work to correct them. _____

5. I actively communicate the organization's values, mission, and vision. _____

6. I have a positive attitude and encourage positive attitudes in others. _____

7. I ask employees for feedback on creating more value and reaching goals of the organization. _____

8. I am aware of internal politics, and I strive to minimize this activity. _____

9. I support and practice work-life balance and a healthy environment for everyone. _____

10. I consistently achieve my personal goals and objectives. _____

Your LEADERSHIP Index Score: _____

Compare your LEADERSHIP Index "Tune-up" Score:

60	Smooth cruisin'—no tune-up required; whatever you're doing, keep doing it!
50–59	Tune-up required—gets you there, but could run better.
40–49	Running rough—inconsistent; call the repair shop.
30–39	Warning light—diagnosis needed for trouble spots.
20–29	Breakdown—stalled; call for roadside assistance.
10 -19	Trade-in suggested—are you driving the right car?

Identify Obstacles

When you have your score, take an objective look at the roadblocks preventing you from accelerating your performance as a leader. Interestingly, leaders themselves often create their own roadblocks again and again. How is this possible? Leaders typically achieve promotions through successes in previous positions utilizing well-established behavioral patterns. It is only natural to continue what you've always been doing—especially if it has worked well in the past. It may not occur to you that indeed, your leadership style may need an efficiency tune-up to produce increased results in today's complex organization.

To identify blind spots you may have concerning your leadership style, consider asking members of your team to rate you by responding to the same LEADERSHIP Index as you used earlier. Simply change the word *I* to the phrase *our leader,* along with additional minor edits to each statement. You may discover roadblocks you have overlooked. Discuss the results with your team members to gain additional insight.

Develop Strategies

As a leader, you take care to drive with strategies that address opportunities and map the most efficient route. But strategies are not the end of the road trip. It is critically important that you prepare a realistic action plan that reinforces leadership strengths and addresses areas for improvement which, if not addressed, may put the brakes on your own optimal effectiveness. Your personal action plan should include *what* you commit to doing, *why* you are going to do it, *when* you will do it, and your targeted *expectations.*

237

For example, commit to openly admitting to your own mistakes and agree that you will do this by encouraging honest dialogue that will lead you to corrective action. Your team must be explicitly told that calling you out is indeed acceptable! The process may not be comfortable for you or others, but if you've given your permission, you and your team can candidly address any detours ahead. You may be responsible for repeatedly creating your own roadblocks. As you honestly seek to enhance your leadership effectiveness, roadway obstacles must be identified and removed.

Measure Results

"What gets measured, gets done!" An integral component of the develop strategies process is to define expectations. These expectations must be revisited and reviewed routinely to be relevant and compelling. Map out when, where, and how the results will be evaluated. Some steps of the action plan may be best addressed at team meetings, some in one-on-one meetings, and some even in all-employee meetings. Once commitments are set, drive toward them to measure success in reaching your destination. Failing to follow through on your action plan commitments will certainly steer you into the ditch!

The Road Ahead

Whether you are a leader in your organization or aspiring to enhance your career, you contribute to driving your organization. Even though the organization may be performing satisfactorily now, there is no assurance that it will continue to run smoothly and successfully in the constantly changing future environment. What high-achieving leaders have done so far in their careers to accelerate success may not be what is required tomorrow and in the future. It may be time for a leadership tune-up to enhance your leadership performance and your career journey!

Reference

Davis, Jocelyn R., Henry M. Frechette Jr., and Edwin H. Boswell. (2010). *Strategic speed: Mobilize people, accelerate execution.* Boston, MA: Harvard Business Press.

BIO

TALENT DEVELOPMENT team™ (TDt) is focused on accelerating performance for *exceptional* results. TDt's highly experienced assessment and coaching professionals assist organizations with their most precious commodity—human capital. Talented employees are high performers, and high performers seek opportunities to further develop their skills and effectiveness, either within the organization or elsewhere. Retaining employees and maximizing their effectiveness must be on any organization's priority list. TDt provides innovative resources—leading-edge tools and processes—for organizations to identify, develop, and retain their top talent. TDt is Ted Szaniawski, Gayla Doucet, John Guettler, and Marti Cizek. Visit http://www.talentdevelopmentteam.com/.

64

Life Balance:
A Powerful Tool for Career Success

Haider Al-Mosawi

You may have been telling yourself for many years now that once you've achieved success at work, you will be able to afford a balanced life, in which you can spend as much time as you like with family and friends or on the hobbies that you've shelved while you were focusing on your work.

However, life balance isn't the result of career success; rather it's a powerful tool that you can use to assist you in moving your career forward. In fact, I'm willing to bet that you've already experienced many ways in which life balance can actually help your career rather than deterring it. Giving your health attention will enable you to experience greater vitality when it comes to getting your work done. Fostering strong family bonds will allow you to alleviate the tension that can accumulate at home when you're not giving your loved ones the attention they want. Taking time out to rest and pursue your personal hobbies will help you avoid early burnout and nourish your spirits.

By delaying your efforts to achieve life balance, you risk compromising your health, relationships, and peace of mind, which can all affect how well you perform at work and therefore your chances of career success. Besides, career progress never ends. You will always find goals and challenges that will drive you forward, so when will you ever give life balance a chance? You can make an effort today to inch your way toward a balanced life to improve not only your performance at work but also the overall quality of your life.

Usually, life balance is seen to consist of balancing personal and professional commitments, but that's too simplistic because it doesn't accurately reveal our human needs. Instead, consider categorizing your needs according to the following life areas:

1. Spiritual

2. Intellectual

3. Psychological

4. Social

5. Professional

6. Recreational

7. Physical

To achieve life balance, you need to make progress in every life area so that each area can contribute to your happiness and success. Follow the subsequent steps to get started in creating a balanced life right now.

1. Visualize what your ideal life looks like. What do you want to be, have, and do? What would a day in your ideal life look like? A week? A month? A year? Think of each life area and what that would look like in your ideal life.

2. List all the ways in which you can improve each life area. Be creative, and don't allow limiting beliefs to hold you back! You can go through your day noting all the ideas that come to mind rather than trying to create these lists in a dark corner of your office.

3. Pick one to three ways in which you can improve each life area. From the lists you've created in step 2, pick out the ways you can improve in each life area. The options have to be available to you right now, and you must be able to incorporate them into your schedule. You can choose to focus on a single life area for a few days before you move on to another life area. A trick would be to choose activities that help you progress in several life areas at the same time. These overlaps will help you avoid feeling pressed for time and will make balanced living much easier than you expected! A discussion with friends can engage you intellectually as well as help you bond socially (as opposed to reading a book by yourself). A team sport, such as soccer, can be a great recreational activity that is also social, with added physical benefits!

4. Repeat the process. As you make progress in creating a balanced life, more and more opportunities will open up to you, and you will find it easier to incorporate changes that will help you improve your life and grow as a person. And because you're giving all your life areas the attention they need, you will experience exponential progress as your success in one life area helps to support and amplify your success in another.

Don't put off your needs as you relentlessly pursue career success as that will compromise your efforts. Balanced living will make your career path much easier to walk and much more enjoyable and rewarding for you and those around you.

BIO

Haider Al-Mosawi writes about holistic growth through balanced living at http://www.PersonalGrowthMap.com/. He's a fan of simple approaches to personal growth, but not of simplistic ones that overpromise and underdeliver. Visit http://www.PersonalGrowthMap.com/ for more advice on how to work toward a balanced life today!

65

How to Enhance Your Career
by Being a Lifetime Learner

✺～✺

Felicia Gopaul

During the last recession, 8.4 million people lost their jobs, and according to Rex Nutting of MarketWatch.com, "this recent recession has been the worst since the end of World War II more than 60 years ago." Especially vulnerable during these times have been the people who had failed to invest in themselves by being lifetime learners. For them, job loss has meant being forced into a world in which their knowledge and experience gained on the job are being measured against another's updated credentials—and have been found lacking.

Why You Need to Be a Lifetime Learner

The definition of a *lifetime learner* is someone who supports "the continual acquisition of knowledge and skills throughout [his or her] life," according to the Computer Language Company Inc. By being a lifetime learner, you empower yourself by taking responsibility to learn the skills and information necessary to be an asset to your current employer as well as any prospective employers.

Additional benefits gained from upgrading your knowledge come from increased self-confidence in your ability to be an asset on the job as well as the feeling of accomplishment gained from updating your skills and knowledge. Being a lifetime learner may also provide the potential to increase your earnings with both your current employer and future employers who need and appreciate the newly acquired skills and knowledge you have developed.

We All Have the Same Time

Some argue that it's hard to find the time to be a lifetime learner. You have the responsibilities of family and work, and when you get home, the last thing you want to do is open a book. But the reality is that each of us has the same twenty-four hours in a day: eight hours to sleep, eight hours to work, two hours for commuting and personal hygiene, two hours supervising homework, baths, and dinner. You still have four hours a day that you could utilize to add to your knowledge. Will you position yourself for opportunities by learning new technologies, software, or industries, or will you let yourself be subject to the vagaries of an uncertain job market?

Why Is Not Updating Your Knowledge Dangerous?

It starts with lack of control. With the changes in technology happening in many fields, many industries are making significant advances in the way things are done. Without that upgraded knowledge, you leave yourself vulnerable to being deemed obsolete. For example, according to the Did You Know Video 4.0, in the technical fields, the amount of information is doubling every two years. That means that half the information you currently know will be obsolete three years from now. If your knowledge is obsolete, you could inadvertently be positioning yourself for a layoff. And if you are laid off, at a time you are the most vulnerable, you are reentering the workforce without the knowledge that is now necessary for doing the job. The colleague next to you was also laid off but found the time to keep up his skills and knowledge, and employers will be more interested in hiring him because he knows the new tools and tactics of the trade.

Summary

It is important to be a lifetime learner. Being a lifetime leaner will allow you to maintain control over yourself and your future by continually renewing your skills and knowledge so that if the misfortune of a layoff hits you, you will have the skills and knowledge for which employers are looking.

Let me end with a story. I had a client who was working on an air force base that was due to close in four years. She decided to take the remaining four years while she was working to complete her undergraduate degree and obtain a master's degree, while her colleague watched her do so. At the end of the four years, when the base closed, her colleague lamented that she was being laid off, had no degree, and didn't seem to have the knowledge and skills for which employers were looking. However, for my client, it was a simple decision to continue her education. She decided she could be four years older with new degrees and knowledge or simply be four years older. It's a choice you have today, and I invite you to decide that you will join the ranks of the lifetime learners.

If you are still employed, check to see if your employer has a tuition reimbursement plan to help cover the cost of continuing your education. And even if your employer does not have a tuition reimbursement plan, you may be able to take advantage of the Lifetime Learning Credit to help pay for your lifetime of learning.

Bio

Felicia Gopaul is the president and founder of College Funding Resource. Based in Bloomfield, New Jersey, we help adult learners become lifetime learners by helping them find the right school academically and financially to update and upgrade their skills and knowledge. Ms. Gopaul has been quoted in newspapers, magazines, and online and has been a featured speaker from California to New Jersey. To download your free copy of the report *Five Critical Mistakes You Are Making in Your Career*, visit http://www.CollegeFundingResource.com/5Critical or call Felicia directly at (201) 453-9875.

66

MOTIVATION

Motivation

❧~❧

Muzaffar Sultan

According to the *Cambridge Dictionary, motivation* means "enthusiasm for doing something." It's the energy that forces human beings to act and achieve goals.

I would like to relate human life to the solar system. Let's consider that the sun is you, planets are important aspects of your life, and everything else is debris in space or other planets in the galaxy. You (the sun) highly influence your environment (planets), and your environment influences you. Here's a graphical representation:

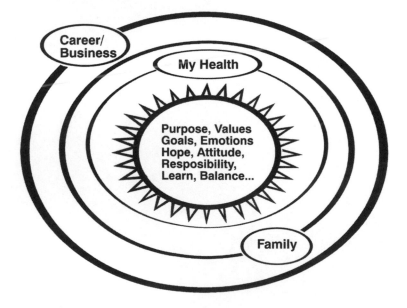

Everybody's priorities are different, and so are their planets. For example, a student might have Education as a planet instead of Career. You can draw your own solar system to understand what's important in your life. This is a very good tool to discover different priorities in your life. Remember, though, that the sun plays an extremely vital role in the solar system.

Let's discuss some energy sources (fuel) that can create powerful motivational force. Your purpose/mission, values, and goals work as a compass to guide you in the best direction.

Internal Energy Sources (Fuel)

Purpose/Mission

> When a man does not know what harbor he is making for,
> no wind is the right wind.
> —Seneca

Purpose is why you do something. Many people don't know why they are doing what they are doing in their lives. They are like lost ships taken in whatever direction the winds blow.

One way to understand your purpose is to ask the question, why do I exist? What's my purpose on earth? What causes am I supporting? There are three kinds of purposes one has to understand:

1. Make this world a better place; understand the laws of nature and understand God

2. Raise a family (part of nature); if we don't do this, humanity will cease to exist

3. Understand and use our unique talents given us by the Creator (or whatever name you want to give)

The stronger our sense of purpose is, the stronger our passion, energy, and commitment will be.

Believes/Values

> The soul attracts that which it secretly harbors; that which it loves,
> and also that which it fears.
> —James Allen

As per the *Cambridge Dictionary, values* indicates the beliefs people have about what is right and wrong and what is most important in life, and these beliefs control their behavior. Most people think they believe what they say they believe, but our beliefs and values are reflected in our thoughts, words, and actions. For example, if I say I value family more than work, and then I spend most of my time in the office and don't spend time with my family, my actions will negate what I say.

We must have a clear understanding of what we believe and value. If we don't know the priorities of different values, we can't make proper decisions whenever we are given choices.

Following are a few ways to identify our values:

- Always be mindful of your thoughts, words, and actions. Prayers and meditation can help in understanding your beliefs.
- Whenever you experience pain and trouble, this will allow you to stop, dig deep, and reflect.
- Imagine (just for this exercise) that you have only six months to live. How will you spend these six months of your life on this planet? What will you do? With whom will you spend your time?

Vision/goals

> The most pathetic person in the world is
> someone who has sight, but has no vision.
> —Helen Keller

We should write our life goals and then convert them into ten-, five-, and one-year goals. Clearly written goals with deadlines show commitment. Review your yearly goals regularly using 3" × 5" index cards, or make affirmations. They bring focus and have power.

Your goals should be your personal goals. They should not reflect the wishes of other people. They should come from your inner self. Each night or first thing in the morning, write your daily task list, which should be aligned with your yearly goals.

A study by the Harvard Business School from 1979 shows that

- thirteen percent of graduates who had goals in their minds were earning, on average, twice as much as the 84 percent who had no goals at all
- three percent of graduates who had clear, written goals were earning, on average, ten times as much as the other 97 percent put together

Positive Emotions

Positive emotions such as love, compassion, and gratitude create powerful positive energy. Avoid negative emotions such as hatred, jealousy, and fear as much as possible.

Hope

Hope and faith are very powerful forces. One of the ways to develop these is first to work on those goals that have an 80 to 100 percent chance of success, then gradually begin to work on those goals that have a 10 to 50 percent chance of success. You will become unstoppable.

Attitude and Perspective

Attitude and perspective are all about how we see and feel about each and every thing in our lives. Do you see a half-empty glass or a glass half full? People with good attitudes always try to find something positive in everything. Other people find negativity in everything and whine. A positive attitude will give you power to make it through troubles.

Blame, Excuses, and Responsibility

> Your potential is limited only by how many excuses you have.
> —Unknown

Some people always blame others or find excuses for all the bad things that have happened in their lives. Highly motivated people take responsibility for their thoughts, feelings, actions, and attitudes. Get rid of all excuses and blame from your life. They drain energy from you. They make you feel powerless and victimized.

Learning Experience

> Our greatest glory is not in never falling but in rising every time we fall.
> —Confucius

Highly motivated people act in spite of fear. They always look at each goal, project, and success or failure as a learning experience. If you approach each project or goal as a learning experience, you will never fear failure. Each failure will be a new learning experience that you can use to make yourself successful next time. Never fear troubles—they make you stronger.

Balance

Balance allows you to give the right attention to each planet in your life. You will lose an important planet if you lose balance. You must give attention to each planet in your system on a daily or weekly basis.

Calmness and Patience

Calmness and patience come with experience and, usually, after going through trials and turbulence in your life. Learn to develop these virtues. A calm person has full control of his or her thoughts, feelings, and actions.

External Energy Sources (Fuel)

Reward

Reward is a good motivator. Whenever you set a goal, also set a reward. Create mini-rewards for bigger goals.

Physical Body

Take care of your body by eating right and exercising physically at least three times a week.

Companionship

Birds of a feather flock together.

Find good companions who will support you in your goals. Avoid those people who whine, blame, and suck energy from you.

Final Words

All your medals, awards, degrees, accolades, wealth, and so on, can be lost, unless you accept what you have become in your life. Always look at the person you will become by achieving something. Your journey will become your goal, irrespective of your final outcome. The most precious thing is *you*.

Enjoy your journey!

BIO

Muzaffar Sultan is a certified coach/mentor, author, and inspirational speaker. His expertise is in project management, subliminal programming, goal setting, laws of attraction, natural and spiritual laws of success, and software development. He's been learning and applying personal development knowledge and spirituality since 1982. Now he's started spreading the knowledge of personal development and spirituality through coaching/mentoring, writing, speaking, community work, and websites. He volunteers in community development work, mentors project managers, works as a project leader, and maintains http://www.spiritualvitality.com/ and http://www.spiritualvitality.net/. You can visit http://www.spiritualvitality.com/ to read articles and download free tools, e-books, and ezSP (subliminal programming) software.

67

Motivation Matters

❦

Susan Lynn Perry

Imagine this scenario.

You are an incredible athlete. You've been training in your sport since you were thirteen years old, and you're on the fast track to being at the top of your game. You're winning race after race and well on your way to being the absolute best you can be. You've also signed a very lucrative contract with a sponsor. You're living your dream, man. Life has never been better.

Now, imagine your world coming crashing down all around you as you're diagnosed with a disease so deadly that your doctor only gives you a 40 percent chance of recovery—and on top of that, you're only twenty-five years old.

What do you do?

Do you stop competing forever? Do you succumb to the deadly disease and let it beat you down? Or do you stay motivated to continue on your path to stardom, beat all the odds, and enjoy the sweet smell of success even that much more?

Well, if you're Lance Armstrong, you certainly pick the latter.

Lance Armstrong has continued to beat the odds year in and year out. He not only beat a very aggressive case of testicular cancer that at one time had spread to his lungs and brain but also won the grueling Tour de France seven consecutive times. It's an amazing story about an amazing man who has always had one thing going for him throughout the good times and the bad. The one thing Lance has that no one can ever take away from him is his *motivation*.

Motivation is the thing that propels us forward into taking action in our lives. It's deep down inside each and every one of us, drives us, controls us, and commandeers our thinking. It can force us to seize the day and make the most of it, or simply to muddle through our usual daily routine. Motivation is the master, plain and simple.

If you're having trouble figuring out what your own motivation is, and more important, how to tap into that motivation, I want you to consider things you've done in the past that were successful. Have you completed your college degree? Have you ever negotiated a nice raise from your boss? Have you started a successful company? What sort of accomplishments have you made in your career so far?

Now, think about *why* you wanted to complete that goal and what really drove you to buckle down and actually do it. *That's* your motivation! That's the thing you need to grab onto with both hands and use to drive yourself to your ultimate success.

Let's turn to your current job for just a minute. If you're not where you think you should be, whether it's on the pay scale or the corporate ladder, or both, think about the reasons why. Do you focus on the most important and hardest tasks first, as soon as you get to the office? Or do you stand around at the coffee machine, the receptionist's desk, or the copier, socializing and wasting time?

The best thing you can do at your job, whatever your job may be, is to always give 100 percent—even when you don't feel like giving 10 percent. I know that may be hard for you on days when your motivation is a bit low. But if you'll take the time and effort to give your absolute best—even on seemingly menial projects—trust me, you will be noticed.

If you don't believe me, I want you to do the following. If you think you should be earning more money, then I want you to start keeping track of the reports you turn in or the projects you manage. At the end of the quarter, sit down and write out all your accomplishments on paper. Then take some time to research what others in your field are getting paid for the same work. Finally, I want you to write a simple letter to your boss.

You should end your letter by asking to meet with your boss the following day at a specific time. Don't leave it to chance. Your boss will certainly not be the one to come to you. After all, you *are* trying to squeeze more money out of him or her. Your boss will most likely appreciate the effort you've put into your written request. Even if you don't get an immediate raise, I'll bet you'll get one sooner than if you had *not* written that letter.

Now I want you to think about Lance Armstrong's story again. It's a true-life story that shows you clearly how strong a role motivation can play in your life. It shows you that even the best of the best don't have it easy all the time. It shows you that hard work will eventually pay off in the end.

Don't hesitate. Focus on doing the things right now to put yourself in motion and start moving forward in your career. *Now* is the best time to start. Just take one small step in the right direction, and no matter what you want out of life, you *can* get it. But you have to want it so badly that you won't quit until you get there. Now get up, go out there, and get what you deserve!

Bio

Susan Lynn Perry is an accomplished freelance writer and best-selling author of fiction (*Hindsight*), nonfiction (*Procrastination Elimination*), and short stories (coauthor in several Cup of Comfort and Thin Threads anthologies). Her latest novel, *Hindsight,* is what she likes to describe as "fiction inspired by true events." As a former corporate executive, business owner, and motivational speaker, Perry delivers her message with her own unique blend of professionalism, humor, and class. A native Texan, she currently lives in San Antonio with her wonderful husband, her amazing son, and an enormous cat named Bobo. For more information, please visit http://www.mothercub.com/.

68

And You Want Me to Be *What?*

A Tactical and Strategic Guide to Moving Out to Move Up!

☙~☙

Jean Mulrine DeMange

After twenty-five years of recruitment and placement of professionals, I have met and had many career discussions with individuals, but in the last few years, things have vastly changed. Mergers and acquisitions have created dead-end positions, which no one could have anticipated. A professional may have started his or her career at the right level, and the position would have taken the person to his or her planned career destination, but events have happened beyond his or her control. The CEO may have left the company; the division was sold; a new company may have purchased all or part of the old company or merged with another division or corporation. Such events will leave you frustrated because your career has been derailed, or left in a position that is substantially lower than your current position, or become a job you hate. When they describe your new role and your response is, "You want me to be what?" don't be shocked or angry. Think strategically and tactically. Let them know you will need a bit of time to assimilate mentally these changes with your role in the company or organization to address them properly.

To review this strategically, look at how the new organization is structured to see if you are on or at the same level, or on a higher level. Have you moved way down in the organizational chart in terms of position or duties? After the dust settles, look internally to see how the "new" internal culture has evolved. If you look around at the new organizational chart and do not see any way to move toward or obtain your career goals, even after some internal preliminary discussions with your manager about career growth or a way through the changed organization, face it: *you need to move out to move up!*

Many people are tied emotionally to their roles in an organization, and sometimes they will put their careers on hold for a while; time, location, and family commitments play a role in this decision as well. If the new organization tells you that your new role is going to be   very different than it was before, or slide you down the organizational chart, don't kid yourself that a miracle will happen if you just hang in there. Don't convince yourself that the new CEO or senior management of the newly formed company will revert to the way things were before. They will be operating with a new vision for the company, and you may not be part of it. Remember, you are from the old, and the new company will be seeking outside talent who will move into roles in the new organization. They will want fresh and new ideas for the new organization, not from the old group. With that in mind, *you need to move out to move up*!

Sometimes, though, people bolt too soon from a company. They may not be able to judge with any accuracy how they fit into the new structure. Bearing that in mind, you should discuss your concerns in a confidential and ethical manner with your recruiter. Here are some tactical suggestions to plan your move out:

- Work with a professional recruiter—not against him or her. Work as a team.
- Make sure that the recruiter is in your niche and has had experience in that area. Top recruitment professionals will tell you if they have no contacts in the specific area of your career growth. It is a waste of time working with someone who has no experience or contacts in your area of expertise, especially for you.
- Listen to the suggestions your recruiter offers and consider his or her advice when you've evaluated your next move. For example, a recruiter may tell you that you will need a master's degree to move up to the next rung on the corporate ladder. Don't ignore the recruiter's advice about furthering your education. He or she knows from experience and market demand that master's-level professionals will be hired for that level of position in an organization.
- Look at companies that appeal to you. Share your list and thoughts about those companies with your recruiter. He or she will most likely know something about the companies' corporate environments and cultures and may already know the leaders of the organizations and what the companies or organizations are looking for in potential employees. The recruiter will share this information with you to evaluate whether your skill set and culture are a potential match.
- Be faithful! Work with the recruiter on a plan to reach your goal. This is a relationship based on trust and can be a long-term, mutually beneficial relationship covering several moves in your career.
- Do not post your résumé on the Internet. It dilutes your chances of being considered exclusive and desired by companies. On top of that, it works against you when you work with a professional recruiter. Fewer than 5 percent of all the applicants who submit their résumés online for positions are hired off the submission. If you are looking for just a job, go ahead and do that; however, if you want a career, don't waste your time.

- Communicate, communicate, communicate. Your recruiter will view your responses as an employer would. How and when you respond is important. The recruiter is viewing your habits in the same way a company would and will be able to determine if you hold good potential for his or her client companies.
- Answer questions with honesty and integrity. *Be realistic.* Stay focused—it is a process that takes time and energy to accomplish, but the effort is worth it.

Many times, people have unrealistic expectations and portray themselves poorly in résumés. Take suggestions from the recruiter, and don't be afraid to brag about the good things you have accomplished as part of your current and previous organizations and *how* you accomplished those specific goals and tasks. If you have exceeded those goals, *quantify* them—but don't over embellish. For example, you may explain that you were promoted into your current role and took over an operation that was in the negative in revenue and growth. In an eighteen-month time period, you turned it around and achieved a margin of growth of 47 percent while lowering operating costs by 15 percent. Once you have quantified this, explain how you achieved it in an interview.

Stay with your plan, but think before you leap! Don't be afraid to ask for a helping hand in a recruitment partner to ease your transition to your next career step. The time, energy, and career-building relationship will help you achieve your goals with a strategic and tactical approach to navigate through the career maze.

Bio

Jean Mulrine DeMange is CEO, president, and founder of Wellington Thomas Ltd., *The Recruiting Experts in Healthcare*, http://www.wellingtonthomas.com, which is based in St. Petersburg, Florida. Her recruitment experience has been in health care, and since 1991, the practice she founded has handled professionals from first-level management to the C- level in corporate, regional, and facility-based opportunities through the United States.

69

5 Networking Strategies That Guarantee Career Advancement for Life

Abbe Lang

If you want to create an immediate, positive, and lasting impact on your career or business, *network*. You can't get to where you want to go without other people, so consider this thought: "Your Network Is Your Networth." The quality of your communication, your relationships, and your network will determine your level of success.

Most professionals think they network and connect well with people, but the truth is that they don't have a goal or a plan to target relationships that will move their careers and lives forward, consistently.

When you apply the following five practical networking strategies, you will turbo-charge your success in your career, your business, and your life.

You can't pick your family, but . . . Studies show that each of us has an immediate contact circle of approximately 200 people that we know on a first-name basis. Do your 200 contacts know what you do to earn a living? Besides your attorney and accountant, everyone from your tailor to your postman and plumber should know what you do to feed your family. Be sure that these people know how they can help you build your business and advance your career. One simple way to convey this to your contacts is by first asking how you can help them in their career or by asking them, "What is a good lead for you in your business?" They may seem stumped by this question at first because it is so rarely asked, but once they give you their answer, they will invariably ask you the same question in return. Be prepared to give a brief response that grabs their attention and gives them a clear understanding of how they can help you. Your excitement about your work, coupled with your positive energy and enthusiasm, will compel them to want to explore ways to help you and possibly refer business to you.

COIs, referral partners, and raving fans. Remember the old adage "It's not what you know, it's who you know"? That statement is no longer true. The new paradigm is "It's not who you know, it's who knows you!" America's foremost business philosopher, the late, great Jim Rohn, said, "We become the combined average of the *five* people we associate with the most." Who are your top five? Are they movers and shakers? Are they people that can introduce you to powerful circles of influence (COIs) in your career field or business? It's critical to your success to "network up." Don't discount your friends and business associates, but get known by people who are doing better than you and whom you aspire to be like. In sports, you don't get better by playing people less talented, you get better by playing with champions, and the same applies in business.

Embrace social media. Social media is here to stay. LinkedIn, Facebook, Twitter, and YouTube are the four dominant social media platforms. The fact is that if your competition is there and you're not, you will lose. If you're in sales, social media is "the new cold call," and if you're not in sales, social media is the new networking group, lead generation source, and online chamber of commerce. These tools are the most powerful, quickest, and smartest way for you to connect with people to help you build your business and advance your career. LinkedIn has more than 75 million business professionals who want to network with you; if you ignore this technology, you will become obsolete.

Social media is your online 24/7 resume. The content you post about you, your career, and your business needs to be consistent with the image you want your clients, employer, and the marketplace to see.

Enthusiasm and likeability are attractive. Your enthusiasm will lead to more sales, higher-level contacts, bigger promotions, better relationships, and a happier life. Enthusiasm is contagious, and when companies decide to hire or promote a candidate, it's not only the most talented who get hired—it's the most talented, enthusiastic, and likeable candidate who most often wins. Start out every day with a big smile on your face. It sounds simple, and it is—when you smile, you look happy and more confident. Most people, including your clients, coworkers, and boss, will be drawn toward you, and they will look forward to being around you. People buy into you first, and then they will buy what you are "selling" simply because you are selling the positive and likeable *you!* Likeability leads to trust, and trust builds long-term, mutually beneficial relationships in business and in life.

Ninety percent of success is showing up. People want to know you are going to be around for the long haul if they are going to do business with you. It's imperative that people know THAT they can count on you. If you have dedicated your time to join an association, a networking group, or a chamber of commerce, show up every week. If you volunteer for something at the office or join a committee, be on time for meetings and follow through. Honor your promises, and do what you say you are going to do. Dependability builds likeability, credibility, and trust, so be dependable. Spend time with your customers and contacts and listen to their thoughts and feelings. When you connect with someone and exchange business cards, write down a few notes about your conversation so that when you follow up with that person, you have some immediate rapport. Ninety percent of success is showing up consistently, with a focused purpose.

Remember, your number one goal in business is to market yourself authentically and consistently. By keeping your face and innovative ideas in front of your network, your clients, and your associates, you will advance your career. I know these practical strategies will make a significant positive impact on your career because they've helped transform my career and hundreds of my clients' careers. The process is simple, but the key is taking consistent action toward building, growing, and maintaining your network. Have a career you love to do, and then fall in love doing it.

BIO

Abbe has enjoyed a lucrative career in the title insurance and mortgage industries. She has owned and sold for the largest insurers in the business. Her talent to market and position herself in multiple industries sets her apart from her peers. Abbe's clients are attracted to her positive energy, dedication, and optimistic outlook toward life. She is very happily married to her husband, Joe, and is the proud mom of three sons, Michael, Robert, and Nicholas. Her love of sales, health, and marketing propelled her to become a Master Certified Coach. Her goal for everyone she touches is to lead a happy, healthy, and more productive life. She can easily be reached at Abbe@AbbeLang.com or online at http://www.AbbeLang.com.

SETTA: A Networking Success Formula

Kim Stacey

Let's stop for a moment and think about what makes networking relationships—both in and out of the workplace—more fruitful. As the executive director of the Association of Women Funeral Directors (AWFD), I spend much of my time engaged in what I call *SETTA*. This is a best-practices model of communication learned during years of working with, and on behalf of, our phenomenal members. Why are they so adept at SETTA? They are adept because, understandably, they have a deeper awareness of human *vulnerability*. So what does SETTA stand for?

- Sensitivity
- Empathy
- Tolerance
- Trust
- Active listening

Essentially, SETTA is a way to treat people as they wish to be treated, not as so-called well-meaning others think they should be treated. Most important, it provides a foundation to facilitate people's *empowerment*. Let's examine each element separately.

Sensitivity

Emotional sensitivity is really just *awareness*—not of our physical surroundings but of the needs and emotions of others. Though many of us can't imagine being insensitive to the emotional plights of others, there are those of us who are blissfully unaware of what others are going through. These folks have to train themselves to be more sensitive to others. Not surprisingly, sensitivity is considered by the funeral consumer to be an essential. In fact, here is a recommendation from the M.I.S.S. Foundation website: "His or her attitude should be sensitive and gentle. If you feel a sense of over professionalism or he seems to be austere, please hang up and try another funeral home. Assuring that the director will be sensitive to your needs as a bereaved parent is the most important factor of choice."

Empathy

Empathy is what you feel when you enter the internal world of another person. Without abandoning your own perspective, you experience the other's emotions, conflicts, or aspirations. The word literally translates as "in feeling" and is the capability to share another being's emotions and feelings. The most successful members in the AWFD have experienced loss and are more adept at empathy—and some are just naturally empathetic. Others—especially our younger members—accept that they need to nurture their empathetic abilities.

Tolerance

Defined as the "capacity for or the practice of recognizing and respecting the beliefs or practices of others," the lack of tolerance in human interactions has long been a factor in conflicts, both major and minor. I think René Dubos expressed the dramatic need for tolerance when he said, "Human diversity makes *tolerance* more than a virtue; it makes it a requirement for survival." Though he may have been speaking of survival on a wider scale, you can easily see that this is true for the narrower realm of business or entrepreneurial survival.

Tolerance is not the absence of personal bias but rather an emphasis on forbearance and acceptance of the differences in others. Once fostered, tolerance allows you to establish trust, the next element of SETTA.

Trust

Establishing trust is about listening and understanding, and a tolerant attitude means that you can listen without judgment. No matter our profession, we must understand what the other person wants and then help him or her to achieve it (which often includes helping them see the way to do it). We must work with people collaboratively to enable them to see what they want and then help them see the ways achieve it. All this is dependent on *active listening*.

Active Listening

This is where empathy really begins, isn't it? After all, you can't put yourself in another's shoes without truly hearing what he or she is saying. But it seems to be harder than we think; depending on the study being quoted, most of us remember a dismal 25 to 50 percent of what we hear. That means you only really hear two and a half to five minutes of any conversation, unless you work at it.

The way to become a better listener is to practice. In other words, make a conscious effort not only to hear the words that another person is saying but, more important, to try to understand the total message being delivered—through words, tone, emphasis, and body language.

To do this, you must pay attention to the other person very carefully. You simply can't allow yourself to become distracted by what else may be going on around you or by your own sensitivity or empathy; you just can't afford to lose focus on what the other person is saying. To enhance your listening skills, you need to

- let the other person know that you are listening to what he or she is saying. Keep eye contact. Acknowledge your involvement through a simple nod of the head or, if the situation allows, a pat on the shoulder.
- respond encouragingly so he or she will continue speaking. Patiently wait for information you need. Certainly asking an occasional question or making a comment to recap what has been said communicates that you understand the message.

Our members know that applying the SETTA model to any networking experience is the preferred strategy, bringing respect and understanding to the forefront. Not only are you gaining information you can use to build your career and a clearer perspective on the experiences of others but you are creating a relationship on which you can build in the future.

Most people you'll meet in your quest for a successful career are hungry for quality information and recommendations, and for innovative thinking. You can offer them what they need through SETTA—it's a model of interaction grounded in respect and authenticity.

Remember that whether online or offline, relationship building takes *mindful* energy. You need to be deliberate with your listening, whether in face-to-face dialogue or in social media conversations, and remind yourself constantly that your goal is to truly hear what the other person is saying. The next time you are face-to-face with someone you feel could become a client, employer, or business partner, the next time you choose to post on a social media site, consider the issue of the person's *vulnerability* and remember to follow SETTA. This will help you bring *sensitivity, empathy, tolerance, trust,* and *active listening* to every conversation.

Bio

Kim came to funeral service with a graduate degree in sociocultural anthropology, specializing in the cross-cultural study of death rituals. She is now the leading copywriter for funeral service professionals. Kim has been published in *American Funeral Director, Mortuary Management,* and *American Cemetery* as well as on many industry-related blogs and funeral service news sites. She is also the founder and CEO of the Association of Women Funeral Professionals, which exists to "strengthen the presence of women in funeral service." The organization provides members with tools and resources to foster their leadership within the industry. You can learn more about it at http://www.wfpconnect.com/.

71

NON-PROFIT LEADERSHIP

The Pathway to CEO for Association and Nonprofit Executives

❧❧

Pegotty Cooper

Association Management Is about Building Relationships

Relationships with the board members, the staff, related organizations, legislative bodies, regulatory agencies, and advocacy groups require the ability to listen without judgment, without adhering only to your position. You need to really hear what others are saying and integrate their needs into the programs and services you are offering.

Command-and-control types of leaders do not fit into today's multigenerational and diverse associations. The democratic process is alive and well in associations, and the top-down, old-school authoritarian leaders are a fading breed. The board and the members own the association, and you had better not forget that!

Association Management Is about Building Consensus among Diverse Constituencies

An association executive who made the switch from a corporate finance position to become executive director of the association representing her peers said that the steepest learning curve came in working with different constituencies of the same profession with distinctly different beliefs. You have to manage your own point of view and put processes in place to make sure that the stance of the organization reflects the members' points of view, and members at the local or state level may have a very different perspective than those engaging at the national or international level. Members have to trust that their professional or business association represents multiple constituencies.

One of the most important qualities in the current political scene is the ability to build consensus among your own membership and with organizations that represent different segments of the industry. The people who are recognized as leaders year after year are those who are straight shooters and can be trusted by politicians to represent the issues fairly. People have to play well in the sandbox, and those who go outside the sandbox and voice dissension will lose their credibility.

Association Leaders Must Be at Home on Main Street, Wall Street, K Street, and Nanjing Road!

The past few years, with all of their political upheaval and changing economic realities, have forced associations to look beyond their traditional operating spheres and now require professionals to be astute in financial management, political negotiations, mergers and acquisitions, technology integration, and global expansion. The stakes are very high in the current political environment, in which new regulations and wholesale public policy changes may affect businesses in every sector. Most associations are affected by the local economics of their members, the impact of market confidence on the industry, the activities on Capitol Hill, and the international labor and trade environment.

Association leaders are finding that their view of international operations as just another U.S. outpost does not fit today's reality. You need to listen to various regions, recognize the standards for doing business in those countries, and adapt to local laws and regulations.

Association Leaders Must be Adept at Governance and Board Relations

Association executives are expected to be astute at managing the affairs of the board in partnership with the board chair—and to be the broker of ideas that will help to formulate the strategic vision to guide the association through the seas of change. At the same time, respect the desire of the board chair and the other members to leave their mark on the organization. Developing relationships with the key players and maintaining the ability to walk the fine line of taking charge and letting go is a challenge that has to be relearned with every new change of board leadership. Using good consensus building processes will strengthen the relationship.

The whole scope of association activities is changing. The association executive must know when to bring in expertise to help to develop structure that meets the governance needs of the association. This executive also must develop buy-in from leaders and members alike to make the changes in decision making at the board level. This will help ensure that the association will be nimble and flexible in adapting to its members' shifting priorities and its political and legislative environment.

Zeroing in on the Best Fit for You and Your Experience

Fit is all about the *culture* of the association, the *issues and activities* that you will deal with on a daily basis, the *people* with whom you will engage—members, staff, and those related to the industry outside of the association—and the *environment* in which you will be working.

The challenge to finding a fit in the "culture" is that culture lies in the unsaid: the hidden assumptions and the unspoken beliefs and attitudes that create the perceptual filters for viewing the future and making decisions about the behaviors that are reinforced and rewarded. To find a fit, you should examine your own values and beliefs. Do some honest assessment of your experience, results, strengths, and areas of greatest success. Add to your list those areas that provide an equal dose of satisfaction and fulfillment.

Know Your Value

It is time to examine your experience and translate it into value and relevance for the association in which you are currently employed or that you are targeting. Focus on where you add the most value and relevance to an organization and illustrate that as your personal brand. Your brand should be visible in everything you do or say. Become known as the expert in that area so that when a recruiter asks his or her contacts for referrals, your name is at the top of the list.

Become Visible

Becoming visible either in the industry or in the association is an important aspect of getting the job! There are many ways to become more visible in the association community:

- Engage in social media conversations in your areas of expertise.
- Publish articles in an association or trade publication—online or in print.
- Do presentations at association meetings, chapter meetings, or special interest group meetings or in webinars.
- Volunteer in the association for which you would like to work.
- Join peer groups and associations and get actively involved on task forces.
- Be involved in charitable organizations where leaders from your targeted associations are engaged.

The way to be visible is as a contributor who brings value. "Givers get" is a mantra in the world of networking, and networking is all about building mutually beneficial relationships with others.

Be Engaged and Engaging

Ask yourself the following questions to evaluate the degree to which you are engaged and engaging:

- When you are with another person, are you paying attention to what he or she is saying?
- Do you engage in active listening, or are you running through your to-do list or thinking about what you are going to say next?
- Do you look for ways to bring value to every conversation or situation, or are you trying to impress people with your knowledge and expertise?
- Are you curious and engaged in learning about what is important to others, or are you focused on moving your agenda forward?

Being real, genuine, and authentic draws people to you because you are not trying to meet some unrealistic standard of perfection. You are comfortable in your own skin and can focus on being engaged with others.

BIO

Pegotty Cooper, MBA, spent fifteen years in senior leadership roles in international trade and professional associations and was CEO of a state trade association. She has completed the Institute program for Association Management, earned her CAE (Certified Association Executive) in 1986, and was designated to the ASAE Fellows in 1994. She has also worked as an executive for a Fortune 100 company. A certified coach for the past seven years, Pegotty provides leadership and career coaching to association executives, plus outplacement coaching and convention career programs. She also facilitates the CEO Dialogue course for ASAE. Visit her blog at http://www.careerstrategyroadmap.com/.

72

Inter*not*

What Not to Do When Protecting Your Professional
Reputation and Personal Privacy Online

❧

Tecumseh A. Jones

"Just because you're paranoid doesn't mean they aren't out to get you." And if you aren't at least a little paranoid these days, then you aren't paying attention. The Internet has grown into a necessary business tool for you—and an irresistible weapon for others to use against you. It's a lot easier to hurt or destroy a business or reputation online than it is to build—or rebuild—one.

Who Is Likely to Wield This Etheric Weapon against Me, My Business, My Reputation, My Personal Privacy, or Even My Family?

- Anyone
- A dissatisfied customer or client
- An envious coworker
- Your competition
- A jealous partner
- An estranged family member
- A Facebook "friend"
- An old flame
- That kid you teased back in high school
- A disturbed neighbor
- A disgruntled salesperson who has your data
- Someone who thinks you owe her something
- A former colleague
- Your impulsive adolescent
- A person who politically disagrees with you

- A stranger
- A mechanized viral Internet hate program

What Kind of Damage Can Someone Do?

- Lift your name and/or photos from your own site and post them on sites that *discredit, embarrass, and even endanger you* or your family, colleagues, or business.
- *Stalk you* from site to site for the sole purpose of harassing you, even if literally a virtual stranger
- "Review" your product or service online as *damaging, illegal, or harmful—* whether or not the person has ever actually used it
- *Incite others* to commit senseless acts, some violent, against you or your business
- Open up e-mail accounts, register on forums, or post free ads all *in your name* (complete with *your picture,* lifted from your own site)
- Access outdated or inaccurate information *you removed from your site years ago* (it's *still cached online somewhere!*) then post it places others will read it now—and in the infinite future—as though it is still your current position
- Set up websites that mimic yours—either to *defame you or to lure traffic away from your business* for his or hers
- Use *all the posts you have made,* such as book reviews, as a platform to *denigrate you* on those same sites with his or her follow-up censure of you
- Dominate the *search engines* with his or her websites that libel you so that anyone searching *your name* finds only his or her propaganda

What Should I Do Now to Protect My Reputation?

First, find out what information about you others have Internet access to; it's more than you think! Press releases; professional and trade directories; other sites linked to yours (whether you want them to!); public records of past and present addresses; property tax records; live Google satellite images of your home; births, marriages, and divorces; probate court records, including wills and adoptions; family genealogies; obituaries of loved ones—the nature of your current Internet presence will imply other places for you to search.

What Do I Need to Do If My Business or I Am Attacked?

Start by telling yourself the truth about what has happened. What are the facts? Unless you are the hot global news topic of the day, the attack *is not* "all over the Internet." It just feels that way; keep it in perspective.

- If you read online even an implied hint of *physical danger* to you or your family or business, even if the threat is disguised in humor, contact your local authorities immediately. Get it on their record. Keep a copy of that record. Upgrade any basic security about which you may have grown lax.
- Assess, then reassess, the weight of the online information.
  - How accessible is it via search engines when looking for you or your business, using a variety of search words?
  - How many sites does it appear on?
  - How many unique visitors view it, and how often?
  - How old or recent are the posts against you?
  - What is the credibility of the site the attack appears on?
  - Are there any legitimate comments that could pose harm?
  - Is enough factual data interspersed with the falsehoods about you so as to confuse the reader or convince the reader that the attackers are to be more trusted than you?
  - What do you estimate the potential damage could be in the next six months, the next twenty-four months, and the foreseeable future?
  - Is it an irritant to your ego or an actual assessable wound to your reputation and/or business operations?
  - Some businesses believe even bad publicity is good publicity as it keeps them in the public eye. Can you safely, legally, and creatively turn the criticisms into free advertising?

Before you directly tackle any online defamation:

- *DO* consult with a professional Internet reputation service, whether or not you retain them to represent you. They know the latest issues and solutions.
- *DO* document everything—keeping dated hard copies of every post, not just links, as the attacker may change, move, or delete items you will wish you had documented. Good documentation also saves you legal fees if you retain a lawyer later.
- *Do NOT* rush to defend yourself. Pause, plan, *then* act.
- *Do NOT* post anything on a forum that has attacked you. Beware that you are entering the attackers' territory, where your power and rights are controlled by those who have already maligned you and may not be amenable to being proven wrong about you!
- *Do NOT* rush in to defend anyone else who is being attacked—especially without his or her knowledge and consent—as you may end up harming the person more; additionally, you may end up exposing yourself to harm and damage.
- *Do NOT* ask others to post in your defense as they are likely to say too much, say the wrong thing, or make it worse merely by interacting with the libelers or assailants, thus fueling the attackers' interests.
- Respond from a place of power—even if you have to back off to find it.

- *Do NOT* give your attackers any more of you to attack, or you risk turning a passing Internet predator into your own personal and obsessed parasite.
- Take the high road. *Do NOT* ignore the threats posed to your reputation. Either hire an attorney or other capable Internet reputation service that will mud wrestle for you, or choose to live above the fray.

The Prediction

The instant connectedness this generation craves via 2-D friendships and bulk business with strangers, and the validation people yearn for via self-exposure and self-promotion, will soon come full circle: privacy will be more rare and valuable than fame and a lot harder to regain. Plan your career accordingly.

The Moral

If you can only be one—rich or famous—choose rich (you can always share). Work to build fortune, not fame. Fortune and fame are relative terms to be determined by you. If your fortune depends on an element of fame, then maintain control of your image and intellectual property, and design your fortress well as you will attract unexpected challengers. In this Internet era of hyperexposure and increasing risk, you can't afford to be famous unless you also have the corresponding wealth to protect yourself. It's not selfish; it's survival.

Bio

Tecumseh A. Jones is a respected writer, consultant, and speaker on numerous topics, including balancing personal and business life in our border-morphing world. Jones's upcoming book is *ASAP's Fables—Fast Wisdom for Tough Times; 50 New Five-Minute Fables for Instant Enlightenment—Guaranteed!* The complete *Inter*note-book on which this book's contribution is based may be obtained via Tecumseh A. Jones's blog (http://TecumsehAJones.wordpress.com/). Contact Tecumseh at TecumsehJones@Live.com.

73

Take Charge and Own Your Career

❧～❧

Brad Federman

"Wow. I can't believe they just announced a restructuring. What is going to happen? What if they decide to outsource our department? What if I get laid off?"

This is all too familiar territory for many people. Unfortunately, thinking about their careers at this point is too late. So I ask you, why do most people wait until their careers are in jeopardy before they think about their next move? Why is it that even then, many of us only think about our next move?

The first thing someone does when he or she has an idea for a business is to write a business plan and create a strategy. Great business leaders revisit that strategy regularly and often to determine if they have made progress, identify any needed course corrections, or set new goals.

Careers are no different. We always need a long-term strategy and a relevant plan. It is imperative now more than ever to take charge of your career. It is time for a paradigm shift when it comes to careers.

Traditionally, career development was something that happened to us. We were told to be good corporate citizens and a company would manage our careers. Years later, career-pathing strategies took over, which were flexible and allowed us to know how to move up in an organization. Over time, for some people, career planning became less about advancing and more about enjoying their work. With the need for advancement and work satisfaction, people began to increasingly shift between companies, reducing tenure and creating challenges for traditional career approaches. However, most companies and employees alike still depend on these same approaches to career development.

Here is the problem: careers are not about your next move. Careers are not about ensuring you get additional money in your next job—although that would be nice. Careers are about ensuring that over the course of a forty- to fifty-year span, you always have options, choices, and the ability to produce your needed and/or wanted income. In other words, it is no longer about your work with a company or your next job. In fact, the word *career* means a path through life. How have you created, developed, or maintained your career path through life? Have you taken the steps to guarantee your future marketability? How long will you be relevant?

Following is a short quiz to help you think through how well you have created a plan:

1. Do you have a plan for demonstrating clear value in the next three months? It is not enough that you know you are doing good work. It must be clear that you are driving the business forward to all of those around you!

2. Are you clear on what your development needs are for the next year? This is not about making a bonus or acing your performance appraisal. You need to know what will help you pass your peers and keep you on the cutting edge.

3. Have you outlined a long-term career plan? Where do you ultimately want to be, and what are the steps to getting there? Of course, this plan will change, and no one knows the future, but life necessitates meaning and direction.

4. Have you defined what your potential development needs will be in twelve to eighteen months? How about eighteen to twenty-four months? Two to five years? You can only define your needs on this timetable if you have mapped out your long-term career.

5. Are you aware of your strengths (what you currently do that makes you valuable), opportunities (what you could do well with practice that would help you add more value), development areas (weaknesses—yes, weaknesses—of which you should be aware and for which you must compensate to guarantee that you do not hold your career back), and career concerns (a career ceiling or terminating conditions that, if not addressed, will definitely create a career detour or catastrophe)?

6. Are your plans built around company opportunities or your life career path? (Your plans should start around your life.) Do you know the difference?

7. To what extent have you thought about economic and industry trends, conditions, and changes? How has that affected your plans?

If, after answering these questions, you feel you should strengthen your career planning, following are a few tips.

Make career planning a regular event. We have physicals each year, companies' budget each year, why not review your career each year? This should be a reflective time and your time. This is not about the company you work for, but about yourself.

Know thyself. Think about your preferences, what motivates and drives you, what you are good at, and what you struggle with on a daily basis. Take any number of self-assessments that are available on communication styles, approaches to conflict, or even job preferences.

Before you look forward, look back. We have a tendency to move to the very next thing. What if you did not make the progress you thought you would make between the last career-planning event and now? What if you made more progress than you expected? Looking back helps you move forward.

Look outside of work. Your hobbies and personal interests can provide insight and possibly new career paths. Many people have turned hobbies into successful businesses. Others have utilized personal experiences to strengthen their work habits.

Track your successes. How can you ascertain if you are adding enough value if you have not tracked your value? Remember to make it real and concrete. Think about how you have added revenue, reduced waste, improved profitability, reduced product launch times, and so on. Use numbers and dollars where you can because these are measurable and capture attention.

Define yourself by your skills, not your role. Many individuals hold themselves back by defining themselves by their roles. If you characterize yourself as an engineer, a reporter, or an accountant, that is what you will always be, and most likely only be. If you relate to your skills and define yourself by your skills, such as writing, negotiating, and researching, many options are possible.

Pay attention to the outside world. Your company is not your world or the world. We live in a time when industries are changing significantly, the idea of work is changing, and technology shifts in a second—all these factors will influence your plan.

Have a fallback position. Life throws us curves, and we must be ready to change our plans at a moment's notice. However, we can have a fallback position or options when things do not work out as planned or the way we want them to.

Network, network, network. Be curious, always learn, and connect with others. Careers are most often influenced by relationships. Do you have the right relationships to grow your career? Do you have an appropriate number of relationships to grow your career? Most people do not. Those who do have the relationships typically do not maintain them. People only help when the relationship is a quality one.

Rely on yourself. Too many employees want their companies or managers to develop them or facilitate the process. Great. Take advantage of those resources and efforts when available, but do not rely on them. Typically, they act in the best interests of the company first and in your interests second.

Remember, it is your career. Take charge and *own it*!

BIO

Author, speaker, trainer, consultant, and entrepreneur, Brad Federman is the president of Performancepoint, a client-driven management consulting firm specializing in employee and customer engagement. Having spent over twenty years focusing on the human impact on organizations, Federman has become a recognized leader in the corporate world and the performance improvement industry. He has traveled the globe consulting in North America, Asia, Europe, and the Middle East, working with organizations of various industries and types. Federman has spoken at international conferences, such as that of the American Society for Training and Development, and has been quoted in publications such as *Fortune Small Business, HR Magazine*, and the *Los Angeles Times*. He is the author of several articles and the book *Employee Engagement: A Roadmap for Creating Profits, Optimizing Performance, and Increasing Loyalty*, published in August 2009.

Brad Federman may be reached by phone at (901) 737-3468 or by e-mail at bfederman@performancepointllc.com. The website for his company is http://www.performancepointllc.com.

74

Living a Passionate Life of Purpose

᪥᪢

Estra Roell

As I was driving down the road with my sixteen-year-old son, I noticed that he was being more glum than usual.

"What's up?" I ventured.

"I just don't know what to do with my life," he replied. "I don't know what I could possibly do to make a living that I would be good at."

"You'll spend most of your adult life at work," I advised, "so do something you love."

"I don't know what that is. I don't know what I like to do that I could make a living at."

"Well, what I notice is that many times when I come home from work thinking I have groceries, I find them missing because you've been cooking for your friends. Every after-school job you've had has been in a restaurant, and you talked the manager into promoting you from busboy to line cook, and you've done really well. Do you think you'd like to be cook?" He brightened and turned to me with an actual smile. "No," he said. "Not a cook. I want to be a chef!"

This boy, who had been a rather bored, lackadaisical high school student, went on to culinary school and was one of the top students. He received accolades from his instructors, his original dishes always sold out, and he even got excited about the papers he had to write. When you are passionate about what you do, everything changes.

Studies by the research company Harris Interactive have shown that 80 percent of working Americans don't enjoy what they do for a living. The highest incidents of heart attacks are on Monday mornings. Clearly something is missing in the lives of most people.

We all come into this life with a purpose. Each of us has a unique contribution to give to the world, and that gift will always be in the form of something we love to do. If you are spending your days out of touch with what you feel most passionate about because you think that's the only way to make a living, you will feel it as stress, boredom, false fatigue, poor health and a general state of unhappiness. How successful do you think you will be under those conditions? With whom would *you* rather do business or have as an employee: someone who is charged up with enthusiasm for what he or she is doing or someone who is forcing himself or herself through each day?

When you are engaged in work about which you are passionate, you are fulfilled. You feel a sense of aliveness, vitality, and joy. Your actions come from a sense of inspiration. Many people limit themselves because they don't believe they can make a living doing that to which they are naturally drawn; they feel afraid, they think they lack the necessary skills, or they are under pressure from family to take a certain path in life. This is your life, and no one else can live it for you. Not only will you be healthier and more fulfilled by following your passions but you will actually be more attractive to abundance and success. Think of Oprah Winfrey, for example. Her passion was talking to people, and look what she did with that!

The first step toward moving in the direction of a purposeful life is to get very clear on what your top passions are. The things that fire you up are your clues to your highest purpose and life's work. Think of how you feel as you are preparing to go on vacation. Now think of how you feel as you get up to go to work. Wouldn't it be nice if you felt the same excitement for both?

The answer for my son was right in front of him, but he couldn't see it because he wasn't asking the right question. He was trying to figure out what a good job would be that would pay the bills and that he might be able to do reasonably well. He wasn't asking himself what it was he really loved. What did he enjoy spending time doing? What fulfilled him? Our highest purpose is not about figuring out what the world needs. It's about what has meaning and is fulfilling for each of us. Sometimes we just need a little help to see what is already within us.

An Exercise to Help You Get Started

Find a quiet place and time where and when you will not be disturbed. Imagine your life as if you were already living it joyfully and abundantly. Let your imagination flow freely, with no restrictions. *Don't judge your answers* or limit yourself in any way. This is just you and your imagination. Allow yourself to drill down until you find the things that light the spark for you!

On a sheet of paper, answer these questions:

1. What kinds of activities am I engaged in and what skills am I using? Think of anything you enjoy as hobbies or volunteer work such as traveling, gardening, painting, writing, cooking, organizing, being with children, singing, meditating, counseling, working with machines, working with numbers, exercising, surfing, reading, teaching, woodworking, and so on. Think of things that have always come easily or naturally for you, and hold nothing back.

2. Where do you like to spend your time? Are you inside or outside? Do you work from home or in an office? Do you travel for work?

3. Who are you with? Do you prefer to work alone or with others on a team? If you are with others, what kind of temperament do they have?

4. Do you have your own business or work for someone else? If you have a boss, what is his or her management style?

5. How much time do you devote to money-making activities, and how much time do you have for family and self-renewal?

6. Are there classes you need to take or people already successful in your area of interest who would be willing to mentor you?

7. Ask yourself, who do I want to be? What kind of person am I, and what do I most value?

Now, using the answers from the preceding questions, imagine your life ten years from today. Imagine you have followed your passions, no matter what obstacles or fears may have appeared to pull you off course. Write a story of your life, including all the juicy details and feelings you have as you look back to see all you have accomplished and the person you have become. By always choosing in favor of your passions, opportunities have opened up for you in ways you could not have imagined!

Now, write another story in which you allow fear, excuses, or well-meaning family or friends to hold you back. How does that life look and feel?

When you step back from your purpose, you not only deny yourself your most joyful life, you deny the world your unique gift. Your purpose could be baking the most delicious cupcakes or making scientific discoveries. All that matters is that it has meaning for you.

BIO

Estra Roell, known as America's Life Purpose Coach, is a Certified Life Coach and Psych-K facilitator. She is the co-host of the weekly radio show "Coach Cafe" on Blogtalk Radio and a member of the International Association of Law of Attraction Professionals. Please visit her website at http://www.AmericasLifePurpose Coach.com/ to receive her free report and audio series on *Visioning and Goal Setting: Perceiving Your Purpose and Heading toward It Today.*

75

Discover Your Purpose and Put It to Work

❧

Sean Cook

"May you live in interesting times."

Though the origin of this so-called curse is debatable, few would argue its applicability to our current era, marked by the failures of institutions we once took for granted—banks failing, companies that were once shining examples of industry and finance being taken over by the government, newspapers going out of business, and even colleges closing their doors. People are losing their jobs, their retirement funds, their health insurance, and their houses. And those of us who still have some (or all) of these aren't happy, either. According to the Conference Board (2010), trends in job satisfaction show a steady decline between 1987 and 2009. People are less interested in their work and don't feel secure in their jobs.

Interesting times, indeed. But is it really a curse to live through them? Or a great opportunity to discover your purpose?

I wish I had spent more time with this process of discovery earlier in my career. After fifteen or so years working as a higher education administrator, I realized that I was living someone else's life. It was a pretty good life—I had a stable job, owned my own house, and had very little debt and a decent amount socked away for retirement. My wife was employed, we lived in a good neighborhood, and our two young children went to a great day care. I lived in one of the safest places in the entire country, with a low crime rate and a decent cost of living. I worked for one of the largest and most respected universities in the world, Penn State, and despite having the itch to move several times, I had found ways to stay in a community I loved and move up to a level in the organization where I had actual influence and could see the impact of my work on the people and the organization. I had it pretty good.

The problem, though, was that I wasn't happy. As I moved up, I moved further from the things I cared about and spent more time managing processes, handling details, training staff, administering budgets, responding to emergencies, and basically covering the university's ass.

I won't claim this is something unique. It's the burden of managers everywhere—you bust your hump, dedicate yourself to doing great work, get acknowledgment and praise, and start to listen to what others say you should be doing. Then it happens: you accept that long-time-coming invitation to join the big kid's table as a manager, and you learn some important lessons, starting with the following:

- Be careful what you wish for—you just might get it.
- There's a difference between doing what you are capable of doing and doing what you are meant to do.
- Other people are well meaning, but they don't know shit about you.
- Unfortunately, neither do you.

If you are like most people, you don't go looking for trouble. You just do what you are doing, keep your head down, do what you are told (or what you think you should be doing), and hope no one figures out that you are making it up as you go along.

But something must be different for you now—you picked up this book and started reading it, so something resonated with you about finding ways to enhance your career. Maybe you were looking for tips on how to be more efficient or more organized. Maybe you were hoping for a few practical strategies for managing your team or improving your professional image.

This article will not deliver any of that. Those are just details. First, you need to step back and see the whole picture. There is no greater way to enhance your career than to discover your purpose. Then you can spend your time and energy on finding ways to align your career choices with it.

What is purpose? It is, at once, the most mythical and most simple concept: *what you are meant to do.* The key word here is *meant.* So many of us spend our lives doing what we *want to do* or *are told to do* or *are capable of doing.* We also do what other people say *we should do, have to do,* or *would be good at doing.* There is a logic to it, and one can certainly keep busy, and earn a decent salary, from all these ways of doing. *But the doing is not the key to happiness in your life or career.*

Doing is repetition. Habit. Routine. It's mechanical and soulless. As technology advances, we create new and better ways to offload these routines to machines and to create systems to manage them, as if anything and everything is multiple choice, programmable, and easy to explain.

Is it any wonder why so many of us are lost in the details, stuck in routines, and feel like a cog in some machine? It's not enough to know your place in how a machine operates, especially when processes and routines are clearly going wrong and the machine is headed for a crash.

The good news is this: you are not a cog. You are more than a well-oiled gear in some engine, and you have more than a function or a routine. You are a human being, filled with potential. You can play multiple roles, and each choice takes you in a new direction, toward yet another choice, and another. The key is choosing the right things: *those that align with your unique purpose.*

All your life, you have been collecting clues to your purpose. Before you got distracted by other people's opinions, a need to feel accepted, or the lure of money, you knew there was a better way. To put your purpose to work, you will need to explore your interests (what you enjoy learning about and doing) and your values (how you treat others and wish to be treated). Spend some time each day thinking about them. Place a weight on each. Rank order them. Know what place they have in your life. Then generate a list of all the options before you at any given moment in time. Test each option against your interests and values, and discard the ones that aren't in alignment.

Once a clear option emerges, make a plan, put it into action, and revisit it often. Measure the success of your plan against the things that really matter (your interests and values), and adjust accordingly.

Sound simple? Ideas usually are. You may need help exploring your interests or giving weight to those things you value. Setting priorities can be difficult; designing a plan for putting them into action is harder; and keeping yourself accountable for your progress is the hardest of all. You may need a partner to help you execute your plans.

But one thing is certain: if you want to be successful in life and career, you'll do best by moving past conventional wisdom and frames of reference. Take the career path prescribed for you and throw it away. Set aside everything other people have said you should do "because you're good at it."Go digging for your purpose. Then put it to work.

Reference

Conference Board. 2010. U.S. job satisfaction at lowest level in two decades. http://www.conference-board.org/press/pressdetail.cfm?pressid=3820.

<u>B</u><small>IO</small>

Sean Cook is a Certified Life and Career Coach from Athens, Georgia. Before becoming a coach, he earned his master's degree at Clemson University and spent over fifteen years working in higher education as a student affairs professional. In his practice, he helps college students make successful transitions from high school to college and from college to career. He also assists higher education professionals in creating fulfilling careers and achieving work-life balance. You can read more by Sean at http://HigherEdCareerCoach.com/ and http://HigherEdLifeCoach.com/. He is currently writing his first book, *Putting Your Purpose to Work,* to be published in 2011.

76

How to Use the Power of Change and Transition to Get the Success You Want

❦

Liz Copeland

So you are ready for a change. Maybe you have had a big change forced on you through job loss or restructuring, or perhaps you are choosing change—you've grown stale and you want to move on, make things bigger, or simply do something different.

Or maybe you are happy with your job, but there is one thing that's bugging you or holding you back, one thing that you can't quite seem to get under control. Maybe others less talented than you are more successful, and you know you could be doing what they do. Or you are letting opportunities slip by, not because you don't have the technical skills needed but because you are just a bit too scared to make a move and put yourself forward. Or you are not even sure what you want to change—you know that you are seeking something more, but you don't yet know what it is.

If any of these descriptions fits you, you can successfully negotiate change and transition if you know how to do the process and shape the future you want to move into. It really doesn't matter whether the changes you want to make are big or small, or whether you are being forced into change (because someone else has pulled the rug from under your feet) or are making changes voluntarily. Change is scary; it can be challenging and difficult. It is a venture into the unknown and a move away from your current safety. I know this because if you didn't feel some kind of dread or anxiety about making the changes, you'd already have made them!

Though most people are afraid to change, *this is where the greatest progress is made, the greatest adventures are to be had, and the greatest success can be found.* So here is a step-by-step process for making the changes for your success (even if, at the moment, you don't know what that success might be). For those of you who like to plan ahead, there are five steps, and you might want a pencil and paper to jot down ideas as we go through them.

1. Discover Your Story

This is where we look at what's going on, how you got where you are, and who you are—and why you're worried about it. Take the time and space to write down what has brought you to where you are now. Write about what has brought you to this point today.

What has made you feel you are making a big decision in your life? Whether you are jumping voluntarily, or whether you are being pushed, something is making you do this—we call this the Big Event. It could be that you lost your job, or you won the lottery and at last have the financial freedom to do what you want. Or it could be that your job is OK but you're not quite getting there—now you want to step up and make a really big move, so you are creating your own Big Event. Maybe you have an opportunity in your career, and this time, you want to make the most of it, instead of listening to the fear that is holding you back.

What is the Big Event? Whether it's come from outside or you have had to define your own Big Event, write down how you got here.

2. Recognize Your Past

One of the things you will want to do in creating change in your career is to take some of the stuff from your past with you. Generally, you'll have to sort the past into four categories:

1. Things you *don't want* to have in your future. You'll know what they are for you, so write them down.

2. Things you *want* to take into your future. These are the clients with whom it was a delight to work, the friendly and productive office in which you worked, the bonus scheme that really incentivized you and made you rich. Work out what you want in your future.

3. Things you feel you *have* to take into your future: responsibilities you feel you can't ditch, but you don't see how they fit into your future.

4. Things you *can't let go of*, even though they will hold you back. This is the loss of your comfort zone. If you feel you could go for the promotion but you might lose your friends—you could make the big money-making pitch, but you'd lose the approval of others; you could strike out on your own but you'd lose your current security—note down what you think you might lose.

Now look at **alternative** ways of meeting the needs of yourself and others, and hold onto all the great things in your past that will go with you and enhance your future success.

3. Embrace Your Future

If, when you look at your future, there is chaos (too many choices to make and too many things you can do) or a void (you see nothing you want to do), this step will be essential for you.

Looking back on your life, notice anything or anyone you liked, any event or activity that made you feel good, any job that inspired you, any person with whom you enjoyed spending time, and ask yourself the following:

- What did I like about it/them?
- What good feelings did it/they generate for me?
- What made it/they important to me?
- What did I value from this?
- What do I want to take into my future?

Note this down. Now you can start to embrace your future!

4. Add All the Resources You Want

To shape your future, you will need outer resources such as money, time, and skills. You'll also need inner resources of confidence, self-reliance, enthusiasm, and so on. Here is one microexercise to help you: note three resources that will be essential for your career success. Now find a guide for each resource—this could be someone you know, a fictional character or a historical figure; he or she just has to represent the resource to you. Picture your resource guide giving the resource to you as you look at your future. Make this visualization as vivid as you can. Do this to set the scene when you are thinking of the changes you want to make, and add additional resources as you wish.

5. Mix and Merge Everything You Have Created

You now know what you want from your past and in your future, and you can look for the things that will enrich and enhance your life and add the resources you need to help you on the way. Helpful questions to ask at this point are the following:

- What do I want from my future?
- What do I most want to do?

- Where do I most want to be?
- What will help me do that?
- When I have done all that, how do I want to feel?

And now write down the *next action step* to take in creating this future success and making the changes you want.

BIO

As creator of the *True Courage Coaching Process*, Liz Copeland is skilled at helping her clients uncover the rich and varied possibilities they have in their lives. Liz shows solo entrepreneurs, business owners, and corporate executives how to use the power of change to get what they want and serve their business with productivity, passion, and purpose. As a lecturer and speaker, she supported others who were developing their skills and starting their own businesses. To receive bimonthly *True Courage Insider Secrets* and Liz's free *True Courage Success Kit*, subscribe today at www.truecouragecoaching.com.

77

PROFESSIONAL REFERENCES

The Art of Cultivating Professional References

Positioning Former Supervisors, Colleagues,
and Other Associates to Help You Get Hired!

Wendy L. Yost

As a former student affairs professional and current university professor, I am frequently asked to serve as a professional reference by former employees and students. Over the last two decades, I have learned what it takes to best communicate what employers want to hear before extending a job offer to a candidate or agreeing to a candidate's desired starting salary. I've also witnessed the pitfalls that often arise when a candidate doesn't adequately prepare his or her professional references to speak positively on his or her behalf—a costly mistake, to be sure. In recent years, I adapted these insights to serve the clients I coach as they manage the various facets of their job searches. It was out of the hundreds of coaching conversations that I have had over the years that the CONNECT Model came into being.

Consider whom to approach about serving as a professional reference in relation to the specific job/s for which you are applying. Depending on the position, it may be advantageous to extend beyond the typical references, such as past supervisors, to include former clients who held you in high esteem, leaders within nonprofit organizations who have seen evidence of your work ethic or character in volunteer settings, or colleagues who know people at the company for which you are applying to work.

Organize yourself before approaching possible references. Your professional references should get to serve as your professional references without feeling called to assist you as career coaches, résumé writers, or personal assistants. Take a few minutes to think through the last time you talked or interacted with each person you are considering approaching, and then think through what they might need to know about you now to serve as a positive and current reference for you.

Never tell after listing someone as a reference—always ask before doing so. I have experienced my share of blind reference checks where I only learn that someone listed me as a reference on receiving the call for the reference check. This is not good—for me, the employer, or the candidate. Also consider that the person you would like to have serve as a professional reference may have changed jobs himself or herself, and therefore the person's contact information may have also changed. When a potential employer is conducting a reference check, you want to avoid his or her call resulting in the discovery that you listed a significantly outdated contact.

Narrow down the information your references need to help you get hired. At minimum, provide your references with the following: a copy of your most current résumé, a copy of the cover letter and/or application you are submitting for the job, a few bullet points about why you are excited about the particular position for which you are applying, the timeline for the selection process, and your current contact information, in case the reference has questions. On a related note, because hiring processes can be incredibly expensive for companies, some companies are now conducting reference checks before inviting candidates to interview—so it is important that you position your professional references with the information they need, early in your job search process.

Expect and accept advice. Connecting with potential references need not be limited to asking "can I use you as a reference?" Make yourself available to your potential references when you first begin a new job search. Who knows, they may be aware of openings or future openings for which you might be perfect, and better yet, they might be able to help you secure them. On the flip side, if there was a performance issue while you worked with a potential reference or a style difference that got in the way of you working together effectively, you might want to have a candid conversation with the reference, acknowledging your growth since leaving the position and your gratitude for all that you learned while in that position. It takes some courage, but I also recommend asking anyone you hope to have serve as a reference the following question: "Is there anything that you can think of, from our time working together that would position you to give me anything other than a positive reference?" Then take a deep breath, allow for silence while the reference considers the question, and await his or her response. If the reference says yes, ask for a specific example of what comes to mind, and see if you can mitigate it. Depending on how the conversation unfolds, reassess whether to list that person as a reference. While this could result in an uncomfortable conversation, it is better that you have it than that he or she has it with a potential employer.

Communicate status. Let your references know how the selection process is unfolding in brief, bulleted e-mails or quick voicemails. If you were invited for an interview or have been informed that you are now a finalist, let them know. You may also want to let them know what you talked about during your interviews so that they can get a sense of the kinds of questions they might be asked. I've personally gone so far as to ask certain references to cover certain aspects of my character, work ethic, or experience so that when pieced together, the two or three calls the potential employer made to my references painted a multifaceted picture of the unique contribution I was positioned to make. I got the job and the salary I hoped for!

Thank them, thank them, thank them. I recommend sending a handwritten card via snail mail thanking anyone who served as a professional reference for you at the following intersections of your job search: when you are offered a job or have accepted a job offer, when you pull your application from a position in which you are no longer interested, and when you are released from a search process by a potential employer. It is particularly well received and remembered when you send a card a few months in on a new job, acknowledging your reference for helping you secure the position and sharing a few things that you enjoy about your new role.

In closing, cultivating professional references is something in which you invest on an ongoing basis, not simply when you are in the midst of a job search. It is also something in which you invest with a variety of people, not just one or two. Given that some job searches can last longer than initially anticipated, it's a good idea to have several possible references who are current on your most recent experience so that you don't rely on the same few people over and over again, possibly burning them out, and perhaps burning bridges in the process.

I invite you to take a few minutes today to reach out and acknowledge someone who has made a difference in your life. Share how your life has unfolded since you last saw or spoke to one another, see if you can stay connected more easily now using one of the many social networking sites available, and express your desire to stay better connected in the future. Who knows, the few minutes invested in reconnecting with someone today might just lead to your next job opportunity!

<u>Bio</u>

Wendy L. Yost, the owner of More Is Available Coaching & Consulting (http://www.moreisavailable.com/), partners with individuals and organizations to assist them in growing through transitions and generating desired change. With a master's degree in leadership and several coaching and spiritual counseling certifications, she possesses nearly two decades of experience helping people achieve desired results faster and with greater ease and enjoyment. Wendy passionately blends her professional expertise with her interest in practical spirituality to lend perspective when clients are going through particularly challenging times. Wendy also delights in teaching classes in leadership, marketing, and entrepreneurialism at California State University, Northridge.

78

Elevate, Enhance, and Enjoy

The 3 Es to a More Purposeful Career and Life

꿵꧁

Bambi Corso

Enhancing your career is synonymous with self-improvement. It takes desire, intention, deliberate choice, and action. Though what you do for a living may not define you, it is still an extension of who you are and therefore requires the same type of attention you would give to anything you might choose to do to enhance yourself. So where do you begin?

You begin with you. Enhancing your career means first enhancing yourself. No matter where you are in your career, all changes begin on the inside and work their way outward. Most people will have several careers over their lifetime, but regardless of what you do, or what you want to do, there is a course of action that, when followed, will bring you higher success in achieving your objective. "Elevate, Enhance, and Enjoy" is a simple, three-step process I developed for combining the inner and outer work necessary for change.

Step 1: Elevate Your Thinking

One's destination is never a place, but a new way of seeing things.
—Henry Miller

Are you aware that your thoughts are the most powerful tools you have not only to enhance your career but also to enhance your entire life? More than your schooling or years in business, your thoughts are the catalysts that create your reality because what you think about expands, and what you then affirm, you create. The way in which you think is so powerful that knowingly or unknowingly, you are constantly creating your reality just by where you place your attention.

Because everything in your life begins with your thoughts, make a conscious choice *only to focus on positive thoughts*.

As you think about enhancing your career, start by noticing where your mind goes. Are you thinking about what you want or about what you do not want? Do you think that something you are about to undertake will be an enjoyable experience or pure drudgery? Notice whether you are spending your time and energy thinking about all the things that are going right in your career and life or on the things that are going wrong. It is your responsibility to choose consciously to elevate your thinking by selecting the higher thought because what you think about expands, positively or negatively.

This is also true for your self-talk. Notice the things you say to and about yourself because the language you use can work for or against you. Focus on your greatest qualities, and find ways to change any thoughts that do not support you because your opinion of you is more important than anyone else's opinion of you. Remember that how you do anything is how you do everything, so elevating your thinking in one area of your life will transform every other area as well.

To do this, begin by looking for the good things that are happening in your life and focusing on those. Have an attitude of gratitude and stay in an appreciative state of mind because appreciation is one of the highest possible thought forms.

Here is a very simple tool that will instantly bring you into a grateful mind-set. The next time you find yourself saying, "I have to . . . ," such as "I have to go to work today," replace the words *I have to* with *I get to*. All around the world, there are people who would do anything to *get to* do any of the routine things you feel you *have to* do. This is selecting the higher thought.

Step 2: Enhance Yourself

A mind once stretched by a new idea can never
go back to its original dimensions.
—Oliver Wendell Holmes

Life is a constant act of evolving, and we are always in the state of becoming. Whether you want to be better at what you do or change your career altogether, enhancing yourself is a win-win opportunity for you to learn something new. Improving yourself and your abilities builds your self-esteem and confidence, allowing you to see talents in areas you may not have otherwise acknowledged.

Enhancing yourself is about realizing your potential. It is about taking affirmative action toward your own growth. Do you have a goal or a dream professionally or personally that you can begin living today by taking a class, reading a book, learning a new trade, or hiring a coach? Perhaps it is your character you want to improve by living with more integrity, honesty, and authenticity. Whatever it is, enhancing yourself automatically enhances your career because you are integrating those desires into your current life right now, which immediately affects the quality of your work.

So go for it! Initiate a change. Expand on things you want to know more about and discover new aspects of who you are. Surround yourself with people who empower, inspire and support your desires. Do not wait until "someday," because "someday" never comes; there is only today. Start by looking at the things in your current career on which you would like to expand, or find something for which you have a passion and start immersing yourself in it. By taking small action steps today that enhance who you are, you will bring yourself closer to the vision you hold for yourself, while at the same time adding excitement to your journey. "The Journey is the Reward." There is no time like the present to start designing your life the way you desire.

Step 3: Enjoy Your Life

The best and most beautiful things in the world cannot
be seen or even touched. They must be felt with the heart.
—Helen Keller

Enjoying life is about connecting with that which rejuvenates your spirit and feeds your soul. It's about experiencing the things you love the most, the things that activate your passion for life. People often put so much of who they are into their careers that they sacrifice the time and space needed to enjoy their families and other personal interests. As a result, they lose the balance needed to stay joyful in their careers, relationships, and lives.

Perhaps you love spending time with your family, your animals, or your friends. Maybe you enjoy taking walks in nature or traveling in your spare time. You might take delight in donating time to your favorite charity or organization because giving helps you feel fulfilled and purposeful in life. Whatever it is that evokes joy in your life, *make it a priority.* This, like everything else, is a deliberate choice. Creating time to enjoy your life sets a precedent for what is truly important to you and allows you to make more genuine choices about how you want to spend your time. Work and career are necessary constants for most of us, but the true beauty of living lies in deepening your life experience by incorporating that which brings you true happiness.

Utilizing this simple, three-step process will assist you in living a more passionate and purposeful life. You are always being given opportunities for growth. It is your responsibility to learn to say yes when they are presented. *The signs are there— follow them.*

<u>Bio</u>

Bambi is the founder of BambiCorso.com, a company dedicated to deepening people's sense of purpose and authenticity by teaching them to connect with and live their lives' passions by making deliberate choices. With over twenty-seven years of corporate experience, Bambi's passion is helping other transitioning professionals to begin living the lives they feel called to live, just as she has. She does this by using her expertise in spirituality, energy and mind-set management; the law of attraction; and dreamwork. Please visit her website at http://www.BambiCorso.com/.

79

Out of the Question

Harness the Amazing Career-Boosting Power of Proactive Questions

❧

Diana Morris

Fresh out of college, Dan was hired into a fast-track program at an insurance company. By the end of his first year, he was doing pretty well. He had finished a few key projects and was earning a reputation for being smart and aggressive. There was just one problem: Dan was also earning a reputation for having a fit when things didn't go his way.

The day he was called into the vice president's office, Dan tried to look casual. He walked in and sat on the sumptuous leather couch in the man's enormous office.

"Dan, you're fired," said the VP right off the bat.
"I am?"
"Yes. Pack up your desk, and security will escort you out. They're waiting outside my office for you. Thanks, and good luck."

Dan managed to stand up on shaky legs and started to walk out.

"Wait a minute," the VP said. "Come back."
He turned. "Yes?"
"You're not fired, Dan. I was trying to make a point. I could fire you right now, like I just did. And you know what? *It would not be fair.* But I could still do it, and you'd still have to figure out what to do next. If you want to be successful, you've got to stop expecting everything to go your way. The sooner you figure that out, not only will you succeed, you'll be happier."

Dan, who is today very successful as the head of a global construction company, left that office a changed person. "I'll always be grateful to that man," he says. "After that meeting, when something went wrong, I'd ask myself a single question: what can I do next that will start to turn things around? Right away, I felt better, stronger. It was definitely a turning point."

No Fair!

When the meeting doesn't go as planned, when the plum opportunity is handed to someone else, when the long-awaited promotion doesn't come, when the project gets derailed, sales slump, or the phone stops ringing, our sense of fair play takes a hit. It's like the kid inside yells, "Hey, no fair! Not after...

- all the work I did."
- how long I've waited."
- how loyal I've been."
- I've been such a team player."
- I helped out every chance I got."
- I took the time to finish my degree and she didn't."

We want to know *why*. We immediately begin to ask the most uninspiring questions possible—questions that rehash and analyze the problem: "Why did this happen? Who's responsible? Why did they do that? Isn't this the third time this year?" Because these questions zero into what's missing, what's wrong, and who's at fault, I call them deficit-based questions.

On the Lookout

Deficit-based questions have a negative supposition built into them. When you realize you overlooked an important detail, for example, a question like, "Why do I always miss critical details?" instructs your brain to be on the lookout for an answer that begins "I always miss critical details because . . . " The question focuses your thinking on what's wrong and who's to blame (in this case, you).

But it also does something more serious: it supposes that you *always* miss critical details. Without realizing it, through the simple act of asking this question, you've limited yourself. You've said, in effect, that you always miss critical details and that you expect yourself to do so again and again.

A question like "what part of the process is broken?" assumes that the process is broken. Your brain is now on the lookout for when and where and who: "The problem started in April when Jack's team . . . "

A few more examples follow:

Deficit-based."When will John realize just how demotivating his attitude is?"

Negative supposition. John's attitude is pulling the team down.

Answer. "John will realize how demotivating his attitude is when . . . "

Deficit-based. "Why is morale so low around here?"

Negative supposition. Low morale is a serious problem for this team.

Answer. "Morale is low because . . . "

Deficit-based questions serve a single, uninspiring, energy-zapping purpose: to look backward and study the problem—closely, for a long time, and with a magnifying glass, if possible. Answers to deficit-based questions analyze the problem, and they name names. At some point, they will identify who's responsible so that person can be called out, humbly accept the blame, and fix things—quick.

What type of mood does this create at work? What beliefs and views does it foster?

- "I better be careful that problems aren't traced back to me. Better send lots of memos to cover myself and carbon copy everyone I can think of."
- "Better not take the risk of trying something new. If it doesn't go well, I'll face the blame."
- "I need to be careful who I trust."

An Asset-Based Makeover

We can take the very same questions and give them an asset-based makeover, like so:

- "What went wrong?" (*deficit-based*)

and

- "What went right, and how can I use that information to make something positive happen tomorrow?" (*asset-based*)

Asset-based questions are proactive; they zoom your mental lens on the positive potential in any situation. You're no longer studying the problem in detail: when it started, who's responsible, or where the process is broken. Instead you're focused on how you can use what you've learned to create a more positive future.

Here's the first sample question again:

- "Why do I always miss the critical details?"

and the answer your brain is seeking:

- "I always miss critical details because . . . "

Now, here's the same question after it gets a proactive, asset-based makeover:

- "How can I be certain to catch all the critical details in my work in the future?"

and the answer your brain is now seeking:

- "Here's what I can do to be certain I catch all the critical details in my work in the future . . . "

When you answer *this* question—which has the built-in positive supposition that you can be more thorough in the future—you no longer waste time rehashing your mistake but instead plan the steps you'll take next time: the additional research you'll do, the people who'll help with fact-checking, the extra time you'll allow, and so on.

What a difference! Same issue; new approach. Totally different outcome: from hopeless to hopeful. From current problem to future potential. Now you're breakthrough-bound!

Let's make over the other sample questions:

Deficit-based. "Where did the problem start? What part of this process is broken?"

Proactive, asset-based makeover. "What steps worked well, and how can we use them to create the best finished product next time?"

Positive supposition. Part of the process worked well, and producing a great finished product is possible next time.

Deficit-based. "Why is morale so low around here?"

Proactive, asset-based makeover. "When was morale high in the past? How can we re-create those conditions?"

Positive supposition. This team knows how to work well together. We can do it again.

Don't be fooled: asset-based language does look for the silver lining and sees the glass as half full, but this is not sugarcoating, window-dressing, or spin. It's a proven way to show your respect for people, empower them—and yourself—and set the stage for your next career breakthrough.

BIO

In the last twenty years, Diana Morris has helped thousands of people at all career stages break through to new heights of success. Her absolute passion is to help people envision and create a powerfully positive future for themselves. Diana has helped thousands of people at companies like American Express, Roche, Rockport, Pfizer, Tommy Bahama, Ralph Lauren, Novartis, and New York Life, building new strengths in success-critical areas like conflict management, confident communication, business writing, active listening, and personal leadership. Diana is an honors graduate of Harvard University and the author of ten books on breakthrough career skills. Find her at http://www.breakthroughskills.com or call (877) 312-5400.

80

How to Ask for Recognition

❦

Tory Johnson

Every employee wants to be recognized for his or her performance, but many don't know how to go about securing that acknowledgment, or they're uncomfortable tooting their horns. They'll either wait for the boss to offer some form of praise, or they'll suffer in silence when it's not forthcoming. Many employers are content with this cycle because they fear that offering kudos goes hand in hand with opening the coffers.

Yet, for many workers, frequent recognition is even more motivating than an annual raise. So instead of allowing recognition to be passive, employers should encourage staffers to tout their skills and accomplishments. A proud workplace is often a more successful one.

Women tend to downplay their successes more so than men for fear of appearing conceited. And though it's true that bragging excessively is obnoxious and frowned on, regardless of gender, that doesn't mean you should stop short of taking credit for your work—and seeking credit, too, at every stage of your career. That doesn't make you a braggart; it positions you as a proud, accomplished professional.

Take this example: a staffer successfully executes a shareholder meeting, and the CEO seeks her out to offer his compliments. He says, "Excellent job. The event came off without a hitch." She should never bashfully say, "Oh, it was nothing," simply because she is too shy and intimidated to accept the credit and praise. Instead, she must accept the praise with pride. "I appreciate your recognition of my efforts. A lot of work went into planning this event. I'm delighted that all the preparation paid off for everyone." This is precious recognition that she has received from the CEO, and it can lead to raises and promotions if she seizes it and uses it wisely.

Though no one should expect a pat on the back for every little thing he or she does well, sometimes it's advisable to ask for recognition even when it's not offered. Always be direct about what you want in the way of recognition.

For example, when you achieve a major task at work, go to your boss right after the project has been successfully completed and say, "I'm very proud of my contribution to the shareholder meeting last week. I was thrilled to play an important role in such a successful event. It would mean a lot to me if you included my contribution in your weekly report to senior management." Your boss should be willing to do this on your behalf. When it's done, be certain to express your appreciation. You are documenting your contribution and making it known to key decision makers.

Recognition should not be reserved for annual reviews; rather department heads should encourage a monthly celebration of successes. Either at an informal gathering or via e-mail or intranet, require each staffer to submit his or her greatest accomplishment of the month. This might range from closing a sale to resolving a customer complaint. It may also include assisting a coworker in a time of need or creating a new filing system. No accomplishment is too big or too small, and staffers will appreciate the opportunity to receive recognition from colleagues and managers alike. It also sets a strong example of results-oriented thinking for the entire workplace.

In the absence of such formal company-sponsored programs, individuals who want to advance their careers should get in the habit of seeking recognition for major accomplishments—or a series of smaller successes—at least three to four times a year. If major accomplishments warrant it, more frequent requests can be made.

When the culture honors achievement through routine recognition, everyone wins. Employees at all levels feel great about facing their jobs each day, and businesses benefit from a satisfied, productive workforce.

BIO

Tory Johnson is all about spark and hustle at work, dating back to high school in Miami Beach where she joined her all-male debate team—and became the first girl to win a state championship. She dropped out of Emerson College for a chance to work at *ABC News* and then jumped to *NBC News,* only to be fired unexpectedly a couple years later. The permanent scar from that experience inspired her to shift from employee to entrepreneur and in 1999, she founded *Women For Hire* from a corner of her New York City apartment. Now in its 11th eleventh year, the company hosts high-caliber diversity career expos across the country, attracting talented women and leading employers, as well as conferences and programs for current and aspiring small business owners. As the workplace contributor on ABC's *Good Morning America,* she is a favorite among viewers who appreciate her no-nonsense career advice. *Glamour* dubbed Johnson the "raise fairy godmother" for her ability to help women ask for—and get—more money. Her fifth book, *Fired to Hired,* follows

Will Work From Home: Earn Cash without the Commute, which was both a New York Times and Wall Street Journal best seller. She and her family live in New York City. Learn more at toryjohnson.com and connect with her at Facebook.com/Tory and Twitter.com/ToryJohnson/.

81

Conscientious Connections

Secrets to Becoming a Valued and Trusted Referral Resource

≈~≈

Patti DeNucci

Ask any successful professional or business owner how he or she attracts his or her best job opportunities or customers, finds his or her most valuable suppliers and resources, and meets his or her most treasured colleagues and advisors. The person will probably tell you these invaluable connections came as referrals from someone he or she knows, values, and trusts.

This tells you something worth noting: referrals build relationships, careers, and businesses, that is, if those who make the referrals know and practice the success secrets I'm about to share with you here.

As valuable as referrals can be, they can also backfire, especially if you're not consistently thoughtful, discerning, and focused on creating good matches and great results for all involved. Perhaps you can think of someone who referred a friend, colleague, business, job opportunity, or product to you and things didn't turn out so well. At best, the referral created some awkwardness, disappointment, or an unwanted distraction. At worst, it may have been a total disaster involving wasted time and money, negative results, undue stress, bitter feelings, or ruined relationships.

When this happens, no one benefits. Trust fades and reputations slip.

That's why mastering the art and science of sharing high-quality referrals, introductions, and connections—the ones that create true value for those you connect—is critical to your success and reputation. It's time to move beyond being just another enthusiastic, well-meaning networker who connects the dots randomly. Keep reading and learn the secrets of becoming a truly thoughtful connector and trusted resource—the person with whom everyone wants to do business.

Understand that referrals, recommendations, endorsements, introductions, and connections create an impact, whether positive or negative. When it's positive, you're the hero. When it's not, you've generated awkwardness, bitter feelings, or negative results. You're the goat. Which would you prefer?

Make every connection with the utmost care and diligence. In other words, be sure before you refer. Strive to be thoughtful, discerning, and purposeful each and every time you make a referral or introduction. Ultimately, the quality of these referrals and those you refer will directly affect your brand and reputation.

Listen to others' needs and requests carefully. Before you make any connections or referrals, listen closely to the person in need. Ask questions. Be sure you understand what he or she is saying and requesting. Take your time, take notes, and above all, take your role as connector seriously.

Offer options. Even if you're totally confident in the people, organizations, or resources you connect or refer to others, consider that no two situations or human beings are identical. What's more, people like options. Offer several suggestions when possible, and be sure to share what you know about each.

Consider whether you're qualified to make the referral. Before you make a referral, recommendation, or connection, be sure you understand the request. If you don't have a solid recommendation to offer or it's not your area of expertise, don't try to fake it. You could simply say, "I'm sorry, I'm not the right person to help you with this."

Develop a list of traits you look for in good referrals. What characteristics must people or organizations exude before you trust them enough to refer them? Professionalism? Integrity? Responsiveness? Amazing customer service and results? Document these traits, keep adding to the list over time, and use it as your guide.

While you're at it, build your Referable List. Once you know what your standards and criteria are, use them to guide you as you create a short list of people and organizations you believe you can refer or connect to others with confidence. This list will become an invaluable asset to you and your business.

Allow your Referable List to grow and evolve. Add more people and organizations to the list as they win your trust. Don't hesitate to delete those who let you down or make you uncomfortable. Notice how your standards become more refined and sophisticated with time, experience, and observation.

Make introductions just as carefully. It can be fun and rewarding to introduce two favorite colleagues to each other. But do them a favor: don't make introductions or connections without a clear purpose. Ask yourself these questions before making any introductions:

- Why do these people need to know each other?
- What do they have in common?
- How might they benefit each other?
- What positive results could result from this connection?
- Will it be a win for everyone?
- What information do I need to share with them to make it a meaningful connection?

Follow up, gather, and learn from feedback. The information you get here will help you fine-tune your referral skills immensely. It will take extra time and effort, but it's where you'll learn what worked out well and where improvements can be made.

Realize that perfection is impossible. Even when you're extremely particular and mindful in making referrals and connections, the results won't always be perfect. Sometimes things just don't work out. It happens. Keep doing your best. At the very least, you will achieve excellence.

Be humble and learn from your mistakes. If things go awry as a result of your matchmaking, apologize and make good as appropriate. Determine what might have worked out better, chalk it up to learning, and vow to do better next time.

Keep upping the bar. You'll soon establish and solidify your reputation as a supreme business matchmaker and top-notch catalyst for great results, making you one of the most respected, trusted, and valuable contacts in your professional circle. Your reputation will grow, as will your own career or business.

Bio

Patti DeNucci is an award-winning communicator, connector, and coach as well as founder and owner of DeNucci & Co. This boutique referral service refers exceptional freelancers and solopreneurs to potential clients, opportunities, and resources. When she isn't writing or speaking on networking, connecting, and business development, Patti is advising her clients on how to reach for the next level of success. She is one of forty female entrepreneurs featured in the book *Fearless Women, Fearless Wisdom* by Mary Ann Halpin. Patti's own book, which focuses on the art and science of seeking, attracting, and leveraging powerful professional relationships, will be out in 2011. Visit her online at http://www.denucciandcompany.com/, e-mail patti@denucciandcompany.com, or tweet @pattidenucci.

82

RÉSUMÉ STRATEGIES

We Are Not in Kansas Anymore

❧

Edward Dellon

On Monday, September 15, 2008, Lehman Brothers declared bankruptcy and, in so doing, dropped a depth charge on millions of job holders; every company in the country now seems paralyzed as it waits to see what will bob to the surface as a result. All our ideas of how safe our careers were and how our lives would progress were affected in ways we are only now beginning to understand. Millions lost their jobs, and we entered the age of the ultimate buyer's market in employment: we were not in Kansas anymore.

To be clear, our expertise for thirty-five years has been the recruitment and selection of senior-level talent on behalf of client companies involved in large, complex real estate development and construction projects around the world, and that may color our perception of the times as those are among the most seriously affected industries. That said, here are some of the ways in which the trajectory of your career changed on September 15, 2008.

The marketplace stopped caring about you and your needs Your world went from "What can XYZ Corp do for me?" to "What can I do for XYZ Corp?" If your mind-set is still the former—and if your attitude, approach, and, yes, résumé reflect that mind-set—your résumé will simply be replaced by one of the eight hundred other résumés on someone's desk in XYZ Corp's human resources office.

So the question is, what can you do to enhance your career in this terrible employment market; who, if anyone, has some sort of an edge; and what can you do to increase your chances of separating yourself from those eight hundred other résumés in the XYZ HR office?

As recruiters in the real estate and construction industries, we have inordinate experience dealing with extreme downturns and recoveries as there is no industry more inherently cyclical. It is predictable that within every ten-year stretch, market circumstances will combine to cause too much capital, too much leverage, too much demand, and, yes, too much greed and will allow developers to overbuild everything, leading to an inevitable crash. We had crashes in the mid-1980s, the late 1980s, and the early 1990s, and here is the good news for many candidates now seeking to find a new home: if your market has bottomed, and is stalled there, older candidates have a distinct edge over younger ones, not only in the real estate development business but also in many other cyclical industries that depend on human creativity and not manufacturing processes—age and the wisdom it can bring can be a plus in these times. Why? Because individuals who have survived a recession or two have valuable experience in dragging an enterprise out of the depths and back into productive rebirth. You need to deemphasize what you developed, what you built, what you bought, and what you sold in the boom times as none of those skills will be called on for a long time and will instead emphasize the strategies you used in previous crashes to help your company survive.

Next, help your family to understand that survival will mean you might all have to make uncomfortable and unhappy choices. When I receive a résumé that says, "I will relocate anywhere within the 212 area code," which happens at least once a week, that résumé is deleted. The mantra today in our business is "Shanghai, Mumbai, Dubai, or good-bye," because that is where the tower cranes are still in the air. We have recently opened an office in Shanghai, and we are about to open in Abu Dhabi. That was not the plan three years ago, but, as they say, "if you are hunting ducks, you need to be where the ducks are," and in real estate, the ducks are in those three places and will be for the foreseeable future. If you want to survive this depression, you will relocate anywhere you need to go—period.

Edit *all* the soft, touchy-feely verbiage out of your résumé. XYZ Corp is as concerned with its survival as you are with yours, and all it wants to hear from you are specific examples of how you made and/or saved money for your former firm. It wants to hear not how you are eager for new challenges, or are a team builder, or are a champion of diversity. It wants to know that you have actually researched the XYZ Corp, that you know who the officers are, that you know what they are working on, that you can tell them specifically how, in your former role, you were x months ahead of schedule and y dollars under budget on similar projects. They want specific examples that relate to their circumstances.

Along the same lines, delete the objective section of your résumé. It can and will only harm your cause. First, it is self-limiting. If it is too general and soft, it is, at best, vapid. If it gets more specific and says that your objective is to increase your experience as a project director, but someone at XYZ was actually thinking about you for managing director of design and construction, you have just shot yourself. Besides, no matter what you say, the reality is that your objective is to get another job so you can keep your house and not have to take the kids out of school.

Also, delete the personal section. XYZ does not care if you are a wonderful human being; they care if you can make them money. When you tell me that you coach Little League, that tells me that you have to be out of the office before five o'clock and that you cannot work weekends. In this economy? And never, ever tell me that you are a scratch golfer or hold the club championship—or, for that matter, sail. No one keeps a low handicap without lots of time on the course, and when you are on the course, you are not in an airplane on the way to Hong Kong for XYZ Corp. Besides, I am an eighteen handicap, and I will reject you for that reason alone.

Finally, get into the gym and stay there as much as you can. It will bring the stress down, make you feel better about yourself, and make you look better, and XYZ will absolutely perceive you as someone with a full tank of gas who is ready to go.

Remember, you were looking for a job when you got your last one; you will get one this time, too. Good luck.

BIO

Ed Dellon is founder and CEO of Edward Dellon Associates Inc. For thirty-five years, his firm has specialized in the recruitment and selection of senior-level executives to develop and build major, and often iconic, real estate projects around the world. Edward Dellon Associates Inc. has been cited by Southwest Airlines' *Spirit* magazine as one of the most "dependable search organizations" in the United States and has been designated by *Forbes* as a "premier provider" of executive search services in the United States. Ed Dellon can be reached at (310) 286-0625 or by e-mail at edward_dellon@yahoo.com. The firm's website is http://www.edwarddellonassociatesinc.com/.

83

The First Secret to Loving Your Job

≈≈≈

Pamela D. Garcy

Lawrence entered my office, sunk into the armchair, and sighed. I noticed a layer of tears forming over his eyes. Averting his gaze and reaching for a tissue, he said, "I feel like there's something fundamentally wrong with me."

He continued to look down as a heavy tear fell on his polished black shoes, making a quiet *thump*. "I don't know why I can't seem to be happy about my job."

I spoke gently, but with conviction. "Well, first, can you explain to me why you think that your unhappiness at work means that there is something wrong with you?"

Sighing and wiping away more tears with an already dampened tissue, he said, "Because anyone else would say I have the perfect job."

"That's from the outside looking in." I paused. "And what would *you* say, from the inside looking out?"

He nodded and said, "I would say that my job is unpredictable. I never know what else will be thrown at me. I'm always working long hours. I never get a break. Now they want me to travel more. My support staff isn't pulling their weight. I get blamed. Other than my salary, my job stinks."

"So, Lawrence, really take your time here. Think about this. Explain to me why *the challenge* that your job presently stinks has to mean that there is something fundamentally wrong with *you?*" I asked firmly, knowing that it was important that he get this clear.

Looking up, he answered, "I guess it isn't something wrong with me. But I can't stand going there lately, so maybe there *is* something wrong with me."

"So," I asked, "if we discover that some parts of the job could be improved, would you enjoy going?"

Lawrence looked toward my desk at a decorative mug that said *Follow Your Heart*. He nodded. "Yeah, 'cos I actually love the work—I feel like I was born to do it. It is just the rest of the stuff that I hate."

"I can understand that. You don't like all of the unpredictable parts, working late, or getting blamed. But your work itself is your craft, and you love it."

"You got it," he half-smiled.

"So, going back to what you said earlier, when you tell yourself that there is something wrong with you, what is the effect on you?"

"I get depressed . . . kinda hopeless and helpless too."

"And how great is your problem solving when you feel like that?"

"Not great."

"And when you don't problem solve very well, what do you tend to conclude?"

"That something is wrong with me." He laughed to himself.

"Wow, sort of sounds like a vicious cycle, doesn't it? So, what might be a lesson from this, Lawrence?"

"I'm realizing that telling myself there's a flaw in *me* isn't really helping me solve my problems."

"Yes, it seems like it's making things worse—you take a normal challenge and then you put *you* down. It makes me wonder if you see the difference between taking responsibility and making yourself wrong for having a problem."

"Not totally," he shrugged.

"When you just take responsibility, you tend to focus on your choices, your actions, your responses—basically you look at your *behaviors* and think about how different actions can lead to different outcomes. Then you make the best choice you can." I paused to check if he was following.

"So I critique my choice, not myself?" he asked.

"Yes. Your outcome is simply feedback about how effective your choice was. Like my hero Albert Ellis used to say, 'Say *it* is bad, not *I* am bad.' Putting yourself down leads to a victim mentality because you start to feel depressed, hopeless, and helpless—it shuts you down and you stop seeing all of the choices that you can make."

"OK, I get that. I'm going to stop putting myself down. I'll just say that the choice I picked didn't work, and then I'll work on solving the problem better."

"That's a great idea, Lawrence. Also, I wonder if it might be helpful to clarify what is in your control and what is not. Sometimes this process opens you to some creative options you might have forgotten. What do you think?"

He smiled and nodded slightly, "Yeah, let's do that."

"OK, so let's start with the parts of the job that are not in your control. Tell me about those."

"OK . . . I guess one thing is that I can't control what kind of mood my boss is in, or whether he decides to add more work on. I also can't control whether people will do what I want them to do."

"You actually can't control what other people do at all—they can ask you to empty your bank account and buy everyone dinner for a month—they can ask you to work every weekend for the rest of the year," I exaggerated to reveal his power to him.

"Yes, but I wouldn't do it," Lawrence insisted.

"Good to know—so you'd assert yourself, which is something that *is* in your control?"

"Yes. I'd probably quit the job."

"So there are limits."

"Damn straight."

"OK," I said, "so let's get back to this, what else is *out of your control*?"

"Working late."

"How so?"

"If I don't get the work done quickly enough, I will get canned, so it is out of my control if I have to work late."

"Whether they decide to fire you is out of your control . . . "

"Yeah—technically, it is really in my control if I decide to work late."

"Excellent! And whether or not you decide to fire them?" I countered, reminding him of his power to choose.

"That's true. I forgot that," he smiled.

"OK, so let's turn to what else is *in your control,*" I continued.

"My attitude . . . hmmmm . . . whether or not I ask for help is one. If I follow up with my staff is another . . . I can't think of anything else."

"Can I ask you about some others?"

"Sure."

"How about whether or not you speak with your boss and set up a better arrangement?"

"Yes, that's true. I haven't ever talked with him about it, so he probably doesn't know how I feel."

"Good—and how about whether or not you hold weekly accountability meetings with your support staff?"

"Yeah, that would probably get them into action. I could make it a contest too!"

"Creative! And if one decides not to do the work—is finding a replacement in your control?"

"Yes—that's in my control too," he beamed.

"So, let's take a step back here. When you focus upon what is *out of your control,* what do you end up telling yourself?"

"That life sucks, my job stinks, I'm a victim, and there's something wrong with me."

"And you feel?"

"Depressed, hopeless, and helpless."

"Alternatively, when you focus upon what *is in your control,* and you don't put yourself down for having normal life challenges, how do you feel?"

"More hopeful, more optimistic, stronger, more positive . . . so much more motivated. It's like I am realizing that there is a lot that is in my control to do! I want to handle things differently. I'm going to talk to my boss and set up a meeting with my staff right away. I want to be able to focus on my work, do a good job, and then go home and relax," he grinned.

"And it sounds like that is what you're on the way to creating, Lawrence," I smiled back.

Note: *Case details were changed to protect the confidentiality of the individual.*

<u>BIO</u>

Pamela D. Garcy, PhD, is a licensed clinical psychologist and coach in Dallas. Pam's private therapy practice helps patients with emotional healing. Pam's coaching practice helps coaching clients to reach specific goals. Pam loves to work one-on-one with select clients, and she invites you to contact her to see if her services might help you. Contact Dr. Pam directly at drgarcy@aol.com or (972) 248-3861. She is a best-selling author who enjoys conducting trainings; you can check out her site at http://www.myinnerguide.com/. Discover the free relaxation audio, listen to teleseminars, register for the online e-zine, and learn about upcoming events.

Secret Weapon

❦

Savannah-Brooklyn Ross

In generations past, it never dawned on anyone to investigate career options. Putting food on the table was the sole objective. You did what you had to do to provide for the family and did not complain. Usually, the men followed in their fathers' footsteps. Having been provided with hands-on education throughout their youth, they were experts at a very young age. They worked long, hard hours and came home to their families hungry and exhausted. Women who were desperate or very brave found jobs as teachers and nurses. The process was not all that complicated.

Oh, how things have changed! Today people spend a great many years planning and preparing for their vocations. They spend money on counseling, aptitude testing, and years of postsecondary education, all with the objective of finding the perfect job.

The new consensus is to find something that you love to do. It only makes sense to enjoy what you will be stuck doing for the majority of your waking hours. The funny thing is that people are more miserable in their careers today than ever before, contributing to many adults changing careers in their forties.

Let's explore three common methods for choosing your occupation. After doing some real soul searching, you decide that your love for dogs should lead to a career as a groomer or pet store owner. (I have yet to meet anyone in these vocations who are wealthy, but hey, you could be the first one.) The same thing goes for writers, artists, and those who love to cook. Whatever it is that you love, fill in the blank. I am concerned with this concept of doing what you love.

You have a passion for _____. You set yourself up to depend on _____ to provide financial freedom. There is never enough money, and eventually, _____ will disappoint you. You begin to resent _____ as it is not living up to your expectations. Now you are stuck in a career that you hate. But the worst part is, you have lost your passion.

Perhaps you took a different road. You got some advice from your high school guidance counselor, who suggested that you go into a growing industry with a high demand for skilled workers. Well, since every guidance counselor in every high school in the 1980s was advising students to get into computers, you found yourself on the less desirable team in the game of supply and demand—too many trained experts and not enough jobs.

Maybe you bought into the big work-at-home dream and began recruiting and/or annoying everyone who ever dared say hello to you. You discovered that there is no "work your own hours," only "work at everyone else's convenience." You rack up your credit cards and neglect your family, hoping that someday, you might make it to the top 2 percent of the company. You visualize yourself walking across the stage to collect the car you have worked so hard to earn (and will have to work even harder to maintain). You imagine your name in the company magazine showing off your $10,000 a month pay check (and desperately hiding the $12,000 a month in expenses that go along with maintaining the image). Now that you see the ugliness behind the mask, you just cannot bear to walk away. You put so much blood, sweat, and tears into this, and you worked hard to convince your family and friends that you were not getting into some get-rich-quick scam. How would you ever save face if you had to admit that you were wrong? What will you do with the garage full of product you bought at wholesale to meet production?

What to do? What to do?

My experience, challenges, and successes have transformed my views and allowed me to develop a new approach that might very well be the best career-planning secret yet. As a result of putting this method into practice myself, I have created ultimate freedom in all areas of my life and live the dreams of many.

Here is the big secret:

Instead of living the lifestyle that your career will afford you, create the wealth that will afford you the lifestyle of your dreams.

Let's dissect this idea together and see if it holds the answer for which you have been searching.

In all these years of planning, you unconsciously decide to live a lifestyle conducive to your career of choice, unrelated to your passions, goals, dreams, or ambitions. If you choose to become a police officer, you do not live the lifestyle of a movie star.

You give away your freedom and become a victim of your own crime. You strip away your choices and alter your life in unimaginable ways, all the time convincing

315

yourself that you have no options. You rebuke responsibility for where you are and refuse to admit that your life is nothing more than a reflection of the choices you have made.

It is too hard to face the truth. You were not the best parent or spouse you could have been because you worked so hard and were often too stressed, irritable, or unavailable. You never had any extra money to help all those charities and were too depressed or busy to volunteer your time. You can't stand to look in the mirror and see what all those years of stress have done to your body.

There is a way out, and it all stems from common sense, one of our most underutilized assets. Try this on for size: what if you were to turn things around for a minute and first determine what kind of lifestyle you want to live instead of focusing on what kind of job you want holding you down?

When I was faced with near-bankruptcy, divorce, and the impending death of my infant son, I knew that I needed not only financial freedom but also time freedom to care for my special-needs child and mend my marriage.

Some careers seem to promise big money, such as the legal and medical professions, but consume your time and bear so much stress that they keep you from enjoying any life at all—not that these opportunities were even an option with my lack of time and money to get educated in these arenas.

Once I took off the blinders, it became very evident that the answer was right before me. Real estate investing seemed to be a common thread among all the really wealthy people about whom you hear and read. I had no knowledge, passion, or desire to pursue the life of a real estate mogul, but I saw freedom. Although I still have no passion for the field, I respect it tremendously and appreciate working only three hours a month to maintain the multi-million-dollar lifestyle that my investments provide. Sure, there are headaches, but try to convince me that you have no obstacles in your job! I have time freedom to do what I want, when I want, and with whom I want. I never worry about bills or getting to work on time or depriving my kids of grand opportunities. I have the financial resources to explore the world and make a positive impact in third world countries. I have the awesome privilege of sharing my knowledge with others and helping them to live the life they never dared even to imagine.

The point is not that I chose to become an investor; it's that we all have the opportunity to create our own futures by changing our perspectives. Focus on the destination before you choose what vehicle will lead you there. What would it serve to buy a boat if you were looking to summit a mountain? Ultimately, what we all want is freedom. You have the option to live a life of passion and purpose; the question is, are you bold enough to be free?

<u>B</u><u>IO</u>

Savannah-Brooklyn Ross is the president of Rich Mom Enterprises Inc., an education-based company dedicated to teaching a down-to-earth approach to creating great wealth through real estate investing. Her system teaches a simple formula to acquire high-equity, high–cash flow properties. Savannah-Brooklyn Ross helps others create ultimate freedom so that they, too, can follow their true purpose. She is dedicated to empowering others to create their own success stories. Savannah and her family enjoy giving back by building homes and feeding families in third world countries. Visit her online at http://www.richmom.com/.

85

SOCIAL MEDIA

Social Media to Enhance Your Career

❧

Lisa Larter

If you are not utilizing the power of social media for your career, plain and simple, you need to! Facebook has become the place employers go to scope out the individuals they want to hire. These referrals to Facebook are known as character checks, and they go hand in hand with your reference check, except often, they happen before you get to the interview.

Here are a few things you will want to do. First, ensure that your privacy settings are set up to showcase the individual your employer will want to hire. Set up your profile in a way that demonstrates professionalism versus partyism. Remove any and all incriminating photos, and ensure that your reputation would be solid if someone from the outside were to take a peak.

Do not lock up your privacy settings to block individuals; instead set them up so that an outside company can see exactly what you want it to see. Use the likes and interests sections of your profile to showcase your talent, experience, education, and volunteer work as social proof for your résumé.

Regularly check sites like YourOpenBook.org—search your name and see what comes up. If someone has tagged you in a way that does not align with your true character, the one in which an employer would be interested, remove the tag immediately.

Use Twitter to build your social influence and help you get connected to hiring managers. Twitter is an amazing way to network and gain access to individuals. If you are creative, you can find ways to get these individuals to notice and pay attention to you.

There are many stories of individuals who have blogged and used Twitter as a platform to showcase exactly why they were the right person for a job. Out-of-the-box creativity like this is not the norm; it is the exception and is often the differentiating factor when it comes to hiring.

Imagine you want to work for a large corporate company, and you write daily about the things you would do to make a difference and link your post to Twitter; furthermore, you ask people to connect you to someone at that company. It is possible for thousands of people to re-tweet or share your message with others, making it possible for the one person who needs to see to see it.

One day I was on Twitter and wanted to get connected to the owner of a large organization. I sent out a tweet and asked if anyone knew him. Immediately, I had three people respond and tell me they knew the individual and could put me in touch with him. Imagine that type of influence when trying to connect with an executive at the company for which you want to work.

Last, LinkedIn is becoming the platform used most by hiring managers. You want to really spend some time on this professional networking site and showcase your talent.

Find groups that are in alignment with your career path, and become an active participant in them. Write recommendations for others on a regular basis, and ask individuals with whom you have worked to do the same for you.

Get involved in the answers section and showcase your knowledge. Participate regularly and answer questions to demonstrate your skill level and get noticed.

Look at the jobs section daily. LinkedIn is known as the networking platform of choice for job postings. Check it not only to find out what jobs are available but to find out the names of the HR managers who are posting the jobs. If you discover the identity of the HR manager at the company for which you want to work, the rest is easy. Find a way to get to know this individual, and stand out. Find out who you know who is connected to this person, and get introduced.

Social media is a game changer when it comes to your career options. It is the one untapped resource that individuals looking for jobs are not fully utilizing because they are too caught up in using it as a purely social platform.

Companies are always looking for great people. They will make room within their organizations for people who bring top-level skills, out-of-the-box thinking, and great interpersonal skills.

If you are serious and consistent about your quest to manage your career through your network, you can't afford not to leverage the power of social media. When you finally get noticed, you will find employers seeking you out versus you going through the traditional path of trying to get hired. When you get your next job through social media, let me know—I'd love to hear about it.

BIO

Lisa Larter is president and founder of Lisa Larter Consulting, an innovative consulting solution firm that gives entrepreneurs a customized blueprint for building solid, successful businesses. A serial entrepreneur with hard-hitting impact, Lisa is known for her no-nonsense approach to helping people accomplish goals through solid business foundations, social media, and customer connections. Lisa has consulted on social media for best-selling authors such as Deepak Chopra, Arielle Ford, and Peggy McColl and has worked with organizations such as Hasmark Services, 20 Vic Property Management, Flowers Canada, and TELUS. To learn more about Lisa, visit http://www.lisalarter.com/, or follow her on Twitter @LisaLarter.

86

Step Up in the Workplace

❦

Mamta Parkhill

It is often thought that if you are not making any career progress with the organization for which you are working, then moving on to another organization is the answer. As part of that process, the CV gets sharpened, the network gets active, preparations for interviews begin, and many phone calls in the workplace start to take place. Does this sound familiar?

Of course, if your organization does not embrace the same values or philosophies as you, then yes, move on and find an organization that does fit better culturally with you as a person.

It is also thought that to have career development possibilities, you need to work for an organization that has defined career paths and structures in place.

But have you often received an internal communication that announces someone in your organization has been promoted to a role that didn't exist before? After this announcement has taken place, the talk on the company grapevine asks how this happened, why the person got this position, and why the role wasn't advertised. Shortly after, further communications will follow, this time from the recently promoted, and the talk this time will cover how the person is so excited with this new position and how he or she cannot wait to get started. Does this sound familiar?

Of course, this opportunity did not come out of the blue. The CEO, divisional director, or department head didn't suddenly wake up and decide to give "John Smith" that role.

So how did John Smith get this career development opportunity? He simply made the commitment to step up and make things happen for him. Stepping up to another level will give you and only you another route to enhance your career.

This alternative route is always available, no matter how large or small the organization. The size of the organization is not an excuse; this route will always be there, providing that two conditions exist.

The first condition is that your organization is financially stable. If your organization is not financially stable, then it will be in either fight or flight mode. Career enhancement possibilities will probably be replaced by job security and, unfortunately, employee survival.

The second condition is that you are happy working for the organization that employs you. You might not yet have your ideal position within your organization, but it does have the right culture for you. In the long term, organizations would rather have staff on their payrolls who fit with their cultures and will see the benefits in investing in these employees to get the best out of them.

Your workplace does have the opportunities that can help anyone enhance his or her career beyond his or her wildest dreams, providing that it is financially stable and is the environment in which the person wants to work. To have access to these opportunities, you have to make the internal commitment to yourself and step up in the workplace, using this approach to enhance your career.

Make a commitment to start doing everything you do so well that your department head, director, or CEO cannot afford to let you go. Stepping up in the workplace will get you on that personality platform so that you become invaluable to your team, department head, director, CEO, and, ultimately, the organization.

To make any commitment seriously means you have to take action. Without any action, there is no serious commitment.

The first step toward your personality platform and to this commitment is to carry out some quick, simple analysis on your own habits and attitudes in your workplace. Ask yourself the following:

- How reliable are you?
- How organized are you?
- How committed are you to your responsibilities?
- How flexible are you?
- How positive are you?
- Do you show initiative?
- Do you think outside the box?
- Do you listen to your colleagues?
- Do you care about your colleagues?

Be honest in your analysis of your habits and attitudes, and give yourself a score out of ten. You should already know how you operate, but scoring yourself will give you a measure and point of reference for improvement.

Next explore techniques and strategies to improve your scores on each habit and attitude. Where you have scored low on a particular habit or attitude, you will be able to find plenty of techniques and strategies for improvement. Take advantage of the many techniques that are available to you, and don't delay—start implementing these strategies straight away and increase your scores. The quicker you implement these strategies, the quicker you will start contributing to your personality platform.

For those habits and attitudes that are already your strength areas, further improvements will need more creativity. But once you have found strategies to improve on what you already do well, it will make the contribution to your personality platform even greater; you will be operating at an even higher level as you are taking those extra steps.

Also, learn to take well-thought-out risks because being unremarkable and unnoticed in your work environment won't get you where you want to go. For example, take the lead in high-visibility projects to improve your initiative score. To improve your reliability score, become even more dependable by analyzing your tasks, and deliver early the tasks that key people in the organization find the most important as inputs into their own tasks. Show that you care about your colleagues in every way—a kind word or a question about their health will go a long way toward motivating them and improving your score. The strategies and techniques available to you are endless.

The average person tends only to perform good enough; true successors always go that extra mile and step up as valuable employees. Don't be satisfied by being another person on the payroll; rather become a key personality on that payroll.

On a formal basis, organizations do provide opportunities for visibility; they can help map out clear developmental goals and support their staff in achieving them. On an informal basis, key organizational leaders need credible advocates who will support them and be seen as a motivating, inspirational personality by their own teams.

By becoming this personality, the door will open up informal networks to you and qualify you for promotion to the next level or a newly created role that you helped shape, as your organization can't afford to let you go. So instead of shopping for the perfect role, create the opportunities by stepping up and letting the perfect role come to you.

B*IO*

Mamta Parkhill is a versatile and successful project manager with over ten years of experience within the insurance, financial, and utility sectors. She holds BA and MSc degrees and a number of professional qualifications in project management, including Prince2 Practitioner. She is a keen world traveler, cooking enthusiast, and badminton player. To get some more tips on "stepping up" your game, visit her website at http://www.mamtaparkhill.com/.

87

Facts Tell, Stories Sell: How Much Are You Selling with *Your* Story?

Kathleen Watson

Storytelling is an activity that's seen in almost all cultures worldwide. Stories are powerful. They not only entertain but inform, teach, and sell—if they're well crafted.

Just what kinds of stories are most important for you as a business owner? The crucial ones fall into two main categories: internal and external. Internal stories are what you tell yourself—your so-called self-talk. You can think of them as your version of reality. These stories can and do cover an enormous range of topics. If you're a business owner, chances are you have stories about

- how you're different from your competitors
- why your product or service or brand is better
- what your customers value most about what you do
- the right way to promote your business
- why you do things the way you do
- why you've succeeded
- why you've failed

External stories, on the other hand, are the messages you share with the world at large, especially with your customers, prospects, business allies, and even your competition. The bulk of these messages have to do with

- your USP, or unique selling proposition
- how you solve problems and add value for your clients
- how you do business: your values, culture, mission, and so forth

"And," you may be asking yourself, "I care about all this . . . *why*?" The answer is simple: the right kind of internal story will facilitate your doing what's necessary for success, and the right kind of external story will get people excited about the outcomes you can create for them.

Successful businesspeople make it a habit to pay attention to their internal stories, knowing how those stories will either promote or hinder their success. When you listen to those negative stories that focus on the "horribleness" of necessary tasks, you hold yourself back. However, when your stories help you stay focused on desired outcomes rather than on what you have to go through to achieve those outcomes, your stories will propel you forward. In fact, this is a crucial attribute of successful business professionals: instead of letting any negative stories prevent them from doing what's necessary—things that may be difficult or unpleasant—they do those uncomfortable things anyway.

Here's an example: you tell a prospect that you'll send information to her then completely forget to do so. Once you realize your mistake, the stories kick in. Some will make it impossible to recover:

- "It's been so long since she asked for that . . . I'm too embarrassed to contact her now."
- "She probably wouldn't have bought from me anyway, so I bet I haven't missed out on anything really."
- "I'll pretend I sent it to her already. That way she'll think it was some problem on her end that kept her from getting my information."

Other, more productive stories will allow you to act with integrity, come from a place of power, and very possibly salvage the situation:

- "It's so unlike me to forget something like that. I'll see if I can hand-deliver the information to her and answer any questions about it on the spot."
- "I'll call to apologize for my mistake and offer such-and-such as a way of making up for my oversight."
- "Ouch! What a good reminder to improve my system for following up with inquiries. I'll put a priority on revamping my follow-up process."

Naturally, the best way to avoid all this storytelling is simply to deliver promised results in a timely manner. (In fact, performance coaches often use the word *stories* to describe the excuses we offer to explain a lack of results.)

Your external stories are crucial for success because, as successful business owners know, *it's not about you—it's all about your customer.* You must keep your marketing and promotional messages focused on how you make life easier for those customers. Your only real value to your clients is as a problem solver, a pain reliever, a provider of value. When you clearly articulate how you solve their problems, *that* is the story that your clients care about—and when you deliver on that story, your business thrives.

What should you look out for to ensure that you're not wasting resources on ineffective external stories? Following are some red flags:

- You drone on about product features without ever addressing what those features *do for* the consumer.
- You fall prey to geek-speak. (This applies to any professional, whether your expertise is in a technical field or not. Every profession has its own jargon.)
- You realize that you could plug a competitor's name into your message and it would still make sense. This is a clear indication that you lack a *unique* selling proposition, which puts your product or service at risk of becoming a commodity.
- You've failed to ask the questions uppermost in the consumer's mind: Why should I care about this? What's it going to get me? How does this solve my current dilemma?

On the other hand, following are some characteristics of powerful messages:

- They acknowledge that no one cares about your product's or service's features; instead, they focus on how that product or service *creates highly desirable outcomes.* In other words, the message clearly tells prospects how you give them what they want.
- They focus on the customer's pain, not on your offerings.
- They appeal to the reader's or listener's emotions first and intellect second. This is important because consumers buy emotionally then justify rational-ly. Appealing to the gut first, then ensuring that the brain is happy, is a very powerful approach.

Consider this example: a copywriting duo talks about how one principal is a published author and the other a popular blogger; how the principals have over sixty years of combined experience in sales and marketing; how they've worked together for over eight years; and how they combine complementary writing styles and perspectives to create a compelling finished product.

Yawn.

How does any of this address a prospect's pain? The answer is that it doesn't! These attributes of the writing team may well appeal to the prospect's brain, but talking about them totally fails to engage the prospect's emotions.

Feel what a difference it makes for the copywriting duo to proclaim, "You have a great story. You deserve great storytellers. Our job is to get more prospects more excited about what you do so they practically *hurl* themselves into your sales funnel." Might this have just a bit more emotional impact than a litany of features?

Facts tell, and stories sell—*if* the stories you tell yourself and your prospects are well crafted and intentionally designed to get the results you and your prospect value.

Some business professionals are willing to work on both their internal and external stories; some aren't. Struggling businesspeople would rather be comfortable than successful; successful ones are willing to sacrifice comfort for results. So here's a question for you: based on your stories, into which category do *you* fall?

BIO

Kathleen Watson, MBA, is a business networking mentor. She partners with her clients to create blueprints that enable them to stop wasting money and networking opportunities, share their value with more clarity and confidence, and better serve their ideal clients. The founder and principal of Client Connections, she is also the author of *Net Profit: Business Networking without the Nerves.* Learn more at http://www.yourclientconnection.com/.

88

The Critical Path to a Great Career

⁂

Kim Seeling Smith

Have you ever wondered why some capable and talented people seem to effortlessly achieve their career goals, while other, equally capable and talented people seem to plateau or even senselessly slide backward as they near their goals?

I have—and I have spent the last sixteen years studying the differences between these two groups of people, first as a recruiter, then as an executive and career coach, trainer, and speaker. What I discovered was that it is not talent, ability, education, personality, political astuteness, or even luck that determines your professional fate.

Whether your goal is to rise to the top of your company, grow a thriving business, manage your career around family, or simply do meaningful work with interesting people in interesting places, your ability to realize your goal will almost certainly be ensured by following the four steps on the Critical Path to a Great Career.

Step 1: Set Your Course

I worked with thousands of people during my fifteen years as a recruiter, and one thing constantly surprised me: the lack of focus that people put on planning their professional lives. It's astounding! Your career is the biggest part of your life outside of your family. However, I estimate that only about 5 percent of the over five thousand candidates whom I interviewed knew where they were headed professionally. Most of them simply walked through the doors that were opened.

The saddest part about this is seeing very capable and talented people walk through doors through which they should not have gone. These are the people who plateau in their careers. Worse still, they may actually start to slide backward as they reach higher and higher levels. Then there are the people who don't walk through the doors that might have led them to greater opportunity, satisfaction, and fulfillment in their professional lives (not to mention in their personal lives). Why does this happen? Because they have not been taught how to manage their careers: how to think strategically about where they are going and how to get there!

The first and most important step on the Critical Path to a Great Career is to set your course. It is essential to determine where you are heading in the next three to five years.

I find that most people simply focus on their next job because they have become unhappy where they are or want additional opportunity or more responsibility. They spend a lot of time trying to decide between two or more immediate opportunities without asking themselves the bigger questions, such as who do I want to be? Where do I want to go? What do I want to accomplish? Questions like these will help you determine how your professional life will support your personal goals. This is a bit like planning a vacation and spending more time trying to decide whether to fly, drive, or take the train to your destination, without asking yourself where you want to go.

Once you've asked yourself the bigger questions and decided on your three- to five-year goals, it's time to assess where you are and look at the gap between there and where you want to go. What skills, abilities, and experiences do you need to mind that gap? Make a plan to get those, and you will be well on your way.

Step 2: Make Your Mark

The next step on the Critical Path to a Great Career is to make your mark. Figure out what your unique value proposition is and exploit that. What makes you unique? How can you apply your uniqueness to your current role?

I'm not talking rocket science here. Maybe you are good at influencing people and energizing them for a common cause. Maybe you can translate technical speak into laymen's terms. Maybe you can see patterns in a jumble of information and can clearly articulate a way forward. Or maybe you have laserlike focus and persistence and are a machine at getting things done.

Why is this important? Because it will allow you to express yourself in your own way, which will lead to great job satisfaction and engagement at work as well as an entire career in which you are doing what you love. And as a by-product, it will make you indispensable to your employer and infinitely more employable throughout your entire career.

Step 3: Master Your Skills

The skills that I'm talking about here actually fall into three categories: career transition skills, job search skills, and the four critical, nontechnical skills that everyone, regardless of function, must master to continue to climb the career ladder.

First, let's consider career transition skills: these are the strategies you need to master to get noticed and to continuously set yourself up for promotion. They also encompass mastering the technical skills you need to keep your options open as you climb the career ladder.

Secondly, consider job search skills. Most people rely on recruiters to find their next jobs. Good recruiters are worth their weight in gold, but even the best recruiters only place between 1 in 8 and 1 in 10 people. See the problem? To really manage your career, you will need to learn how to create a value statement (your thirty-second elevator pitch), write a killer résumé (although, if you truly understand and live your unique value proposition, you will never need a résumé again), and definitely learn how to network (virtually and in real life) and, potentially, how to approach companies directly.

Then there are the four critical, nontechnical (i.e., not related to your particular function or role) skills. My experience in working with thousands of people taught me that everyone, and I mean everyone, needs to become proficient at these four skills to maintain an upward career trajectory throughout his or her life. The four skills include technology (as it relates to your function), communication skills, managerial skills (people, time, resources, etc.) and most important, the ability to think strategically and solve problems.

Step 4: Condition Resilience

Every career will have setbacks, times during which things don't go according to plan or happen as quickly as you'd like. Companies are bought and sold, go out of business, and relocate. Market conditions change. Your own personal circumstances change.

Your ability to pick yourself up and dust yourself off will, in many cases, be the ultimate test for how high you can climb or how happy and fulfilled you will be, both personally and professionally. It's therefore essential to be able to condition resilience. This isn't about keeping a positive attitude, it's about having a robust set of psychological strategies to be able to handle anything that comes your way.

Those are the four steps on the Critical Path to a Great Career. If you follow them, I guarantee that not only will you be able to accomplish all your professional goals but your professional goals will support your personal goals, and you will truly live a life you love.

<u>Bio</u>

Kim Seeling Smith is an international speaker, trainer and author on Career Management and Employee Retention issues after having spent 15 years as a recruiter in the United States, Australia and New Zealand. During that time she worked with thousands of individuals and studied the differences between those capable and talented people who successfully reach their career goals and those equally capable and talented people who plateau or senselessly slide backwards as they near them. Kim shares these distinctions with her clients in her *Critical Path* series of programs, helping them to reach their personal and professional goals. Visit her online at http://www.MyCriticalPath.com/.

89

Managing the Moment

❦

Relly Nadler

Careers can be advanced or destroyed in moments. In an interview, you are asked a challenging question, and your interviewers are hanging on your every word. A colleague in a meeting is upset with you and begins to call you out. A direct report makes a major mistake with your best client. Your responses in these moments are examples of your emotional intelligence and especially your emotional self-control. Top 10 percent performers excel in these moments, and their careers advance because of it. What follows is an explanation of this competency along with examples of the stress–EQ–IQ interrelationship and a tool to help manage these moments.

What Is the Emotional Self-Control Competency?

Emotional self-control is demonstrated by a leader being able to manage impulsive and/or distressing feelings. Leaders who are competent in emotional self-control are able to stay composed, calm, and unflappable in stressful situations, regardless of the environment. They have control of their emotions versus their emotions controlling them. Leaders with emotional self-control think clearly while under pressure. Their IQ and executive functioning stay intact. One reason why emotional self-control is so critical is that it is fragile and thus can be lost in a second, with devastating effects.

Emotional Intelligence Research Examples

Case studies of wrecked careers were examined by a consulting firm in the course of testing 4,265 people from all levels in the organizations studied. These employees all had a lack of impulse control, with little ability to delay gratification.

Stress, EQ, and EI

Henry Thompson has been studying the effects of stress on EQ and IQ since the early 1980s. In one study, he exposed people to the stress of a baby crying and found that the higher the stress, the less emotionally intelligent participants behaved. Thompson did another study with sixty-two participants, taking their EQ under normal and simulated "stressed out" mind-set conditions. He found that the stressed-out mind-set participants scored twenty points less than the normal participants. This was one standard deviation less than the norm. These results suggest that "stress may reduce the leaders' access to his or her full EI ability."

When stress is high, as it is in most organizations, it is critical that the leader be able to manage his or her stress as well as the team's. Thompson has stated that a "high stress environment would be expected to restrict leaders' access to their full EQ and IQ potential."

We have all had the experience of doing something in the heat of the moment that we regretted later. We ended up saying, "How could I do that, what could I have possibly been thinking?" Well, in reality, we weren't thinking clearly; we were overwhelmed with an emotional reaction. We were *hijacked*.

The *amygdala hijack* is a term coined in Daniel Goleman's *Emotional Intelligence,* his first book on the subject. The amygdala is the emotional part of the brain and regulates the fight-or-flight response. When threatened, it can respond irrationally. A rush of stress hormones floods the body before the prefrontal cortex (PFC) can mediate this reaction. The PFC regulates executive functioning, which includes understanding, deciding, recalling, memorizing, and inhibiting. It is essential for thinking things through versus being on autopilot. The PFC is relatively slow in making decisions (one hundred milliseconds), whereas the amygdala is quick (fifteen milliseconds). This means we feel before we think! The amygdala can override the PFC with uncontrolled automatic responses.

Joe Wilson: "You Lie" Outburst

Representative Joe Wilson, the GOP congressman from South Carolina, shocked many observers when he shouted, "You lie!" after the president denied that health care legislation would provide free coverage for illegal immigrants in a 2009 speech.

After the speech, Senator John McCain of Arizona, the Republican presidential candidate last year, called Wilson's outburst "totally disrespectful" and told CNN's *Larry King Live* that there was "no place for it in that setting or any other." "It was crude and disrespectful," said Senate Majority Whip Dick Durbin, a Democrat from Illinois. "I think the person who said it will pay a price."

Wilson said his outburst wasn't planned, again another example of a hijack that he wasn't able manage. "It was spontaneous," Wilson said. These few seconds of lack of emotional self-control and not thinking have defined his career and possibly arrested it.

Self-Management: How to Regain Your IQ Points

The good news is that this loss of IQ points is temporary. Self-management is a leader's ability to be aware of what he or she is experiencing as another data set of information and to be able to accept, manage, and adjust his or her emotions. These emotions are just as important as our thoughts, if not more, given their power to overwhelm us.

The Emotional Audit

A leadership tool that can help with both self-awareness and self-management is called the *emotional audit*. It is designed to ask strategic questions—and that can change the focus when a person is emotionally charged or about to get hijacked. When you are counting to ten to calm down, ask these questions to better direct your brain's thinking.

This audit is helpful, especially if you are feeling triggered by someone or something. Wait five seconds until you get an answer to each question. To build your self-awareness and self-management, use the audit numerous times during the day. You may notice certain patterns you have to what triggers you, how you are feeling, and how you get in your own way.

Following are the strategic questions and hypothesized brain components that may be accessed with these questions in order. The goal is to refocus activity away from the amygdala and light up other areas of the brain to gain more cognitive control and give you constructive options and direction. The first two questions access and label your thoughts and emotions. The third question makes conscious your intentions. The fourth question evaluates your actions in line with your intentions. Patterns of how you get in your own way may emerge. The last question takes in all this new conscious data and allows you to better direct your brain and actions toward the goals you want to achieve.

The more you practice the emotional audit, the easier it will become, and you will see patterns emerging. I imagine you will get the same two or three answers to questions 1 to 4. This acute awareness will give you more information, control, and self-management to generate better solutions with question 5. Making a few subtle changes can move you into the top 10 percent of performance:

- *What am I thinking?* (basal ganglia—integrates feelings, thoughts, and movements)
- *What am I feeling?* (basal ganglia—integrates feelings, thoughts, and movements; temporal lobes—emotional stability, name it to tame it, labeling affect)
- *What do I want now?* (cerebellum—executive functions connecting to PFC, cognitive integration)
- *How am I getting in my own way?* (PFC—learning from mistakes)
- *What do I need to do differently now?* (PFC—the boss supervision of life, executive functioning, planning, goal setting, insight; anterior cingulate gyrus—the brain's gear shifter, sees options, goes from idea to idea)

Taking time to pause and ask these strategic questions can reengage your PFC, bringing back your IQ points and helping to advance your career versus having the moment destroy it.

BIO

Dr. Relly Nadler is a licensed psychologist, executive coach, corporate trainer, and author. His books, *Leading with Emotional Intelligence, Leaders' Playbook: How to Apply Emotional Intelligence—Keys to Great Leadership,* and *Leadership Keys Field Guide,* are full of emotional intelligence (EI) secrets, strategies, tools, and profiles of leaders. Relly has coached CEOs, presidents, and their staffs and has developed and delivered innovative leadership programs and facilitated team trainings for Fortune 100 companies. He is recognized around the world for his expertise in applying EI for top performance. Go to http://www.truenorthleadership.com/ for more information and free EI secrets.

90

Creating a Stress-Free Career Journey

Ann N. Gatty

Is there such a thing as a stress-free career path? Probably not, but at least we should try to minimize stress while working as much as we can. It is a fact that most of us have to work to pay the bills. We invest a lot of our time making a living, so doesn't it make sense that if we are going to invest so much of our precious time earning money, we try to find work we enjoy? Can a person develop a life that is fulfilling of professional ambitions, personal enjoyment, and family connections? Following is a list of strategies to build a successful and stress-free career.

1. Know thyself. You really cannot know what type of career to choose until you take an honest look at yourself. Identify the strengths that you can bring to a job, the weaknesses that need to be improved, and your genuine interests. Be honest with who you are. As you set your goals in life, make certain that they are *your* goals, which you are trying to accomplish for your own self-worth, not for family members, friends, or colleagues. Choose a career because it is the right fit with your personality and a career in which you believe. There is nothing worse than working in a job you hate. Be able to identify your competencies knowledge-wise; the skills that you use with job performances; and the abilities you can add to your organization. This unique combination that you possess is your competitive edge and indicates why an employer should hire you.

2. Know your passion. As you consider a career path, ask yourself what you love to do. Where is the passion in your life? Have you considered how you can make money pursuing this passion? When you identify what you really love to do, then pursuing the passion will bring you the most satisfaction and allow you to stick with the learning curve and the ensuing tedium without losing your enthusiasm. Remember that doing exceptionally well is the result of obsessively focusing on one thing and getting passionate and inspired by it. Pursuing your passion means that you will shine—and people will notice. They will notice competency, self-confidence, and a smile.

3. Enjoy the journey. Learn from the people you meet and the experiences that occur. Learning is a lifetime activity. It never stops. With your career path, strive to enjoy the process, and use all these components to enrich your perspective and continue toward your goal. Find the benefits in the work you are doing *now* that can make positive contributions moving you forward. Be optimistic and keep looking ahead. Change the path if you need to, but keep a forward perspective. Know when to move on and when to stay and keep your head up, looking forward. The experience needs to be enjoyed.

4. Play nice. As you keep moving up in your career path, take care of the people behind you. Let them have the benefit of what you have learned. Help women climbing below you on the corporate ladder. Give back to those who helped you. Don't make enemies. You may need them and never know where they will end up in their career paths. It is much better to work together to accomplish goals. And this work strategy doesn't just apply to the military. It applies to all facets of life. This is a good networking tactic. People notice whom they can trust and on whom they can rely to get their work done.

5. Read. Yes, you need to read and read different types of news and different types of books. If you read the *New York Times,* then read the *Wall Street Journal.* Get different perspectives. Know what is happening in the world around you. The more you read, the more you will shape your personality—and the more interesting you will become to your colleagues.

6. Keep a portfolio of your work. Put aside materials that you have produced reflecting relevant skills and accomplishments. These can be work assignments that you have produced in various phases of your career or projects that are reflective of different job capacities. Choose about five examples of your very best work that make you proud. Keep these works as a reminder to yourself about what types of assignments and tasks you prefer. Women tend to downplay their accomplishments and are not boastful by nature, so having concrete reminders is helpful for your self-confidence and will allow you to sell your capabilities to future employers when job interviews come along down the road.

7. Develop a game plan. What is your dream? I have talked about the journey, but really, a journey is only as good as the plan that creates it. Your plan should provide a sense of direction but leave your doors of opportunity open so that you can make changes when appropriate. Your career plan is developed with a sketch of information as you start, and then it becomes more detailed as you learn and experience more. You become more knowledgeable, and your expertise actually comes from your many contributing experiences. Yes, it is OK to fail, as long as you learn from it. As a matter of fact, I don't know anyone who has not failed at one point or another when building a career. Keep your eyes on the prize, and don't lose track of the big picture.

8. Your life is not always in balance. Work, family, community, and you are never in balance. Sometimes there is a trade-off. I have found that you cannot wait for time to be exactly right to make a decision. You are always living in the present, not waiting for some future event to occur. Emotions can only be felt in the present. Past is a memory and future is unpredictable. So live now, listen to others, and know who you are and what you want to do. Then do it.

BIO

Ann N. Gatty, PhD, is a life coach infopreneur, author, and organizational strategist. She has taught in classrooms and organizational training sessions and works as a life coach for professional and personal development. Dr. Gatty has developed curricula for college courses, organizational training, and personal development. She finds a continuous need among women, of all walks of life, to find a life balance between professional goals and personal responsibilities. Her website, http://www.stress-management-4-women.com/, offers stress-management strategies, life skill development, and a means of finding your true passion in life. She has authored *Discovering God's Recipe for a Healthy Body, Heart, and Soul.*

Success and Motivation: Understanding the Relationship

❧

Valerie Parson

People from all walks of life strive to obtain so-called success. For some, achieving success is almost as easy as breathing, while it seems to be the most elusive state to achieve for others. But what does success really mean? Why are people struggling just to consider themselves successful? What are the key factors that would make success an attainable state? If there were an easy way or a shortcut to achieve success, what would it be?

These are just some of the thoughts that play around the heads of those whose main aspiration in life is to attain a social or financial standing at which things are more comfortable and easier to get. This article will discuss what success is and the key factors that contribute to its fulfillment.

What Is Success?

The meaning of *success* varies from one person to another, depending on the individual's personal goals and aspirations. As an example, if a person's greatest aspiration is to land a corporate job for which he has been aiming, getting that sought-after career spot would mean success for him.

To define what success is for you, you should try to reflect and look into the depths of your being because only you can define what success will be for you. For others, success means gaining material wealth, while for some, success is about being happy and contented with what they have, with where they are, and with whom they are with. If what you have aspired to is already in the palm of your hand and you intend to stop, settle with it, and maintain that contented and calm feeling, then perhaps you can consider yourself successful.

The Elements of Success

There are several ways to achieve success, but according to some of the most successful individuals, success is easier to realize when it is used with the following guiding principles:

- **Know yourself.** What do you really want? How do you want your life to go? Know your core values and personal targets, and work your way toward achieving them. You might not get it the first time, or you may commit mistakes along the way, but keep going. Be comfortable with your choices, and forgive yourself for your mistakes. Learn the lessons of the past, and look forward to a positive future.
- **Set your goals.** Write down what you intend to achieve, and work for it. By writing down your aspirations, you will see that your life has more direction because your goals are clear and you are fully aware of the path you have taken and where you are headed.
- **Get a support system.** Success can hardly be obtained if you try to climb the ladder on your own. Obviously, things will be a lot easier if you have people behind and ahead of you who will give you a nudge when you are getting slow or who will advise you to slow down when you are getting too fast.
- **Choose your path.** Everybody needs something to hold on to, whether a religious belief, an ideology, or a political philosophy. Whatever it is, know what your belief is, and be guided by it in your journey toward success.
- **Be practical.** You should understand that you cannot reach your goals with pure theory. Use modern technology and communication tools to get what you want and to reach the intended destination that will define your meaning of success.
- **Have self-discipline.** Discipline means not wasting time. It means waking up when it's time to prepare for work and going home to attend to other important things when it's time to do so. It's about accomplishing things that can be done today and not putting them off for tomorrow.

What Is Motivation?

The definition of *motivation* is simple. Motivations are those things that drive a person to obtain his or her goals and ultimately achieve success. Just like success, motivation also comes in different forms. Whereas some feel motivated to work to meet their families' needs, others are motivated to work hard for the comforts and financial gains they will obtain. In other words, motivation is what compels you to do things. It is your driving force. It is what fuels your passion and pushes you toward your end goal. You must determine your purpose and have a specific target to get yourself moving; otherwise you won't see why you should push yourself to the limit.

The Motivated Individual

How will you know that you are a motivated person? What do you usually do when you encounter problems while you are working really hard for the fulfillment of your dreams? Do you wallow in frustration or strive harder to conquer the challenge? A motivated person is one who sees obstacles as opportunities to work harder and be better to achieve his or her targets. A motivated individual is a happier person who sees life with zest and passion and will do everything to achieve his or her goals, positive that, in the end, he or she will attain his or her goals while maintaining enthusiasm along the way.

Understanding the Relationship

Motivation and success are two different things with two different meanings, but they are greatly interrelated. You cannot be successful without being motivated, and motivation will be deemed futile if it did not gain success as an end result. Although motivation and success are two different things, they have one important key element: passion. Being motivated means having a burning passion that you carry with you while reaching for your dreams, and passion is what you need to appreciate and maintain your success in life. In other words, the relationship of motivation and success is a cycle. You need motivation to achieve success, and when you achieve your idea of success, you need motivation to continue experiencing that successful state.

Summary

The idea of success and what motivates individuals to attain what they want in life may vary from one individual to another, but at the end of the day, you will know that you are successful when you feel at ease with the choices you have made and when what you have—all the accomplishments, your personal relationships, and your career—provides you an avenue to continually express your passion in life and fulfill your dreams as creatively as possible.

Whatever you do—whether you are making millions out of a multinational company or are doing volunteer work for the needy—what counts is whether you can sleep at night knowing that you made the right decisions and the right choices in life. What matters is not where you are right now and where you will be when compared with others but rather whether you are contented with where you are, whether you have that satisfying feeling that you would not want to be in any other place. Success is about being happy and contented with what became from your decisions in life.

B<small>IO</small>

Valerie Parson is a personal development coach and author of an e-book titled *Emotional Intelligence*. In addition, Ms. Parson is the owner of a self-improvement website, "Personal Development Worksheets" (http://www.personaldevelopmentworksheets.com/). Her website provides information to assist those who are on a journey to improve their personal development in developing positive time management skills and to encourage them on their course of self-improvement. In her free time, she enjoys reading and playing tennis. Hamilton, Bermuda, is her home.

Look, Listen, Learn, and Love Your Way to a Successful Career

❦

Tiffany Crenshaw

Individuals who are happy and successful in their careers have similar qualities. They look for opportunity, listen to others, thirst to learn, and love what they do. Here's how you, too, can look, listen, learn, and love your way to a successful career.

Look for opportunity in everything, including triumphs and setbacks. If you give a presentation at work and receive rave reviews, why not explore other speaking opportunities within and outside your company? If you are the go-to person in your office for technology problems, is there a position for you within your company's IT department? Or perhaps with a software company specific to your industry? If your company is selling off or dissolving your division, is there an opportunity to start your own business to meet the needs of customers who will be affected? Don't let opportunities pass you by unnoticed—identify what opportunities are in your path, consider how you can approach them, and then take action. One of my favorite mantras is "the greatest risk you will ever take is the risk of regret." How many opportunities have you let slip by because you didn't notice them, didn't know what to do with them, or were afraid to act on them?

Listen to those around you. It's a given that you can enhance your career with lessons learned from others. Yes, conferences, workshops, classes, speakers, podcasts, and webcasts are great ways to learn from others. But tuning in to everyday people is just as effective, more affordable, and sometimes a more pleasant experience. Listen to the success and failure stories of those in your own network: friends, family, colleagues, superiors, neighbors, and mentors. What opportunities did they seize? Ask for their advice about a particular situation, or ask them for a critique of you. Listen thoughtfully to their responses, even if you don't agree. Peer groups are one of my favorite places to listen and learn. Seek out other professionals in your field to meet with periodically over dinner or for overnight retreats to share successes and discuss issues with which you struggle. The advice you give and get back will be invaluable.

Learn from mistakes. Early in my career, I was drawn to successful employers, but I had a knack for selecting personalities who had contentious relationships with team members, customers, and vendors and who ran very high-stress, deadline-oriented companies. I wouldn't trade these experiences for anything. They made me who I am today, and I learned more from their flaws than I ever did in a classroom, conference, or training session. Purposefully tuning in to the way they conducted themselves professionally and seeing the results in action helped me set my own standards for how a company should operate. As a result, our company's practices are vastly different from my former employers' practices, and those practices work well for us. Yes, I've made plenty of my own mistakes, and you will, too. But it's what we do with those mistakes that can elevate our careers.

Love what you do. Your work hours take up far too much of the day to be doing something you don't love. And believe me, I know what it is like to love a job, and I know what it is like to hate a job. I spent the first five years of my career counting down the minutes until five o'clock, the signal to break free from my cubicle prison—and then I found recruiting. Most days, I truly look forward to getting into the office. Rarely do I think twice about working long hours that may consume evenings and weekends, because for me, it's a passion. If you don't love what you do, you need to ask yourself two questions: how content am I with my current career? and if I were to make a career change, what three things have to be in my next job or career to take it seriously? Reflect on your answers to these questions, and then seek out career options that align. The result should be career contentedness, at the very least, and passion for your career, at the very best.

If you are committed to enhancing your career, I urge you to ignite your career senses, including your common sense, by looking for opportunity, listening to others, learning constantly, and loving what you do. When ignited, you'll find career happiness and success.

<u>Bio</u>

As chief development officer and cofounder of CareerMoxie, Tiffany uses her nurturing approach to coach and guide candidates throughout the job interview process and their careers. Beginning with her own career in advertising, she moved into recruiting following an unfavorable experience with a headhunter who piqued her interest in the industry. Since then, she has dedicated the past thirteen years to the profession. She is president and founder of Intellect Resources, a search firm specializing in health care IT. A graduate of Peace College and UNC, Tiffany now lives in Greensboro with her husband, two children, and the family golden retriever. Visit http://www.linkedin.com/in/tiffanycrenshaw/.

93

The Telephone Interview

❧～❧

Lauren Kurbatoff

The purpose of the initial telephone interview is to try to screen you out. Though this first interview will tend to be more high level than to test detailed technical professional skills, this twenty- to thirty-minute interview has a distinct purpose—and it is not to automatically assign you a telephone interview with the hiring authority or to set up a face-to-face interview.

Usually a representative from the human resources department will be making the first call to you. This individual will be looking for you to answer a lot of why questions: why are you interested in making an employment change? Why did you leave each of your places of employment? Why are you interested in working for the company? Why this position? Other pertinent questions to anticipate will be about salary, relocation, personality and cultural fit, and what you view as your greatest strength and biggest weakness.

Think of the telephone interview as verbal sumo wrestling. The objective is simple: have a lively and articulate exchange with the interviewer so you can advance to the next round.

Prepare before your interview. Complete due diligence on the company, gather salary information for the position, get your résumé and paperwork in order, and prepare answers to the expected questions—writing answers to the why questions in the margins of your résumé.

During the interview, have a copy of your résumé in front of you. If you are being represented by a recruiter, make sure you are working off the same copy the recruiter sent to the company. The résumé will keep you from hesitating through the interview on such things as dates from a job you held ten years ago.

When you answer the phone and your interview is beginning, move forward and sit on the edge of your seat. Really, please do so. You will be more engaged and focused when your body posture is alert.

If you are talking on a cell phone, stay in a good reception area. Poor phone reception, or, even worse, a dropped call, will break the flow of an interview.

While you are speaking, smile at different points in the conversation. The physical act of smiling animates and warms the voice naturally and keeps you from falling into a monotone speech pattern. Personality and cultural fit are important within a company. An inviting voice will leave a positive impression.

Do not smoke.

Stay germane to the questions asked by your interviewer. If you are asked what time it is, tell her the time and not how to build a watch. It is natural to want to expound on your knowledge, but refrain from long-winded answers. That doesn't mean your responses should be short and clipped. Find the right balance. Once you answer a question, stop. No more filler words. No rambling. Don't feel pressured to fill the silence. Let the interviewer pick up the lead.

When you are being interviewed, and this is true for all interviews, use *no negatives*. Your glass is not only half full but overflowing.

You will be asked why you left each of your previous employers. You must answer without hesitation. Even if you were terminated by an employer, answer honestly, succinctly, and move on.

When asked why you're interested in a position with the company, use the opportunity to answer several things at once. First, answer the why question in a positive light. Second, show that you're sincerely ready to accept a new job with the company and are not wasting their time. Third, you can showcase your due diligence homework on the company and that you know something about it.

Now, putting it all together, consider the following:

> interviewer: I see you're a department manager at Big Widgets. They're larger than us. Our open position is for a widget production manager on the night shift. Why would you want to leave your current company? And would working nights be an issue for you?
>
> you, *as your mind conjures up the troll to whom you report and how he'll remain in his position until he retires; having collected your thoughts (no*

negatives), you smile and answer: I have worked at Big Widgets for six years and have enjoyed several promotions within the company, gaining expertise in several operational departments. The person to whom I report is locked into his position, and continued promotional opportunities appear limited. I'm intrigued by the night shift assignment and look at this as an opportunity to pull all of my previous departmental responsibilities into play at once, functioning as the lead manager at night. The quality of your company's products is highly rated, and your company's last quarter growth exceeded that of Big Widgets. I find a smaller company has its advantages; bigger isn't always better. I believe I could be challenged at your company and at the same time make a positive impact on your production runs.

The question of will you relocate for a position knocks candidates out all the time. Even if the locale is not your first choice, you must, without vacillating, answer that relocating is not an issue. Make it clear that your career comes first.

The topic of salary will come up in the conversation. It is best to let the interviewer broach the subject first. Companies have a clearly defined salary range for each position. There is a low, mid-point, and maximum assigned to the position for which you are interviewing. Usually, an employer will want to hire at the mid-point.

If you are working with a good recruiter, you will know the salary range offered. If not, a quick Google search for the salary base of your position within your industry and geographic area will provide you a range within which to work.

Remain flexible at this early stage when asked about salary expectations. Firm figures can be negotiated at the offer stage. If you are being represented by a recruiter, your answer can reiterate that the recruiter presented the salary parameters to you and that you find it to be an acceptable range.

If you are representing yourself, try the following: "I'm assuming your organization has a salary range for this position. Based on the industry standard, I'm confident a mutually agreeable compensation package can be reached."

Shy away from a response that salary is not important and that you are more interested in the job. Money is always important. To say otherwise often sounds insincere.

When the interviewer asks if you have any questions for him or her, ask insightful ones gleaned from your earlier due diligence on the company. Common questions include the following: Why is the position open? How long has it been open? What key strengths are you looking to find in the right candidate? This last one is important—if you have those key strengths, make sure you mention them.

If you realize you didn't answer an earlier question correctly or fully, and Klaxon bells are going off in your mind that you blew it, don't panic. When appropriate, readdress the issue by stating that earlier you said something and want to correct (add to) your statement. The important thing is to correct the mistake during the call while you still have the chance.

Still interested at the end of the call? Let the interviewer know you want the job. In closing, offer, "I want to conclude by saying that my interest in this position is *even greater* than when we started this conversation."

Don't let yourself get knocked out of contention by the telephone interview. With thorough preparation completed before the event, ready answers articulated smoothly throughout, and a strong concluding reaffirmation of your interest in pursuing the job, you should gain access to the next round.

<u>BIO</u>

Lauren Kurbatoff is the cofounder of Black Leopard Inc. executive search agency, which specializes in nationwide recruitment and placement services for the food processing industry. Lauren possesses twenty years of experience as a recruiter serving the staffing needs of Fortune 500 clients. If you have an employment-related question, please feel free to e-mail Lauren at blackleopardinc@aol.com. Black Leopard Inc. can be reached at http://www.blackleopard.com/ or via telephone at (800) 360-4191.

94

THE UNKNOWN

Fearlessly Charging into the Unknown

The Ancient Wisdom of Life

❧

Sandy Paris

In the midst of difficult times, the best way to enhance a career is to become the champion of your life by fearlessly charging into the unknown. The unknown holds the ancient truths to success, especially in trying times. When we take charge of our lives, we become a lighthouse of peace, confidence, success, and tranquility.

When I was enhancing my business, surrender was the only key that pushed fear aside and replaced it with hope, courage, and an adventuresome spirit. Building unlimited bountifulness in a career in challenging times may be easier than you could ever imagine if you wade into the ancient wisdom pool. Within the hollows of the unknown lies ancient wisdom that has been hidden from the masses. We were all born with the inner seeds of success, health, and happiness. However, most of these precious seeds are lying dormant within us.

So what do we do? We open the door to courage and fearlessly charge into the unknown and discover the ancient truths that are our birthright. The following techniques made it happen for me:

1. I faced my fear and embraced joy, excitement, and adventure.

2. I opened my heart to creativity, which is very powerful yet simple to use.

3. I opened my invisible side, my soul, and my thought pictures came alive.

4. I used these detailed pictures to form the career of which I was dreaming.

5. Each night, I took this vision into my dream state like a treasure hunt.

6. Every morning, noon, and night, in contemplation, I gave gratitude to the Source of all life.

How to Attract to Yourself the Things You Desire

The power within you which enables you to form a thought-picture is the starting point of all there is. In its original state it is the undifferentiated formless substance of life. Your thought-picture makes the model, so to say, into which this formless substance takes shape.
—Genevieve Behrend, *Your Invisible Power*

Today I know that I cannot control the ocean tides. I can only go with the flow. . . . When I struggle and try to organize the Atlantic to my specifications, I sink. If I flail and thrash and growl and grumble, I go under. But if I let go and float, I am born aloft.
—Marie Shtilkind

A very short time after I began to use this technique, I received an e-mail out of the blue from a book reviewer at Amazon who liked my books. He told me that David Riklan had asked him if he knew of any great writers who would like to write a chapter for his book *101 Great Ways to Improve Your Life,* volume 2. This editor then said that I should contact David and say that he had referred me to him.

Through this connection, I became classified as an expert with the likes of the Dalai Lama and Wayne Dyer, among others, on Self Growth.com, the largest self-help company on the Web. It also placed me as a coauthor with all the other famous authors in the book.

This bold, inspired journey into the unknown, working in harmony with the Source of all life, catapulted my business to heights beyond my wildest imagination. These simple ancient techniques that I use are not commonly taught here on earth. The Source of all life reveals to us this invisible power, containing hidden treasures and gifts only available to the true seeker.

Joy, success, profits, and personal dreams are within each of us, not outside of us. These are the powerful secrets hidden within the toolbox of our hearts. Using this toolbox can transform our lives in the blink of an eye.

The toolbox is the key to physical and spiritual liberation hidden in simplicity. However, with the passing of time, ancient truth has been hidden because of our vastly complicated world! Complication hides the treasures of success.

Each and every day, 99 percent of people wake up and greet life from the *effect* side of duality. The magnitude of the effect of such an influence is overwhelming. Therefore we see its devastating effects in our everyday lives as wars, tornados, hurricanes, floods, fear, anger, sickness, job loss, recession, and depression.

However, this leaves an opening for open-hearted people like you. It can enhance your career and open doors for people crying out for help.

Most modern-day self-help teachings state that using positive energy is the way to create the world you want. However, this is a form of manipulation of the original creative force of Wholeness. We mistakenly try to separate the Wholeness of pure spiritual unchanging energy into duality. This is working from "My Will Be Done."

Pure Spiritual unchanging energy comes from "Thy Will Be Done," where we gain love, guidance, and protection from the Source through the toolbox of our hearts. Unfortunately, our educational system does not teach us the hidden ancient wisdom of unlimited bountifulness. Even in the university of hard knocks, it takes many lifetimes of lessons before we accept the treasures that are our birthright: physical and spiritual freedom.

Enhancing Your Career from a World of Wholeness

Humanity is born with the gift of Divine Imagination through our thought pictures. If we choose them carefully for the good of the Whole, then our dreams can become reality. *Moral and ethical values are essential! Love for all life is essential! Love for ourselves is essential!* That makes a great recipe for creating a career from the world of Wholeness—a beautiful career that can last for eternity.

The Maybury laws ensure a healthy career. Richard Maybury bases his work on common law, namely,

1. Do all you have agreed to do.

2. Do not encroach on other persons or their property.

3. Ancient Wisdom replaces the usual filler, fluff, and fancy dance with purity!

- **Spiritual energy.** An endless supply of energy makes up the universe and everything within it. There never has been nor will there ever be a shortage of unlimited bountifulness and wholeness created by the Source of all life.
- **Pure energy.** Pure energy comes from an unchanging world of Wholeness. This energy created everything in these physical, material worlds through Light and Sound. This includes everything we see and hear.
- **Secondary energy.** When pure energy enters the physical universe, it splits from its Whole, pure state into its changing state of positive and negative energy. Now it has become secondary energy. This transformation affords the opportunity to learn the lessons that we came back to earth to learn, mainly, about divine love. We create everything in our personal, physical

lives through our words, thoughts, and deeds. There are no victims! This division of energy sets up a stage for the constant battleground between the two conflicting energies to keep us infatuated with material distractions.

Fearlessly charging into the unknown, through the ancient wisdom of life, opens doors to the mysteries of the invisible world. There we can manifest unlimited possibilities in everyday life. May the blessings be.

BIO

Sandy Paris is a lover of life. She goes beyond traditional self-help teachings and charges fearlessly into the ancient wisdom of the unknown. She has devoted thirty-nine years of tireless service to people around the world who have declared that their lives have been transformed by her keynote speaking engagements and books. She has spent her entire life living the principles she shares with others. She is also a coauthor with Jack Canfield, Alan Cohen, Richard Carlson, and John Gray. Sandy Paris has been classified as an inspirational expert with the likes of the Dalai Lama and Wayne Dyer. Contact her online at http://www.sandyparis.com/ or e-mail sandyparis@mac.com.

95

The Good News Is, It's All in Your Head

≈⌒≈

Elizabeth Brown

Did you know that the average person has sixty thousand thoughts per day? We can't possibly be aware of every one of our thoughts as most of them wiz through our minds so rapidly. The truth is that our thoughts run on autopilot. This is significant because our thoughts also affect our mood—our emotions and how we *feel* on a daily basis. Our feelings are another thing that runs on autopilot. Our thoughts and feelings are a by-product of our belief systems. Both our thoughts and our beliefs have many layers. I call them the inner and outer layers.

Mathematically, it looks like this:

- Our Thoughts + Beliefs + Emotions = Our Expectations

and

- Our Expectations = Our Results.

So if you want to change the results in any area of your life, you first have to change your expectations. To change your expectations, you have to change the way you *think* and *feel*. You have to understand how your belief system is affecting how you think and feel.

The scientific laws of metaphysics teach us that what we think about expands. For those of you who are not familiar with the laws of metaphysics, these laws are as real as the laws of gravity, physics, chemistry, and a dozen other disciplines. I encourage you to Google metaphysics and find out more. I am not a scientist, but I can tell you that these laws come from the understanding that everything in this world is made up of energy, including us. I say, especially us! This energy has different vibration points. As it relates to our belief systems, what these laws confirm is that what we think about grows. Like attracts like. If we have a negative thought or belief about an external event, that will translate into a negative expectation and, ultimately, into a negative result.

Here's the good news: no matter where you are today, and no matter how far you think you are from where you want to be, if you're willing to make an adjustment to the way you think and feel about things, you can absolutely positively get there, guaranteed. *It will be an amazing ride, and your whole life will open up for you.*

Born into a challenging environment where most experts would say that the odds were against me, I broke every survival statistic out there. I did this through the power of my intentions. My life has been a journey of using the power of my thoughts and emotions to carry me into my visions. I would like to share a few key steps for helping you enhance any area of your life, be it your career or some other area.

Step

You have to get clear about what you really want. There are many ways to do this, but one of the quickest ways is to make a list of what isn't working about your current situation. Then, for every item on your list, describe the "turnaround"—how you would like that part of your situation to be. An important aspect of the turnaround step is to know that *you cannot change another person*. The only thing you can change is yourself—how *you* react and deal with external circumstances—so the turnaround has to be focused on you. For example, let's say your current situation is that your boss doesn't appreciate you. Your turnaround would look something like this:

CURRENT SITUATION	TURNAROUND
My boss doesn't appreciate me.	I feel valued and appreciated

Step 2

Most probably, if there is a situation in your life that really isn't working, then it's likely you're not feeling very good about it. In fact, your thoughts and beliefs around this subject are probably not very positive. You may in fact see no possibility of the situation changing. Step 2 is therefore to start to change the way you think and feel about the situation. Remember our equation: Thoughts/Beliefs/Emotions = Our Expectations = Our Results.

Using the preceding example, find ways to tap into feeling valued and appreciated. Make a list of every area of your life in which you do feel valued and appreciated. Spend at least ten minutes a day making a list and feeling gratitude for these areas of your life. Start seeing the cup as half full instead of half empty. This is a very powerful practice and can have a tremendous impact on your ability to refocus your attention from what isn't working in your current situation to what is. Do this every day, and I promise you, over the next several weeks, you will feel lighter and happier. Despite the inevitable struggles and curve balls that life presents us, if we take the time to tune in, we will find there are so many uplifting things around us that we can take into our hearts with an attitude of gratitude.

Step 3

You've gotten clear about what you want. You have identified the turnaround and have begun to tap into what that *feels* like. Step 3 is to start acting as if the situation has actually turned around. Yes, that's right. I want you to pretend, to daydream, to let yourself go into the space of possibility! You need to condition your mind and your energy body into seeing and feeling the end result. Using our preceding example, here is what that would look like. You wake up in the morning, and before you get out of bed, you spend five to ten minutes daydreaming. You see and feel yourself excited about going to work. You're smiling and skipping about. You see and feel yourself arriving at work. You feel light and airy. You pass your boss in the hallway, and you're genuinely happy to see him or her. You can feel how much your boss appreciates you, and it feels great! See and feel yourself going about your day confident and empowered. Nothing throws you off. Imagine your boss coming up to you during the day, complimenting you on your work, telling you what an asset you are to the team. Go into your heart, and feel the shift in every cell of your body. Do this every day, and within a couple weeks, you will start to notice changes—*big changes*! Do this for a couple months in any area of your life you want to shift, and you will start to transform the external conditions of your life. I guarantee it!

BIO

Elizabeth Brown is an empowerment life coach, motivational speaker, CPA, and workshop facilitator who specializes in helping her clients understand how their inner beliefs affect their lives. To learn more about the breadth of Elizabeth's work, go to http://www.cpa-lifecoach.com.

96

Managing Your Time

Brian Tracy

Perhaps the greatest single problem that people have today is "time poverty." Working people have too much to do and too little time for their personal lives. Most people feel overwhelmed with responsibilities and activities, and the harder they work, the further behind they feel. This sense of being on a never-ending treadmill can cause you to fall into the reactive-responsive mode of living. Instead of clearly deciding what you want to do, you continually react to what is happening around you. Pretty soon, you lose all sense of control. You feel that your life is running you rather than you running your life.

On a regular basis, you have to stand back and take stock of yourself and what you're doing. You have to stop the clock and do some serious thinking about who you are and where you are going. You have to evaluate your activities in the light of what is really important to you. You must master your time rather than becoming a slave to the constant flow of events and demands on your time. And you must organize your life to achieve balance, harmony, and inner peace. Taking action without thinking is the cause of every failure. Your ability to think is the most valuable trait that you possess. If you improve the quality of your thinking, you improve the quality of your life, sometimes immediately.

Time is your most precious resource. It is the most valuable thing you have. It is perishable, it is irreplaceable, and it cannot be saved. It can only be reallocated from activities of lower value to activities of higher value. All work requires time. And time is absolutely essential for the important relationships in your life. The very act of taking a moment to think about your time before you spend it will begin to improve your personal time management immediately.

I used to think that time management was only a business tool, like a calculator or a cellular telephone. It was something that you used so that you could get more done in a shorter period of time and eventually be paid more money. Then I learned that time management is not a peripheral activity or skill. It is the core skill upon which everything else in life depends.

In your work or business life, there are so many demands on your time from other people that very little of your time is yours to use as you choose. However, at home and in your personal life, you can exert a tremendous amount of control over how you use your time. It is in this area that I want to focus.

Personal time management begins with you. It begins with your thinking through what is really important to you in life, and it only makes sense if you organize it around specific things that you want to accomplish. You need to set goals in three major areas of your life. First, you need family and personal goals. These are the reasons why you get up in the morning, why you work hard and upgrade your skills, why you worry about money and sometimes feel frustrated by the demands on your time.

What are your personal and family goals, both tangible and intangible? A tangible family goal could be a bigger house, a better car, a larger television set, a vacation, or anything else that costs money. An intangible goal would be to build higher-quality relationships with your spouse and children or to spend more time with your family going for walks or reading books. Achieving these family and personal goals are the real essence of time management and its major purpose.

The second area comprises your business and career goals. These are the "how" goals, the means by which you achieve your personal "why" goals. How can you achieve the level of income that will enable you to fulfill your family goals? How can you develop the skills and abilities to stay ahead of the curve in your career? Business and career goals are absolutely essential, especially when balanced with family and personal goals.

The third type of goal is the personal development goal. Remember, you can't achieve much more on the outside than what you have achieved on the inside. Your outer life will be a reflection of your inner life. If you wish to achieve worthwhile things in your personal and career lives, you must become a worthwhile person in your own self-development. You must build yourself if you want to build your life. Perhaps the greatest secret of success is that you can become anything you really want to become to achieve any goal that you really want to achieve. To do so, though, you must go to work on yourself and never stop.

Once you have a list of your personal and family goals, your business and career goals, and your self-development goals, you can then organize the list by priority. This brings us to the difference between priorities and posteriorities. To get your personal time under control, you must decide very clearly on your priorities. You must decide on the most important things that you could possibly be doing to give yourself the same amount of happiness, satisfaction, and joy in life. However, at the same time, you must establish posteriorities as well. Just as priorities are things that you do more of and sooner, posteriorities are things that you do less of and later.

The fact is that your calendar is full. You have no spare time. Your time is extremely valuable. Therefore, for you to do anything new, you will have to stop doing something old. To get into something, you will have to get out of something else. To pick something up, you will have to put something down. Before you make any new commitment of your time, you must firmly decide what activities you are going to discontinue in your personal life. If you want to spend more time with your family, for example, you must decide what activities you currently engage in that are preventing you from doing so.

A principle of time management says that hard time pushes out soft time. This means that hard time, such as working, will push out soft time, such as the time you spend with your family. If you don't get your work done at the office because you don't use your time well, you almost invariably have to rob that time from your family. As a result, because your family is important to you, you find yourself in a values conflict. You feel stressed and irritable. You feel a tremendous amount of pressure. You know in your heart that you should be spending more time with the important people in your life, but because you didn't get your work done, you have to fulfill those responsibilities before you can spend time with your spouse and children.

Think of it this way: every minute you waste during the waking day is time of which your family will ultimately be deprived. So concentrate on working when you are at work so that you can concentrate on your family when you are at home.

There are three key questions that you can ask yourself continually to keep your personal life in balance. The first question is, "What is really important to me?" Whenever you find yourself with too much to do and too little time, stop and ask yourself, "What is it that is really important for me to do in this situation?" Then make sure that what you are doing is the answer to that question.

The second question is, "What are my highest-value activities?" In your personal life, this means, "What are the things that I do that give me the greatest pleasure and satisfaction? Of all the things that I could be doing at any one time, what are the things that I could do to add the greatest value to my life?"

And the final question for you to ask over and over again is, "What is the most valuable use of my time right now?" Because you can only do one thing at a time, you must constantly organize your life so that you are doing one thing, the most important thing, at every moment. Personal time management enables you to choose what to do first, what to do second, and what not to do at all. It enables you to organize every aspect of your life so that you can get the greatest joy, happiness, and satisfaction out of everything you do.

BIO

Brian Tracy is a top business and motivational speaker, consultant, and best-selling author. In the last thirty years, he's consulted for more than one thousand companies, including IBM, Ford, Federal Express, and Hewlett Packard, and has spoken to over five million people worldwide on the subjects of sales, business, leadership, self-esteem, goals, strategy, and success psychology. He's the top-selling author of over fifty-five books, including *Eat That Frog!,* and has produced more than three hundred audio-video learning programs, including the worldwide best-selling *Psychology of Achievement.* He's one of the most sought-after success coaches and has transformed the lives of millions of people. For more information on Brian Tracy, go to http://www.briantracy.com.

97

Become a *TRUE Leader*™ and Success Will Follow

Erik Therwanger

The art of leadership has been studied for centuries. Countless theories exist, and thousands of books have been written on the topic. People pay top dollar to learn leadership skills at seminars to enhance their careers. Businesses invest millions of dollars annually to train their employees to become better leaders. Why so much focus on leadership? It's simple: success follows leadership.

I learned the meaning of being a leader at the age of eighteen, when I enlisted in the U.S. Marine Corps. Unparalleled leadership skills are taught to all marines, not just a select few. These skills helped us to follow orders meticulously, accomplish our mission, and stay alive. In business, a lack of leadership can cost money. In combat, it can cost lives. By developing leaders, the U.S. Marine Corps has been the most elite organization in our armed services for over 230 years.

Imagine the growth you could experience in your career as you develop the leader within you. In today's uncertain job market, you need an edge to *survive*, but you will need more than that to *thrive*. To enhance your career, enhance your leadership skills. Every organization benefits by having a leader on board, regardless of the job for which he or she was initially hired. A leader will exceed the expectations of his or her position, inspire others to do the same, and be promoted to higher levels of responsibility.

Although most would agree that becoming a better leader would enhance their careers, many do not know where to start. You're probably not going to enlist in the U.S. Marine Corps to enhance your career, so let's look at a few fundamental ways to develop immediately your leadership skills.

To achieve something, you must first define it. Leadership can mean different things to different people. That's why you may experience various styles of leadership from various types of leaders. To guarantee that success, I have defined leadership in a way that I can apply to all areas of my life, personally and professionally. I call it *TRUE Leadership*™.

TRUE Leadership is the process of influence in which a TRUE Leader can enlist the support of other team members in the successful accomplishment of a common goal.

To further enhance your career, you can immediately change your perception. Leaders view their organizations as a team, not just as a company. Businesses, both large and small, need team players, not employees, if they plan to succeed. Every organization will experience challenges, but a leader will perceive these times as opportunities for growth.

It is during these times that your door of opportunity opens as a leader. Employees tend to walk away from a challenge, but a *TRUE Leader* will walk right through the door and discover solutions. Finding solutions to any problem is a key objective of any leader. Employees often say, "This is why it can't be done." A *TRUE Leader* always says, "Here is how we can accomplish this."

Next, choose leadership over management. I don't believe that the concept of management is bad, but I know that the impact of leadership is greater. Every organization wants to experience the benefits of leadership, but most suffer from the effects of management. I have worked for managers and I have worked for leaders. Managers made me feel obligated to get the work done. Leaders made me feel inspired to get it done.

People do not like being managed—not micromanaged, macromanaged, or even properly managed. They prefer to be led—by a *TRUE Leader*. By choosing leadership in your career, you will move away from "managing the people" and start "leading the team." Remember, lead the team and manage the work!

Leaders are essential for growth. Any organization that is focused on growing will seek out those who can understand and apply the Four Characteristics of a *TRUE Leader*:

1. **Trustworthy.** Takes on tasks.
2. **Reliable.** Accomplishes objectives.
3. **Unwavering.** Stays the course.
4. **Exceptional.** Exceeds any expectations.

A *trustworthy* leader instills faith in others that important tasks will be completed with the highest level of integrity. A *reliable* leader displays the ability to accomplish the overall objective (the big picture) of the organization. An *unwavering* leader will remain on target with tasks and objectives, no matter what circumstances arise. An *exceptional* leader will deliver results that not only hit the goal but raise the bar.

Those unique individuals who can masterfully combine all four characteristics into one seamless behavior become *TRUE Leaders*. I have successfully applied these characteristics in the fields of military duty, financial services, media solutions, and self-help. Leadership makes the difference, no matter what career you are practicing.

Leadership skills are seldom tested during the good times. They are put to the test during the challenging times. I have spent far more time in a suit and tie than I have in a camouflage uniform. But the leadership training I received from the U.S. Marine Corps has provided me an unparalleled edge in the business world. As a civilian, I have come to rely exclusively on my leadership skills, especially during challenging times, regardless of my field of work.

Ten months after my marriage, my wife was diagnosed with cancer. I became her caregiver and could no longer dedicate the time I needed to my job in the entertainment industry. I was forced to switch careers. Without formal sales training or experience in the financial services industry, I started my new job selling financial products. I earned money solely from commissions. I didn't want to enhance my career; I *needed* to!

The only thing I transferred to my new position was my leadership skills. During my wife's battle with cancer, I tapped into every aspect of the Four Characteristics of a *TRUE Leader*. Despite our challenging times, I became a top producer and recruiter. Even though this new career was foreign to me, the basic principles of being a *TRUE Leader* allowed me to achieve high levels of success. Years later, I returned to the entertainment industry and accepted an entry-level position to get my foot back in the door.

My job may have been entry level, but my leadership skills were not. I took initiative when others took breaks. I remained positive when others focused on negativity. When a coworker presented a problem, I presented a solution. I did more than was asked, and often more than I was paid to do. By focusing on *TRUE Leadership*, success followed. I received three promotions, including a promotion to vice president. I implemented a culture of growth, launched a sales team that continually exceeded expectations, and developed a leadership team that overcame any objective. Within eighteen months, the company (my team) had nearly doubled its revenue.

When you enhance your career with leadership, success will follow in your personal life as well. Anyone can be a *TRUE Leader*. Although some people seem more natural at it, no one is born with it. Like everything else, leadership is a learned behavior. It will not happen on its own. Starting today, make the choice to become a *TRUE Leader* and enhance your career—success will follow.

BIO

Erik Therwanger is a leading authority on accomplishing life-changing goals, building teams, increasing sales results, and enhancing leadership skills. He has uniquely combined his four years of service in the U.S. Marine Corps, over ten years of sales experience, and his responsibilities as his wife's caregiver during her battle with cancer to create the Think GREAT® Program. Erik is dedicated to helping people achieve a greater life, no matter what circumstances they face. As the author of the *Think GREAT Collection*, Erik's wide array of strategies and techniques encourages people to accomplish life-changing goals. Erik's workshops outline the 5 Steps to Accomplishing Goals: Goals–Reasons–Expectations–Actions–Tracking. He has worked with individuals, teams, businesses, and organizations to achieve greater results. His inspirational and motivational approach has inspired people to take more initiative, create additional sales opportunities, and build stronger leaders. Erik's website (http://www.thinkgreat90.com/) provides countless resources and solutions for individuals and organizations focused on achieving greater results. His "GREAT Thought of the Week" is a free, inspirational message designed to help people begin their weeks with motivation and direction. Also available are video and audio clips of Erik's workshops and speaking events. *Think GREAT* and achieve a greater life!

98

What Is True Success?

❦

David Muraco

Depending on whom you ask, success could mean any number of things. Some measure it solely based on results. Others claim that it's all in the action steps you take. In my opinion, it's more than that. Success cannot be measured solely by results or the amount of action put forth. *True success* comes from the heart. It's how you feel when you finish, and more important, how others feel after you finish. I find it hard to believe that an artist is more concerned about how much time it will take to paint a masterpiece than about how he or she feels when the painting is complete. This is very similar to when a sports figure wins the championship game and, when asked the question "How does it feel?" answers, "What an amazing feeling this is!"

Why is it that books, articles, and personal training systems talk more about how to measure success, or how to create action steps to success, than about how it feels to be successful? Now it stands to reason that in business, in some form or another, things continually need to be tracked and regulated. This, however, cannot be the sole focus of how we measure *True Success*. Empowering our employees, creating great relationships, or making a difference in our communities: these are the ways truly to measure our successes within our business and personal lives. After extensive research, I've found that following a great achievement, the most successful people and organizations rarely talk about the system or game plan that brought them there but instead about how they felt after they got there.

Think of the most influential speeches given throughout history: "The Gettysburg Address" by President Lincoln, "I Have a Dream" by Dr. Martin Luther King Jr., or President John F. Kennedy's speech "Ask Not What Your Country Can Do for You." Were these speeches, given by these amazing men, measured by anything other than feelings? To this day, their words ring true from the power of the men delivering them, not because of how well they would go over in some poll result. These speeches were delivered with passion and feeling, not according to how they were going to be measured.

Visit Amazon.com and search the term "success": this should bring about 141,967 results. Quite an overload, wouldn't you say? I'm illustrating the point that even the books we read more often than not look at success as something measured by numbers. Trying to pinpoint exactly when this happened is challenging. It's as though every time we have a major collapse in our economy, more and more, we see the writing on the wall. It seems the only way to fix this is to measure this or measure that, and only then will we truly have our answers. What a joke! Some of the greatest accomplishments ever made were based on a feeling far greater than the results. You can measure ideas, systems, and training all you want, but you can't measure the size of someone's heart. You can't measure his or her commitment level to a cause. And because of that, most businesses as well as individuals miss the mark of *True Success*.

I can just imagine some of the readers out there saying, "This guy is crazy. He has no idea what he's talking about. I have been extremely successful in my life, and it had nothing to do with feelings."Maybe that's true, maybe not—let's test it. You have to ask yourself how you got to where you are now in your personal or professional life. What event or idea helped get you there? You may even say a particular system got you to where you are in your life. Good! Now for the big questions; are you ready? When things were not going your way, or went badly, how did you feel? When you were at a point of what you define as success, what was it like? And even as you are asking yourself these questions now, how do you feel?

Now let's review, shall we? First, when things were not going your way or went badly, how did you feel? Were you angry or upset? Perhaps the system you were using wasn't working, or maybe you had this burning feeling deep inside to keep going, not to quit. Which one do you think served you the best? You guessed it: it was your feelings. The second question was, When you were at the point of what you define as success, what was it like? Did you recall the system that got you there? Did you recall all the work put in? Or did you recall the feeling of being successful?

All too often in life, as well as in business, we put all the emphasis on measuring success instead of on understanding what success feels like. We can teach most anyone a system to be successful, whether it is in real estate, financial services, or hotel management. When we teach what *True Success* really feels like, we empower a person to be successful. By doing that, he or she can teach someone else, and then he or she can teach someone else, and so on. With that, *True Success* will not be a system that we measure; rather it will be a feeling that we embody.

Remember: be positive, be real, and live your life in the Zone.

BIO

Meet president and CEO of "In the Zone" Professional Coaching Solutions, David Muraco. David is a sought-after speaker and coach and has led numerous leadership and communication seminars across the country. Prior to starting his own coaching practice, David spent over sixteen years in the corporate setting working in the areas of management, sales, team building, and leadership. Armed with a mission and a passion for empowering others, David is committed to empowering one million people to live the lives of their dreams by January 1, 2017. To find out more about David, please go to http://www.in-the-zone.biz.

8 Secrets All Millionaires Have in Common

Lisa Christiansen

Then indecision brings its own delays, and days are lost lamenting over lost days.
Are you in earnest? Seize this very minute; what you can do, or dream you can do,
begin it; Boldness has genius, power and magic in it.
—Goethe

One of the quickest ways to build wealth is to learn from those who have achieved great wealth and mirror them. You must first make a decision to be resolved in your commitment. To decide is to cut off, to sever, leaving no other option or alternative.

1. Make Certain It Is *Your* Dream

I know I will do far more for others than for myself. Do you know anyone like that? Maybe even you? More often in our lives, we spend more time on someone else's goals than on our personal internal passionate desires. Make sure it's your passion to succeed in whatever course you chart; make certain it's your commitment to succeed in life! You define what success is, so choose and be happy.

2. Do Not Call It a Goal

Referencing the book *What They Don't Teach You in the Harvard Business School*, Mark McCormack shares a study conducted on students in the 1979 Harvard MBA program. In that year, the students were asked, "Have you set clear, written goals for your future and made plans to accomplish them?"Only 3 percent of the graduates had written goals and plans; 13 percent had goals, but they were not in writing; and a whopping 84 percent had no specific goals at all. Ten years later, the members of the class were interviewed again, and the findings, while somewhat predictable, were nonetheless mind-boggling: the 13 percent of the class who had goals were earning, on average, twice as much as the 84 percent who had no goals at all. And what about the 3 percent who had clear, concise, written goals? They were earning, on average, ten times as much as the other 97 percent put together. Even with evidence of this proven method of success, most people don't have clear, measurable, time-scheduled goals written down toward which they work. Write it down with a pen and paper while in a state of anticipated expectancy. Emotion is motion. Amazing insight? There's more, so keep reading.

3. Clearly Identify Your Commitment

Begin to see your future in the present—feel it with fervent passion, see it crystal clear—this is what it takes to achieve your outcome. Clarity is power! To quote Tony Robbins, "If you talk about it, it's a dream. If you envision it, it's possible. But if you schedule it, it's real."

4. Use The Tools around You

We must begin to use the tools around us. Whether he or she is a positive or negative motivator, you must have someone in your life who is holding you accountable for reaching and achieving your goals. More often than not, the negative motivators are the most compelling, as I know from experience; I moved more mountains to prove to myself that I could do anything against all odds because of the people who didn't believe in me. For example, a negative motivator is someone who has told you that you will never succeed, or maybe he or she laughed at you when you said you were going to quit your job to begin your own business. I've had many versions of this happen to me over my lifetime, and it moves me every time. Thank you to all those who didn't believe in me; I am sincerely grateful.

Write this person's name down as if you were writing a thank-you card, and say, "I am so grateful for [whatever your outcome is]" in the present tense on an index card or sticky note, and post this on your wall, in front of your computer, in your cubicle, in your vehicle, or in your locker, if you have one. When times are tough, look at that card, and it will motivate you to keep going until you are there. The most important part of this is to celebrate the outcome as if it were already real, with all the energy and enthusiasm of a child. Passion is knowing that those who pushed me forward will soon be behind me—those who didn't believe in me will soon be my strongest supporters. There are equal positives to every negative.

5. Know Your Outcome and Plan It

- *What* is it you want? What is your outcome? What will you sacrifice to get it?
- *Where* will you be?
- *When* will you accomplish it? What month, what date, what year?
- *Why* do you want this? What is the consequence if you do not accomplish this?

- *Whose* help do you need? Who will help you? Who will you reach out to?
- *How* will you make this happen? How will you get the help you need?

In your life plan, you need to outline each of these specific characteristics of identifying at a crystal-clear level. Remember that clarity is power!

6. Review, Plan, and Commit on a Daily Basis

For twenty minutes every day, you need to review and reread and note your progress on this life plan. If you do not have twenty minutes, that is a complete lie. There is a special reading place we all have where we spend fifteen to twenty minutes sitting down. Make every *should* a *must*— don't just *should* all over yourself . . .

7. Tell Yourself You Have Succeeded

Speak your gratitude for your outcome in the present tense. Live in the gratitude of your success now: what you can do, or dream you can do. Boldness has genius, power, and magic in it. "The size of your success is determined by the size of your belief and the fervency of your passion." Emotion is motion. Pay attention to your subconscious thoughts every day; you must guard the doorway to your mind and allow only positive thoughts to enter. Observe how you communicate with others about your business and where you stand as a networker. Always speak with positive verbiage to convey your message in every arena of your life.

8. Share with Others the Conviction and Certainty of Your Commitment

Go out and share with the world your outcome and where you are headed. Don't sit back and try to keep it a secret. Have people laugh at you, then write their names down on a card and stick it on your wall! Envision the results, and make them bigger and brighter than you ever thought possible . . . then be grateful for their fruition.

To *your* success.

BIO

Creator of extraordinary lives, Lisa Christiansen has served as an advisor to leaders around the world for the last two decades. A recognized authority on the psychology of leadership, organizational turnaround, and peak performance, Lisa has consulted Olympic athletes, world-renowned musicians, Fortune 500 CEOs, psychologists, and world-class entertainers. Lisa's strategies for achieving lasting results and fulfillment are regarded as the platinum standard in the coaching industry. Her expertise and guidance have enriched the lives of icons such as pop superstar Kelly Clarkson, Olympian Dara Torres, and the members of the rock band Journey. Visit her online at http://www.lisachristiansencompanies.com/ or e-mail her at lisa@officialwealthcreation.com.

Define Your Attitude at Work

A Critical Step to Career Success

☙ ❧

Long Yun Siang

One of the most important things to do in your career is to define your attitude toward work. How will it contribute to your career success?

How do you define *attitude*? According to the *Advanced Learner's Dictionary of Current English,* attitude is defined as "a way of looking at life; a way of thinking, feeling or behaving." Therefore an attitude is not just the way we think but the way we think, feel, and do.

You may have your entire career plan worked out, but if you do not define your attitude to build its foundation, then before long, your plans will crumble. That's not to say a career plan is not important. In fact, it is very important in achieving career success.

What you need to understand is that a positive attitude is even more important. To define your attitude at work means deciding the values that would guide you in your working environment.

Somewhere in my career, after the tons of self-improvement books I have read, I decided that I needed to define my attitude toward my career. These three values would be my clear, defined attitude toward my career.

Pride

I know this is a tricky word. It connotes arrogance especially when one has too high an opinion of oneself. Personally, in defining my attitude, pride is taken to mean self-dignity. Pride prevents you from doing just enough to get by. If you know everything you do at work has your name and signature on it, then you will give it your best shot and nothing less.

Passion

Just a simple plain interest in any work or career you choose isn't enough to carry you through the tough times. And trust me, there will be tough times. It could be an unreasonable client or an impossible timeline. However, a burning desire will pull you through these. An intense enthusiasm for all things worth doing will pull you through the toughest times.

Belief

To generate that passion, it is important to believe. Only a deep belief will create the vigor and force that will give you the fuel to charge. Know that you can achieve all you set out to do for yourself. You only need to start believing in yourself.

But are these three values enough? They are not. They are part of a bigger equation that includes Skills/Knowledge, Direction, and Action. How do these work together?

Pride and Skills/Knowledge

Pride by my personal definition means "self-dignity." It means the realization that everything you do has your personal signature on it.

However, there is a danger here. That danger is excessive pride without the necessary skills and knowledge, which is arrogance, so Pride – Skills/Knowledge = Arrogance. Pride and skills/knowledge have to be in good balance. What about doing your work with just skills and knowledge and with no pride? Well, you end up with mediocre work. You get it right, but it isn't the best. Hence Skills/Knowledge – Pride = Mediocre Work. When you add this set of positive attitudes in the workplace together, pride and skills/knowledge, what do you get? Pride + Skills/Knowledge = The Best Work Each Time.

Passion and Direction

Passion is the burning desire and love for the work that you do, which will pull you through the tough times. However, it needs to be balanced by another factor—direction. Your enthusiasm and burning desire must be harnessed to focus on the objectives at hand for them to show positive results. Passion without direction would just mean wasted energy.

- Passion – Direction = Wasted Energy

What about direction without passion? Well, what if you know where you want to go but do not have the fuel for it? It just means success takes longer to achieve, if ever.

- Direction – Passion = Success Takes Far Longer, If Ever

When you add direction and passion as a positive attitude in the workplace, you get goals galore!

- Passion + Direction = Goals Galore

Belief and Action

My last equation of positive attitude for career success involves belief and action. A deep believe in yourself will create the vigor and force that will fuel your journey of seeking career success.

This belief must be balanced with action. Action means making your plans work. It means doing, working. A belief that is not backed by a plan of action is just fantasy.

- Belief – Action = Fantasy

What if you work your plans without a belief? Anyone without belief in himself or herself and his or her dreams but who continues to work his or her plans is a fool at work.

- Action – Belief = Fool at Work

When you are able to synergize belief and action into one, your dreams come true!

- Belief + Action = Dreams Come True

A Critical Step to Career Success

When you are able to harness these three sets of positive attitudes in the workplace into one, you will increase your chances for career success.

BIO

Long Yun Siang, or Long, as he is popularly known, runs http://www.career-success-for-newbies.com/ with his wife, Dorena, as their way of paying it forward. Their website—based on their real-life experience—provides tips, tools, and advice for newbies and veterans alike in pursuing career success. Visit the website to download their popular free e-books—*Career Success Recipe for Newbies, SHINE at Work: Your 30-minute Guide,* and *52 Things You Can Do to Improve Your Work—a Week at a Time.*

101

Kisses & Hearts
Career Advice for Young Women

Be Dumb, Be Fickle, Be Superficial

Len Sone

I am here to talk to you girls about careers and to give you some advice. It's slightly ironic because for so long in my own career as a life coach, I resisted choosing this niche (saying that I work with young women specifically). I see myself as a deep thinker, and true wisdom is for everyone. Well, this is what I told myself. The real reason was that I didn't want to be less respected intellectually or read any less in my beloved fields of spiritual metaphysics and personal development because everyone saw me only as a life coach for young women. For longer than needed, I was a life coach for everyone, and my career wasn't evolving. I became irritated and resentful.

The obvious question here is, why did I believe that I would be taken less seriously if I were to work only with young women? Clearly I had beliefs about what society thought about this group (which, by the way, I belong to as well).

This is what I believed society thought:

1. Young women are dumb. They think about dumb things like buying shoes, and they buy too many things.

2. Young women can be easily manipulated and sold things they don't really need and that aren't of value.

3. Young women don't make good decisions.

4. Young women are too emotional (especially on their period).

5. Young women are needy and obsessed with getting, having, or keeping a romantic relationship.

6. Pretty young women are just decorations—they are charming but don't have much to say.

7. Young women are spoiled brats and unprofessional.

8. Young women are fickle and change who they are too often.

9. Young women are superficial.

All in all, my belief was that *people think that coaching young women, that is, girls, is more about bonding over superficial things than having serious intellectual conversations and that it takes less wisdom or intellect to coach them. Hence people in my field won't see how brilliant I truly am or read my books*—or something to that effect.

I discovered that my young female clients battle with the same ideas in their careers. They fear they won't be taken seriously and make career decisions based on those fears. They either cover up their perceived flaws and project a different image professionally while they pursue their career goals, or the opposite—they accept inferior treatment and don't pursue their career goals because they base their entire identity on being not good enough. One example of the latter case that easily comes to mind is a young woman who kept saying, "I never get an A. My boyfriend gets As, but I'm not as smart as him." As a result, she would always sabotage herself in some way academically so that the A she could have easily gotten, she didn't. When her boyfriend applied to a nearby university, she only applied to a community college, keeping with her belief that her boyfriend should be ahead of her. There was nothing wrong with her intelligence or creativity, nor was her boyfriend truly smarter or even particularly impressive academically, so it was odd to hear and see this bright woman make such statements and make such decisions.

Whatever our own defense mechanism is, it became apparent to me as a life coach and as a young woman that something had gone wrong here in our thinking and interpretation. This is the solution. What I'm about to say is going to shock you, but . . . *all nine of the preceding things are true about us young women!* Before you throw stones at me, let me explain: we must allow ourselves as young women to be dumb, fickle, shallow, emotional, bad decision makers, obsessed with looks and relationships, vain, weak, easily manipulated, spoiled, lazy, and unprofessional, or our careers and our lives will never be comfortable and genuine.

First of all, being those things does not mean that we are not also their opposite. We young women can have a deep intellectual conversation one minute and the next talk about something trivial like shoes. The truth is that we young women can cry about how our boyfriends broke up with us and how we felt lost without them for years, yet also be totally aloof and calculated about other boyfriends. The truth is that sometimes we can easily be manipulated and can make bad decisions, but other times, we are the ones who step up as the most level-headed, smart, clever, strong decision makers in situations in which anyone could lose his or her cool. We can look pretty and love that kind of attention of our physical beauty, then lose ourselves completely in some purely intellectual project, forgetting our physicality and forgetting to shave for weeks. The truth is that we are *all* of these things, usually in the same day! And it's all fantastic and valuable because every trait is positive in the right circumstances. You just have to make it work for you! We have to accept and celebrate all these sides of ourselves and realize that it's not to our advantage to pretend that we are one-dimensional when it comes to our careers.

But how is this career advice, Len? OK, the advice is actually the following. Very simply:

1. do what makes your heart sing, even if you truly believe people will take you less seriously for it or judge you negatively for it
2. create your own career custom-made for you

This is the secret hint—the right career for you as a young woman will let you do all these things and much more:

3. be stupid
4. make mistakes
5. be all about your looks
6. be emotional
7. cry
8. talk about stupid things
9. act young and clueless
10. obsess over your relationships and be needy
11. make bad decisions and be foolish
12. be spoiled and vain
13. be unprofessional
14. be reckless and impulsive
15. change yourself often
16. be crazy

In my newly redefined career as a life coach for young women, I can do all of the preceding, and my clients love me for it because I free them to do the same. I don't try to make myself or them into perfect zombies who say and do all the things of which people will approve. I actually help them come out of dark rooms of shame to see the beauty of all of who they are. This is the kind of career I wish for you, my dear. I wish for you a career in which you are free to be all of yourself and in which you don't have to feel embarrassed about any part of your personality. The idea that your career (whether school or a job) should be what you love is not new; however, to get that kind of career, you have to love all of who you are.

Visionaries have always been people who were brave enough to create careers taking full advantage of their infinite inner dimensions. With time, others catch on. Trust that the same will happen to you.

I invite you to create a career that is as abundant and multidimensional as you are. I also invite you not to be taken seriously and to be OK with that. Remember that nothing is permanent. I promise you—your career choices will someday be understood and celebrated by the right people if you're courageous enough to care more about what makes you happy than about what others will think of you.

I love you,
Len Sone

BIO

Len Sone is the owner of Kisses & Hearts Coaching for Young Women. She offers private coaching sessions for young women everywhere. Her focus is helping sensitive girls transform into the women they always wanted to be—beautiful, powerful, and fiercely independent. Beyond that, Len is a mystic, a wisdom seeker, and a happy recluse. She currently lives in downtown San Jose. You can schedule a private coaching session with her by e-mailing Len@KissesAndHearts.com. Visit her online at http://KissesAndHearts.com/.

About SelfGrowth.com

SelfGrowth.com is an Internet super-site for self improvement and personal growth. It is part of a network of websites owned and operated by Self Improvement Online, Inc., a privately held New Jersey-based Internet company.

Our company's mission is to provide our website guests with high-quality self improvement and natural health information, with the one simple goal in mind: making their lives better. We provide information on topics ranging from goal setting and stress management to natural health and alternative medicine.

If you want to get a sense for our website's visibility on the Internet, you can start by going to Google, Yahoo, America Online, Lycos or just about any search engine on the World Wide Web and typing the words "self improvement." SelfGrowth.com consistently comes up as the top or one of the top websites for self improvement.

Other Facts About The Site

SelfGrowth.com offers a wealth of information on self improvement. Our site:

- Publishes six informative newsletters on self improvement, personal growth, and natural health.
- Offers more than 100,000 unique articles from more than 18,000 experts.
- Links to more than 50,000 websites in an organized directory.
- Gets visitors from more than 100 countries.

Contact Information

ADDRESS: Self Improvement Online, Inc.
           200 Campus Drive, Suite D
           Morganville, New Jersey 07751
PHONE: (732) 617–1030
E-MAIL: webmaster@selfgrowth.com
WEBSITE: www.selfgrowth.com

Author Index

A

Allan, Laura, 77-80
Al-Mosawi, Haider, 240-242
Aparicio, Anna, 197-200
Attwooll, Leslie, 51-55

B

Bilanich, Bud, 85-88
Bressler, Helen P., 92-95
Brown, Elizabeth, 354-356

C

Cabanel, Mary-Jeanne "MJ", 117-119
Cabral, Stephen, 38-41
Christiansen, Lisa, 368-371
Cook, Sean, 281-284
Cooper, Pegotty, 265-268
Copeland, Liz, 285-288
Corso, Bambi, 292-295
Cottringer, William S., 183-186
Crenshaw, Tiffany, 344-345
Cullen, Susan, 120-123

D

Daniels, Nancy, 104-106
Davis, Susan Crampton, 159-161
DeCarlo, Laura, 208-212
DeMange, Jean Mulrine, 255-257
de Liz, Monica, 194-196
Dellon, Edward, 307-309
DeNucci, Patti, 304-306
DePolo, JoAnn, 144-146
Douglas, Cherry, 61-65

F

Federman, Brad, 273-276

Frazier, Craig, 81-84

G

Garcy, Pamela D., 310-313
Gatty, Ann N., 337-339
Georges, Colleen, 177-179
Gopaul, Felicia, 243-245
Goruk, Randy, 224-227

H

Hamid, Ayman, 111-113
Hansen, Brock, 114-116
Howard, Jennifer, 228-230
Hyland, Rita, 155-158

J

James, Sarah, 131-133
Johnson, Tory, 301-303
Jones, Tecumseh A., 269-272
Joyce, Judith, 73-76

K

Kerrison, Helen, 165-168
King, JoAnn Youngblood, 180-182
Kraft, Cari, 69-72
Kreisberg, Bob, 14-17
Kurbatoff, Lauren, 346-349

L

Lang, Abbe, 258-260
Larter, Lisa, 318-320
Loeb, Natalie, 231-234
Loving, Vikki, 204-207
Lurie, Sunny Klein, 134-137

ABOUT MICHELLE A. RIKLAN

Michelle A. Riklan holds a B.A. in Theatre, English Literature, and Speech Communications from Hofstra University. While beginning her corporate career, she pursued and completed a M.A. in Speech and Interpersonal Communications from New York University where she also served as an Instructor in Voice and Diction/Public Speaking. Utilizing her education and presentation skills, she continued a career path in Human Resource Management. Her generalist background is all inclusive, but her areas of expertise include employment, employee relations, and training and development.

With a combined 20 years of in-house corporate and targeted consulting experience, Michelle services large corporations as well as small businesses and individuals in all aspects of Human Resources and Career Management.

As an International Award Winning Certified Professional Résumé Writer and Certified Employment Interview Consultant, Michelle has written hundreds of résumés and coached clients through all phases of the job search. Her résumés get results! Individual services include:

- Résumés that land on the *top* of the pile!
- Coaching that puts you *ahead* of the competition.
- Training that ensures career *advancement.*

Memberships:
American Society of Training and Development
Career Director's International
National Résumé Writers Association
Professional Association of Résumé Writers/Career Coaches
Society of Human Resource Management

Certifications and Training:
Certified Professional Résumé Writer
Certified Employment Interview Consultant
DiSC Administrator
Myers-Briggs Assessment Administration
Michelle is also a co-founder of Self Improvement Online, Inc.
www.selfgrowth.com

About David Riklan

David Riklan is the president and co-founder of Self Improvement Online, Inc., the leading provider of self improvement and personal growth information on the Internet.

His company was founded in 1998 and now maintains four websites on self improvement and natural health, including:

- www.SelfGrowth.com
- www.SelfImprovementNewsletters.com
- www.SelfGrowthMarketing.com
- www.NaturalHealthWeb.com

His company also publishes nine email newsletters going out to more than 950,000 weekly subscribers on the topics of self improvement, natural health, personal growth, relationships, home business, sales skills, and brain improvement.

David's first book—*Self Improvement: The Top 101 Experts Who Help Us Improve Our Lives*—has been praised by leading industry experts as the "Encyclopedia of Self Improvement." That book's success motivated him to continue publishing books which, like the one you're reading now, seek to improve the lives of others.

He has a degree in chemical engineering from the State University of New York at Buffalo and has 20 years of experience in sales, marketing, management, and training for companies such as Hewlett-Packard and Dale Carnegie Training.

His interest in self improvement and personal growth began more than 20 years ago and was best defined through his work as an instructor for Dale Carnegie Training, a performance-based training company.

David is a self-professed self improvement junkie – and proud of it. His house is full of self improvement books and tapes. He took his first self improvement class, an Evelyn Wood speed-reading course, when he was 16 years old, and his interest hasn't ceased yet.

He lives and works in New Jersey with his wife and business partner, Michelle Riklan. Together, they run Self Improvement Online, Inc. and are raising three wonderful children: Joshua, Jonathan, and Rachel.